The Dust of the Road

A Translation of *Gard-e-Raah*

The Dust of the Road
A Translation of *Gard-e-Raah*

AKHTAR HUSAIN RAIPURI

Translated by
Amina Azfar

OXFORD
UNIVERSITY PRESS

OXFORD

UNIVERSITY PRESS

Great Clarendon Street, Oxford OX2 6DP

Oxford University Press is a department of the University of Oxford.
It furthers the University's objective of excellence in research, scholarship,
and education by publishing worldwide in

Oxford New York

Auckland Cape Town Dar es Salaam Hong Kong Karachi
Kuala Lumpur Madrid Melbourne Mexico City Nairobi
New Delhi Shanghai Taipei Toronto

with offices in

Argentina Austria Brazil Chile Czech Republic France Greece
Guatemala Hungary Italy Japan Poland Portugal Singapore
South Korea Switzerland Turkey Ukraine Vietnam

Oxford is a registered trade mark of Oxford University Press
in the UK and in certain other countries

© Oxford University Press 2007

The moral rights of the author have been asserted

First published 2007

Originally published in Urdu by Maktaba-e-Daniyal, Victoria Chambers,
Abdullah Haroon Road, Saddar, Karachi under the title *Gard-e-Raah*
by Dr Akhtar Hussain Raipuri in 2000.

ISBN 978-0-19-547215-8

The translator wishes to acknowledge the help of
Mr Uffan Seljuk and Dr M. Reza Kazimi in translating/interpreting
the *ashar* or poetical couplets in the book.

Typeset in Minion Pro
Printed in Pakistan by
Mas Printers, Karachi.
Published by
Ameena Saiyid, Oxford University Press
No. 38, Sector 15, Korangi Industrial Area, PO Box 8214
Karachi-74900, Pakistan.

To

Hameeda

Contents

A Tribute

Dr Akhtar Husain Raipuri was an extraordinary person, a man of many qualities. It is essential to study his life and work seriously, for by doing so we can acquaint our society with the bright lights of values and thoughts which seem to be gradually fading away from it, without any sign of replacement.

I had read Dr Akhtar Husain Raipuri's *Adab aur Inqilab* in the mid fifties, but had never met him, for I learnt that he was abroad, busy with the United Nations' assignments. During this time I met Muzzaffar Husain Shameem who was Akhtar Husain's elder brother. In 1962 I became editor of *Nai Jamhooriat*, a weekly paper published in Karachi. Meanwhile Shameem Sahib's field of activity had become limited to Urdu Bazaar, Sultan Husain & Sons, and Aftab Kirmani's shop. For a time he was my neighbour, as he had taken up residence in Nazimabad. Many thefts were committed there during his absences, causing him to be left with nothing but the clothes that he had on. However he was a man of great patience and forbearance, content and enterprising. Slim of person, clad in a *sherwani* and Aligarh style *pajama*, a cloth cap on his head, and shoes with laces enclosing his feet; his eyes behind dark glasses with round frames, long haired, cane in hand, such was his style. He was a heavy smoker of cigarettes or *biris*. An experienced writer and journalist, he had lived in Calcutta, Hyderabad, Bombay, Delhi, Banaras, Lahore and other places. He used to speak with great affection of Agha Hashar Kashmiri, Maulana Chiragh Hasan Hasrat, Maulana Abul Kalam Azad and Abdur Razzak Maleehabadi. A collection of his poems entitled *Naginay* had been published. He was the author of short stories, criticism, translations, and had compiled books. But none of his works can be found now, even in bookshops which stock old or used books.

Muzaffar Husain Shameem Sahib used to say to me, 'Involve yourself just enough in scholarship to have people believe that you are a learned man. There is no advantage in going deep into it or making oneself wretched in the pursuit of journalism or literature. I am an example of this. Learn a lesson from me!' Three times he insisted on bringing me forms for the Superior Services (CSS) examination, saying, 'Just fill these. I will be responsible for the rest.' Each time I quoted to him:

جانتا ہوں ثوابِ طاعت و زہد
پر طبیعت ادھر نہیں آتی

*I know the rewards for obedience (to God) and abstinence
But what can I do, for my heart is not in it.*

'I don't want to be a bureaucrat. I prefer to live a life of freedom.'

Muzaffar Husain Shameem Sahib used to treat me with great affection. When he learned that during his stay in Aurangabad, my father, who was the Treasurer for the district of Aurangabad, was a friend of Maulvi Abdul Haq, he came to visit him, and for a long time they talked about old times.

When I joined the faculty of Karachi University, Shameem Sahib had died. Dr Akhtar Husain Raipuri was back in Pakistan and was attached to the history department of the Karachi University as an honorary Professor. Those were interesting times. Dr Mahmood Husain was the vice chancellor of the university, and we were all privileged to have Professor Majnoon Gorakhpuri, Professor Ahmed Ali and Dr Akhtar Husain Raipuri join the university. One day, when Akhtar Sahib happened to stop at the toll gate, I too stopped, and introducing myself, mentioned my close friendship with Muzaffar Husain Shameem. Dr Raipuri embraced me and quoted, 'No wonder, "I get a whiff of the loved one."' From that day onwards, until his death, he always held me in warm affection.

Since 1958, I had remained associated with the monthly, *Afkar*, in the company of Sehba Lucknavi. With great warmth and trust he used to involve me in the editorial responsibilities and consultations. One day the focus of the deliberations was the introduction of new themes in the magazine. It was decided that autobiographical writing would be serialized. A list was prepared of the preferred authors, and heading the list was Dr Raipuri's name. When the proposal was made to him on the phone, he agreed after some hesitation, and a day was fixed on for us to visit him and talk about the proposed work in more detail.

Dr Raipuri's house is close to the 'Cheel wali Kothi' or the Eagle House, and Tariq Road. When Sehba and I arrived there, Dr Raipuri, to our great delight, held out some pages of his writing to Sehba Sahib and said, 'Here you are sir, on your persuasion I have put down some random material.' I read out the whole document aloud. Wherever some changes seemed to be called for, they were made by altering a word or two.

At the end of the session we were treated to a repast which was no less than a feast. Hameeda Bhabi (Mrs Raipuri, who is the daughter of Zafar Omar, the author of the famous *Neeli Chatri*) lavished warm hospitality on us. Her face seemed to be blossoming with happiness at her husband's renewed interest in writing.

After that first time it became a monthly practice to go to Akhtar Husain Sahib's house to collect instalments of his memoirs, *Gard-e-Raah*. Professor Anjum Azmi and Mohammad Ali Siddiqui too would now accompany us. In addition to collecting the instalments we would enjoy some wonderfully interesting and informative conversation. Moreover, each time we were treated to an elaborate repast. In those days the cook in Dr Raipuri's employ was one who had worked for Prime Minister Liaquat Ali Khan, and both the food he prepared and its layout and decoration were quite exceptional.

Akhtar Husain Sahib would sometimes be seated in the lawn and sometimes in his drawing room. The conversation would begin. He was a widely read man with an extraordinary memory. Well-travelled and experienced, he had spent years in France and Africa at a time when people here knew very little about those places. He would recount anecdotes from England, Germany, Iran and Spain. He had close friendships with important personalities of the subcontinent. From a very young age his exploration of knowledge had taken him into its obscure and esoteric pathways, which few writers have ever known. His insights and analyses were therefore very accurate and his thoughts lucid. He had complete command over Sanskrit, Arabic, Persian, English, French, Gujarati and Bengali, while Turkish and German were no strangers.

In his early youth he was immersed in the environment of Calcutta, which was the seat of modern knowledge in India. Revolutionary concepts were coming into being. Akhtar Husain was one of the few writers and intellectuals who had the opportunity to study socialism directly from the publications which were its first sources. Moreover he was exposed to company such as the principled, practical, and exemplary personality of Maulvi Abdul Haq, and these people left an agreeable stamp on his life. Akhtar Husain's article *Adab aur Zindagi* was the first piece of documentation in India to set down the theory and fundamentals of Progressive literary criticism, and it is improbable that any other work, subsequent to Hali's *Muqaddama-e-Sher-o-Shayari*, influenced Urdu criticism as much as did *Adab aur Zindagi*.

In 1936, before the Progressive Writers' Association came into being, Akhtar Husain prepared a 'proclamation' in connection with modern literature which carried the signatures of Maulvi Abdul Haq, Munshi Premchand, Pandit Jawaharlal Nehru and Acharya Narendra Dev. This document was another testimonial to Raipuri's insight and prescience.

He left for France before the Second World War. In Paris he made the acquaintance of writers and intellectuals such as Andre Malraux, Jean-Paul Sartre, Russia's first Nobel Laureate Ivan Alekseyevich Bunin, Romain Rolland, Francois Mauriac, Khalida Adeeb Khanum and Alexander Kuprin. His sources of information about Stalin were exiled Russian writers. What he gained from reading Western newspapers like *Le Monde, Le Figaro, Observer, London Times* and *New York Times*, were knowledge and ideas of which subcontinental intellectuals of the period were unaware. Consequently, when Akhtar Husain highlighted some principles, close-minded Progressives in this part of the world were displeased, and rumours were circulated about him. However changing times have borne witness in his favour. He was indeed a man of extraordinary insights. Being a historian as well as a man of letters, his vision spanned the past, present and future simultaneously. His analyses were always scholarly, objective and scientific, and there was never any hint of emotionalism and superficiality in them.

Among his regular visitors was the intellectual and poet, Aziz Hamid Madani. The latter was a relative as well as a compatriot. After Akhtar Husain lost his eyesight, Madani used to spend most of his time in his house. Akhtar Husain's son Salman acted as his father's eyes, reading out newspapers and books to him. Madani had translated French poetry and wanted Akhtar Husain to write an introduction for his compilation. I am told that there was some progress on the project, but neither Madani nor Akhtar is alive now to tell the tale.

When *Gard-e-Raah* was published it was enthusiastically received. People had read the instalments in *Afkar*, but they were interrupted on account of Akhtar Husain's failing eyesight. The book comprised whatever had been serialized, and its publication was celebrated with a function where it was launched. *Afkar* brought out a special issue on Dr Akhtar Husain.

Autobiographies are not new to Urdu, and many have been published in the language. Josh Maleehabadi's *Yadon ki Barat*, Ehsaan Danish's *Jahan-e-Danish*, Dr Yousuf Husain Khan's *Yadon ka Karwan*, Mirza Adeeb's *Mitti ka Dia*, Ishrat Rehmani's *Ishrat Fani*, Aal Ahmed Suroor's *Khwab Baqi Hain*, and Hameed Naseem's *Namumkin ki Justuju*, are all works that were well regarded, but *Gard-e-Raah* had a distinctive style and quality, while the episodes it described were all its own. There is in it a harmony between the writer and his times, offering a canvas in which the times are manifested in all their reality, while the presence of the writer who is no mere chronicler of events, can be felt as a thinking mind and a compassionate, humane and conscientious heart between the lines.

Mr Nazeer Ahmed of Punjab Book House is not just a bookseller; he is also a discerning and alert reader, and possesses a superior taste in books. He read *Gard-e-Raah* as soon as it came out the first time, and thought highly of it. The second edition of *Gard-e-Raah* was also published by Maktaba-e-Afkar, and even that is not available. While Akhtar Raipuri was still alive, Nazeer Sahib had expressed to me the desire that if Sehba Sahib was not going to publish the third edition of the book, he would be happy to do so. However matters were postponed, one of the reasons being that Dr Raipuri had informed me that he was dictating to someone material which was to be included in the book. Shortly thereafter, on 2 June 1992, Dr Raipuri died. Nazeer Sahib again expressed his desire. I took him to see Hameeda Bhabi, who immediately agreed to the scheme. However I stipulated that she should write a piece for the third edition, giving it a proper conclusion, a task for which death had not allowed time to the author. Also, with her in the picture there would be no uncertainty about the authenticity and legitimacy of the volume.

Hameeda Bhabi is an exemplary woman. By observing her and listening to her conversation one gets an idea of how closely her heart and her mind were tied up with her husband. Some poet has declared that 'No husband is a hero to his wife'. Had he met Hameeda Bhabi he may have been forced to revise his opinion. In no time at all she had written her piece, every word of which is witness to the love she bore to the entirety of her husband's personality and art. Said Nazeer Sahib, 'If some more of Dr Sahib's writing could be found, the new edition would gain in importance.' His sincerity bore fruit: when Hameeda Bhabi began to look through Dr Raipuri's papers she found the work he had dictated with the intention of including it in *Gard-e-Raah*. It is now a part of the third edition.

On 8 December 1989 Dr Raipuri had dictated with sadness, 'No writer is happy when concluding his last work; in fact he feels the kind of sorrow one endures when losing a dear friend for ever.' He then dictated some episodes.

On 14 December 1989 he dictated the date and the title of his next essay, In Memory of Faiz, but the opportunity for penning his impressions under it never came. However, whatever material has been secured is a memento of him, and helps to elucidate his thoughts, the state of the subcontinent, and changes in the world.

The events Hameeda Bhabi has described in 'In Memory of Akhtar' highlight many aspects of Dr Raipuri's personality: his habits, his aversion to property, his humanity, his great love of music, his determination, contentment, self-respect, his sea of knowledge and his courage and dignity in the face of death. They are all qualities that proclaim their possessor to be a great and noble individual. We hope that in future Hameeda Bhabi will be writing more about her husband, and will see to the uncovering and compilation of more of his works—such as his letters—that will shed light on other aspects of his personality.

Seher Ansari
23 December 1992

In Memory of Akhtar

Seher Ansari Sahib, you are being very unfair to me! You have stipulated that you will take on the responsibility of publishing the third edition of *Gard-e-Raah* only if I write something about Akhtar in it. How can these hands and this pen produce anything worthy of *Gard-e-Raah*? It is only my longing to see the third edition of the book materialize that gives me the courage to pick up my pen.

All of you have generously and with much respect acknowledged Akhtar's contribution to literature and society. All I can add to this is my observation of the numerous aspects of his personality that were hidden from the public eye. It was against his temperament to discuss his personal life with anyone. Neither I nor the closest of his friends were ever admitted into those innermost chambers.

There are people who on occasion publicly accused him of being hostile to religion, of being a communist, etc. When such rumours reached him, he would laugh and say, 'To speak one's mind is the birthright of every individual'. Akhtar was immune to such talk.

Akhtar was a true believer, for there was no contradiction between his speech and his actions, whether in his religion or in his humanity. He considered that socialism if practiced correctly was the cure for human suffering. He was no pessimist; on the contrary, he believed in the enhancement of the world and of the human being. His humanity and love for humankind was apparent, in the highest degree, from every aspect of his life. He followed the constructive path, both, in his thoughts and in his actions. He respected and honoured those who were older than him, and his kindness to those who were younger was such that he treated them as his equals. During all the vicissitudes of life experienced by him, me, and our boys, he was like a great shady tree, enveloping all of us in his fragrant being. He treated his sons and their numerous friends as though they were his equals. He chose the middle path whenever there were discussions; his arguments were characterized by depth of thought and a universal breadth of view, so that his interlocutors were won over, with no misgiving of being imposed upon or influenced. When they left his presence, they invariably carried with them new ideas and plenty of food for thought. In his speech he would quote poetic couplets aptly. Moreover, he possessed a deep understanding of history, philosophy, the literatures of several languages, sociology, economics, the fine arts and many other fields of knowledge. In addition he had studied in depth various religions, especially Islam, and always impressed his listeners with his well-grounded and measured conversation.

He was never impressed by the worldly status of anyone. For him the criterion for greatness was goodness, quite independently of religion, age, or education. He treated people of lesser status as well as his servants with humility, and as equals.

He used to fast frequently in Ramzan, though less often after he lost his eyesight. However on the 7th and 27th of Ramzan, dates on which the death anniversaries of his brother and father fell, he never neglected to fast. On Eid-ul-Fitr and Eid-ul-Azha he would be the first to get ready for prayers. He looked good in the black *sherwani* and black cap he wore on those occasions. The servants and our boys would accompany him to the mosque for the Eid prayers. On last Eid, for the first time I was superstitious when he was taking his four sons and his grandson Shakir for Eid prayers. My mother never let her five sons and my father leave by one door. I too tried to stop Akhtar and the children from leaving together, but Akhtar only laughed at me and my fears.

In his day-to-day life, Akhtar's personality carried the stamp of Maulvi Abdul Haq. This was reflected in his custom of carefully planning every step that he took in his life, and in his habit of taking regular morning walks and exercise. Even towards the end of his life, when he did not have to go anywhere in the morning, he would get ready and come to the breakfast table punctually at eight, as though he were going to his office. In the afternoon he would change his clothes and listen to the radio. At 4.30 p.m. he would take a bath and change again. By 5 o' clock he would leave his room, have tea, and go for a long walk. By the time he returned, his visitors or the children's friends would be waiting for him. He would be the centre of their attention. Such interesting conversation would follow! Sometimes the children and their friends would have heated discussions; but Akhtar would have an answer for each one of them. He would go to the source of the problem and take it from there. He would analyse the reasons for a conflict and its likely consequences. His vision penetrated deep into the future about which his forecasts would generally come to pass.

For several months he had been deeply affected by the breaking up of the Soviet Union. Restlessly, he wanted to write something on the reasons for the break up, and for a long time he continued to discuss it. When Sardar Jafri came from India on his last trip, I sat listening to the exchange of views between the two of them. Akhtar said to him, 'As you know Jafri Sahib, for a long time I have been taking a dim view of certain practices, and as a consequence everybody was displeased with me. Now look what has happened.'

'You tell me that,' replied Sardar Jafri, sorrowfully, 'Why has it all happened and how?'

In Akhtar's view a deep conspiracy against socialism had existed for a very long time, and its true beginnings, going back into the past, needed to be grasped. He would say, 'I wish I could write about it, or find someone who could write it down for me. It is necessary to write about this tragic event right now. If time is allowed to pass and history takes over, things are never recorded as they happened.'

Sardar Jafri then read out the poem he had composed on the disintegration of the USSR. Akhtar was enraptured.

Akhtar never told anybody that he was blind, always that his eyesight had weakened. He avoided going to see people, or presiding over meetings. Whenever I insisted that he go out he would reply, 'Why don't you understand? When people see me helpless they will pity me. I don't like that.'

However there were occasions when he would go, perhaps because he thought he was fulfilling a moral duty. He always spoke extempore, whether addressing meetings, giving lectures or making speeches. His utterances would be models of precision and brevity, yet they carried great weight for they invariably provided his audiences with food for thought. He was gifted with exceptional powers of retention. If he read something even once, it would be secured in that computer of a mind that he possessed. One could converse with him for hours on history, whether of Asia, Europe, America, China or Japan. He would span centuries, from the past into the present, providing dates as he went along. He could discuss for hours, music, whether of the East or the West. Mention of tourism delighted him, and he could recount the strangest facts and episodes. When the conversation turned to food, he could hold forth on the cuisine of different countries. About the religions of the world he was well informed in the highest degree. When he spoke on spiritualism, Islamic jurisprudence, or mysticism, great religious scholars would listen to him quietly. Many times, I have witnessed occasions when after an international conference people from different countries would be seated at dinner at the same table; for example an Indian may be seated next to a Pakistani, who would be flanked by a Bengali and facing a Frenchman or an Iranian. Akhtar would carry on a conversation with them in all their four languages with such fluency that I would be astounded. Sometimes, in a mischievous mood, he would speak to an Indian in high-flown Hindi studded with an inordinate number of Sanskrit words. The poor man would comprehend nothing, and finally plead with Akhtar to speak in everyday Hindi. Akhtar would laugh and say, 'In your country Hindi is being loaded with so many Sanskrit words that the poor public is bewildered. They can comprehend neither radio programmes nor television news. They cannot understand even their textbooks.'

Akhtar loved animals. His pets included many kinds of birds, parrots, pigeons, dogs and rabbits. At one time he had a tortoise as well. He would pray from 5 a.m. to 6 a.m., and then go out to feed the birds, throw food bit by bit into the fish tank and watch the fish eat. He would give the dog his milk. Like Maulvi Sahib he would make the morning cup of tea for himself. Gargling with salt water, morning and evening, was another habit that came from Maulvi Sahib. The habit of reading until he fell asleep persisted to the end. There was a book by his pillow every night. His hand would be resting on it and he would be listening to the radio as he dropped off. He used to say that to assess a person one should observe how he treated children and animals, and what kind of relationship he had with his neighbours.

His endurance and self-control used to astonish me. Once, in Somalia, the Indian Ambassador was dropping us home. First Akhtar sat in front, then the Ambassador shut the door, got in, and started the car. Akhtar's thumb was caught in the door but he said not a word. When we got down at the gate of our house and the car with the Ambassador drove away, Akhtar fell unconscious on the road. The bone in his thumb was broken, and the flesh was like mincemeat. The UN's doctor was called, and he took Akhtar to hospital. The next day when I asked him, 'Akhtar why didn't you say your thumb was caught in the door?' he replied with a laugh, 'I don't want the Indians to think that we Pakistanis lack courage.'

He observed the utmost simplicity in his dress and his daily life, and I abided by the dictates of his temperament. Everybody who came to our house must have noticed how simply it was equipped.

All his life he enjoyed entertaining his friends. Whenever they came to our house, I used to personally cook the food. Earlier, he used to organize music parties either at home or in a ship standing in the harbour. He went to concerts, ballets, and plays, and took a deep interest in the museums of whichever country he happened to be posted in. Mountains, the sea, forests, and waterfalls put him in such a happy frame of mind that for many days he would talk about them. He often expressed the wish that he were a warden in an African jungle and so had the chance to spend his life close to nature.

He hated owning property. In 1948 when I had a large, two storied mansion on Britto Road allotted for my school, I showed him the allotment order from the Chief Commissioner and the key of the house, saying, 'My tiny home school will now become a very large one. Here is the allotment order. I have already sent some of the furniture there.' His face was ablaze with fury. He took the document from my hand, and tearing it up, threw it away with the key. He said, 'Go and return these pieces of paper and the key first thing tomorrow morning. Have we come to Pakistan in order to plunder it?' Alarmed by his fury I did as I was told the very next day.

When orders were issued for G.M. Syed's arrest, he arrived at our house in the dead of night, wrapped in a shawl. He introduced himself, and told us that he was going to be sent to prison, perhaps for a long time. He added, 'I have come to you with this request: I own a large printing press on Bunder Road. Please take it. Whatever I have read and heard of you makes me certain that you will put it to good use. It was my ambition to bring out a newspaper, but you can create a better newspaper than I. I have stocked enough paper for a year's publication needs.'

Akhtar refused to take the press. G.M. Syed said he would come again the following night so that Akhtar would have a chance to think over the offer and change his mind. I opined that he take it, since it would give him a chance to fulfil his dream of bringing out a paper.

My suggestion infuriated him, for he said he found it unthinkable to take advantage of somebody who was in dire circumstances.

G.M. Syed came again the following night, but once more Akhtar expressed his inability to oblige him. The poor man went away, depressed.

Sulaiman Sahib was the Chief Engineer of the Pir Elahi Bakhsh Colony Scheme, when the scheme was established. He was a close friend of my father. When he came to visit my father he said to me, 'Why don't you book two adjacent houses. If the dividing wall is knocked down you will have one large house.' After I had acted on his suggestion I told Akhtar about it. Furious, he raged 'God protect this country if people like us begin to usurp the rights of those whom the government could not give a house to live in. Go and tear up the membership forms you have filled.' It made me feel ashamed of what I had done, and so once more I obeyed his command.

During the days of Ayub Khan, when the last date for entering claims was announced I filed claims for Akhtar's father's house in Patna, his orchards, and land. When I gave them the forms to sign, both Akhtar and his brother Shameem were enraged. 'We came to Pakistan out of our own free will. Why should Pakistan have to pay for it?' They wouldn't listen to my pleas, and so, seeing their angry reaction I tore up the claim forms.

Once when Akhtar was away on an official tour, I bought a thousand yard plot near Urdu College. On his return when I told him about it, he was so angry that the land was sold off within a few weeks. For some time after that episode he would shake his head and say, 'How could you do such a thing when we already have a house to live in!' Despite the mortification I suffered, I made a similar mistake yet again. When commercial plots were being offered in Block 6, I had one allotted to us. When he found out about it, Akhtar promptly returned the allotment papers, but did not bother to retrieve the allotment fee that had been paid.

Akhtar was fully in control of his thoughts and his speech, as well as his habits. Five years ago, at his doctor's bidding, he gave up his sixty year old habit of smoking cigarettes; and he never mentioned a cigarette after that. He liked food to be of the highest quality. A minute drop in quality was immediately noticed, and the cook was summoned for an inquiry and instructions session. Yet he himself ate very little.

When he was in hospital for ten days, during his last illness, although he had lost large quantities of blood through his mouth, and three fourths of his intestine had been eliminated during an eight-hour operation, as soon as he regained consciousness it was as though he had woken up from sleep. Blood and oxygen were being supplied to his body, but in the midst of it all if a friend or acquaintance came to see him, he would talk to him of matters that interested that individual. When the visitors were poets, and asked after him, he described his condition to them in numerous couplets of poetry. The night he died, he was reciting Persian mystic poetry to his son and explaining the meaning of it until an hour before his death. After his operation when he was not allowed even a drop of water, he never asked for a drink. And finally, on 2 June 1992, a great man departed this life and went to meet his Maker.

At this moment, I am reminded of Akhtar's last sentences in *Gard-e-Raah*: There is now no difference between dreams and awakening. When I look at the sky at dawn, the morning star smiles at me and whispers 'The Greek myths are right in supposing that when the spirit leaves its earthly attire it takes the form of a star in the heavens. Come close to me, you burnt out star, a place has been chosen for you.'

Hameeda Akhtar Husain
12 November 1992

Preface

بیا ورید گر ایں جا بود زباں دانے

غریب شہر سخن ہائے گفتنی دارد

If there is one here who knows the language, bring him
For this stranger in your town has much to tell.

The Ismaili Imam, Hasan II once said to his followers, 'Today is the Day of Reckoning. Come, let's don shrouds, and prostrate ourselves before the Lord of the Judgment Day.' He then preached a sermon to them, bade them rise from their prostration, and announced, 'You are now reborn. You are free from the restraints of the overt, common religious laws, and a new charter of laws has been created for you.'

This century too has seen the rise of many an Imam, who created great upheavals. Living through those upheavals, how far have we arrived from our starting point!

کفن بیار تو تابوت و جامہ نیلی کن

کہ روزگار طبیب است و عافیت بیمار

Bring the shroud and dye your garments blue (the colour of grief),
For time is the physician and well-being the patient.

When the day is ending, there is darkness before us, time lags behind, and the past wraps itself around our feet like a shadow. At the age of sixteen, I left my home to pursue knowledge. It is only now that the voyage has ended and one may sit back, brushing off the dust from the road. Every individual is usually wrapped up in himself. Nevertheless, whether consciously or unconsciously, he absorbs much from his age and environment. My friends insist that once again I pick up my pen, and write down the story of my life. I hesitate to comply because I am by nature a private person, and don't like to make the world my confidant. Yet, like others, I too am a witness to my times. I have confidence in my observation and reading, and have associated with many movements and personalities who have influenced the world in one way or another. The spectacles I witnessed through my interest in nature and history, the political and cultural gatherings of the East and West with which I became acquainted, and my experiments in thought and action, all of these are matters not lacking in interest.

When Buddha was nearing the end of his life, he asked his disciples, 'Is there a question that I have not answered?' One of them replied, 'You've told us everything, but the mystery of what there was before the Creation of the universe and what will happen after death, is still unsolved.' Buddha said, 'Man does not have the key to this secret. His lot is only to understand and solve the issues of this transient life.' As Karl Marx said, philosophers have thought hard enough about life, the real issue now is how to change it.

How insignificant is our earthly life compared to the vastness of infinity, and how short is our time on earth in comparison with perpetuity! Hundreds of thousands of years ago, either through the agency of miraculous creation, or evolution, a two-legged animal was created on earth, who spent all his time in satisfying the demands of hunger, sex, and the lust for land. The story of this struggle is known as history, most of which has melted into mankind's unconscious, and his essential disposition, while whatever remained was secured in the writings and inscriptions of a few thousand years. So what is the sum of it all? In the words of Gibbon, author of *The Decline and Fall of the Roman Empire*, 'History is indeed little more than the crimes, follies, and misfortunes of mankind.'

The present age too is writing its history in the same ancient tradition. Man is so mired in the clashes of religion and views, the struggles of colour and race, the conflicts of class, and national and linguistic prejudices, that the veneer of civilization has been washed away and he lies prone in the domain of life where his earliest forebear had found himself when he left the Garden of Eden or his cave in the hillside.

However, two pillars remain in the midst of this devastation for the building of humanity. They are democracy and communism. Great sacrifices have gone into erecting them, and the future depends on their continuation. Democracy means people's control over government, and communism means people's command over the means of production. The two concepts are interdependent. The primary aim of both is the welfare of the people. My mind rejects democracy dominated by capitalism in the same way as it discards communism controlled by dictatorship of any kind. There is no fundamental contradiction between the two systems, and if an inconsistency is visible the reason for it is that contrary to Karl Marx's prognosis, communism was established not in advanced industrial nations but in backward agricultural ones. Industrial countries have a preponderance of people who are workers in either the physical or mental capacity, so that the question of suppressing them under a dictatorship does not arise.

History is the appraisal of man's struggle in every direction, and current politics is a mere portion of it. All my life I have approached my studies from this perspective—not just my studies, this approach has been central to all my thoughts and reflections. Awareness of history reveals the impulses that drive personalities and movements, and bestows on the mind insight into the future. A chronicle of past events that is devoid of it is no more than history's raw material.

But does not some logic direct the process of history? Does evolution take mankind stage by stage in the direction of a pure idea, as Hegel would have it, or in accordance with Karl Marx's view, does it take it towards a classless paradise, to get to which mankind must pass through a revolution, which is like traversing a bridge as fine as the blade of a knife, and then halt in the purgatory of dictatorship? And is the rise and fall of civilizations an act of perpetual rotation, as Toynbee suggested? According to the religious view of life it is none of these; rather, history is a drama depicting the continual conflict between good and evil, the culmination of which will be manifested in the form of the Judgment Day which is being heralded by underground nuclear explosions acting as the trumpet of the angel of death announcing doomsday to the world.

Ignorant of the secrets of the beginning and the end, a spectator of the world as it exists at this point in time alone, what answers can I supply to these questions?

سنی حکایتِ ہستی تو درمیاں سے سُنی
نہ ابتدا کی خبر ہے نہ انتہا معلوم

I heard the chronicle of life from the middle
I have no knowledge of what happened in the beginning, nor what the end will be

Man's greatest invention is language; and literature, whether prose or poetry, is the creative expression of it. Ever since my childhood I have been interested in literature, and my proficiency in several languages enabled me to satisfy this interest.

The development of a language is tied to the progress of the society in which it is employed. To conceptualize the progress of the society we need to evaluate it, and to do so is the function of prose. When we speak of the backwardness of a country, it is not only the economy that we mean—it is much more than that. Analysis shows us that the root of the problem is mental apathy. The cause of this is the evasion of analysis.

The Oriental mind in general and the Islamic mind in particular, have been harmed by Islamic jurisprudence and poetry, owing to the fact that the one put an end to the ability to analyse and the other stopped the expression of criticism. The vocabulary of poetry is limited, because it is not the vocabulary of the wakeful mind, but of the world of dreams. Its purpose is not to converse, but to whisper. As long as invention was confined to tribal and agricultural societies, the melody of poetry could be mistaken for music; it could claim to be the intimate of God, woman, and nature. But when, a few centuries ago, the age of modern science began, and with it industry and the media came into their own, the world of meaning expanded to such a degree that the scope of poetry became shrivelled, to the extent that from the middle of the twentieth century until now, no language of the world has produced a great poet.

This is not true in the same degree of creative prose, because only in prose can the account of the skeletons in civilization's dungeons, and its chained prisoners be given. If we see little of such narratives in Urdu, the main reason for it is the partition of the subcontinent, for it took place just as Urdu prose was nearing its finest moment.

The truth of the matter is that this is the age of decline for literature as it is for all other arts. Much has been written on the reasons for this. In my view, unlike scientific knowledge, art does not depend for its progress on evolution, which is to say that art does not advance with time as scientific knowledge does. Epic poetry was taken to its summit by Homer 3000 years ago, by Valmiky 2000 years ago, and by Firdausi 1000 years ago, and they have never been surpassed. Who can vie with Kalidas in the immortality he conferred on the beauty of nature as he captured it in words 1500 years ago, or the status Hafiz bestowed on passionate love six hundred years ago? When will a sculptor like Michelangelo or a painter like Rembrandt be born again? The gist of what I am saying is that art, including literature, is not a captive of time, and is not bound by the principles of logical progression that apply to scientific knowledge. Another way of putting it would be to say that scientific knowledge is a boundless ocean, on whose shore stands a scientist as peerless as Newton, lost in wonder. And, art is a mountain range in which there are peaks of various heights. The range of mountains has become shorter until it is level with the ground.

Another viewpoint is that the ability to create never dies, but the modes of expression become poorer with time. When the classical tradition in art reached its pinnacle, and could grow no further, Impressionism and Expressionism endeavoured to take its place, but in a very short time, when their resources came close to exhaustion, the connection between shape and line, voice and music, word and meaning broke, and we have now entered an age of no music, no colour, and no meaning.

There are other reasons also for this disintegration. When God became displeased with man, and man with Him, poetry fell from the height of perfection where Rumi had taken it. When woman descended to the level of ordinary humans and the West not only divested her of her veil but also of her garments, the mystery that had woven a spell of beauty and love around her could hardly remain intact. Similarly, when crushing despotisms in the present age seal the pen, who will voice the burning cry of the individual and who will pay heed to it?

It is true that I cannot hear the silence of the night, nor can I see what lies beyond the horizon in some transcendental world. Joy, that is the harvest of life, I cannot put into words. Yet I can see clearly those problems of human life that have been mentioned above.

Thirty years of my life were spent in education and related activities. This phase began in 1942, with a professorship at the MAO College in Amritsar, and ended in 1972·when I retired from my employment with UNESCO. During this period I served as Assistant Advisor for Education under the British government of India, as Deputy Advisor, Education, in the Pakistan government, and as Advisor, Education, to the governments of Somalia and Iran in the capacity of a UNESCO Representative. Over this period I had the opportunity to make a good deal of constructive input in the course of carrying out my duties.

The function of language is to make the animal a rational being. The purpose of education is to make the animal a human being. The awareness that ignorance is a curse not only for the individual but for society, is not new. What is new is the view that it is the duty of the state to compel every citizen to be appropriately educated, and make the necessary arrangements for this. The rule of compulsory primary education was put into effect in some Western countries about one hundred years ago. The need for it arose due to the demands of the industrial revolution. Before this, society paid little attention to education, for only the rich, the scholars and the nobility indulged in it. As a matter of fact it would be correct to say that education was a means to preserve intellectual dominance over the masses. In Hinduism, the laws of Manu dictated that molten lead should be poured into the ears of the lowest caste who dared listen to the Vedas, while in Greece and Rome eternal ignorance was the destiny of the slaves.

Nowadays every state acknowledges that education is the birthright of an individual, and every government arranges for it according to its own perceptions. In other words, the kind of education that is imparted is basically a political decision. The curriculum is seminal to education and the whole structure of the educational system is shaped by it. How many qualified people are needed every year for the advancement of society and what role they are expected to play, how much knowledge can be assimilated at every educational level, and at what level can pure literacy and primary education be said to end; all these matters are judged in the course of preparing the curriculum. More important than the curriculum is the teacher, but the efforts of the school are of no value without the assistance of the family and environment of the student.

What can one say of developing countries which lack experience in curriculum-making, suitable textbooks, and conscientious teachers, when even in developed countries where these resources are not wanting, the educational system is facing a crisis? There are many reasons for this: one reason is the growing ambition of individuals in burgeoning populations. Other reasons are, the conflict between individuals and society, students' disregard for parental and pedagogical control, the custom of seeing financial gains as the main purpose of education, etc.

Education is imparted through the medium of language, and its benefits are either more or less according to the scientific and literary capital the language possesses. Everybody loves his mother tongue but choosing it as the medium of instruction should be a rational rather than emotional decision. One reason for the fact that newly independent African states are already on the first rung of progress in a matter of twelve or fifteen years, is that they voluntarily chose to adopt English or French rather than their backward tribal vernaculars as the medium of education.

I have come to the conclusion that the world is most harmed by semi-literacy. If from the very beginning the educational system is unable to mould the mind in such a way as to incline it towards the service of society, individuals will remain caught in egotism, a spectacle that we see all around us. Much can be learnt from the experience of communist countries in this regard.

In Urdu, my literary reputation began with the short story, *The Tongue of Speechlessness* (published in *Nigar*, 1933). The story commenced with the following words:

'I am an old banyan tree. I have been standing alone and silent for an immeasurable period of time, calm and restless, speechless and full of song. Countless times have I pushed aside curtains of mist with my leafless branches during bitterly cold winters, and cried out my plaint. How often indeed have the scented breezes of spring sent tremors through my numb body! But now for some days in the past, wrinkles have appeared on my face. I have become insensible to physical sensations. Winter and summer have become one for me.'

It is ironic that I had the boldness to write the story of old age in my early youth; and now, when I ask my pen to chronicle the past, I am not sure for how long this aggrieved friend will accommodate me.

When it stumbles, I soothe it, asking it to assist my memory, but to decide for itself what is worth mentioning and what is best left unsaid.

یادِ ماضی کے ابھی نقش بہت باقی ہیں

حافظہ دِل کی طرح زُود فراموش نہیں

There still remain many images from the past
Memory is not as fickle as the heart

Dr Akhtar Husain Raipuri

It is said about Al Mansur, the vizier of the ruler of Andalusia, Abdur Rahman III, that whenever he returned from a campaign he would shake off the dust from his garment into an earthen pot. At the end of a life spent in combat, when he died, the accumulated dust from the pot was sprinkled over his shroud.

Where can I find so much dust from my own path in life? But whatever there was has been shaken over these pages...

1

The Early Years

When I peered into the enchanted realm of my memory, I found some of my earliest years smiling, some weeping and some, bewildered.

I was born on 12 June 1912, in Raipur, a town in the Central Provinces, India. The population of this town is now almost three hundred thousand, and because of its proximity to the Bhilai Steel Plant, not only has it become a centre for industry and commerce, it even has a university. It was very different in my childhood. The population of the town was then not more than forty thousand, and it boasted no industry; it did not have even electricity. There were no more than five or ten motorcars and as many telephones in the whole town. There were two high schools, where the medium of instruction was English. It need not be added that nobody had ever heard of the radio or television.

Most of the population consisted of Hindus, who lived in separate neighbourhoods according to their castes. There were eight to ten thousand Muslims, most of who, had come to Raipur from north India and Mysore or Madras, in search of employment or business, and settled there. They were comparatively more prosperous and educated, and among them there were some landowners. Due to their long rule, Muslims still commanded some respect, and if an influential Muslim happened to visit the market, the shopkeepers would stand up and bow in greeting. Although the two communities showed tolerance towards one another, their style of living was vastly different, and because of the Hindu belief in untouchability, there was little social interaction between them. Yet they participated enthusiastically in each other's festivals. Lamps were lit in many Muslim homes during Diwali, and Hindus joined in bringing out the traditional Muslim *tazia* procession during the Islamic month of Muharram.

My father, Syed Akbar Husain, came from an old family of Patna. He had been educated at the Aligarh College and the Thomson Engineering College. When the work of constructing a canal began near Raipur, he found a good position there in the department of waterworks. Then he married my mother who hailed from the same place. My mother, Mumtazunnissa was highly educated by the standards of the day. Despite the strict *purdah* that she observed, she had full command over English, Urdu, and Hindi, and her articles used to be published in magazines such as *Tehzeeb-e-Niswan*, and *Zebunnissa*. Unfortunately, she died at the age of twenty-six. I was then just three years old, and my brother, Muzaffar Husain Shameem was three years older.

The two of us had inherited two villages and ample property in the town from our mother, the yield from which was enough to support us. But taking advantage of our father's absence from the scene, our relatives used age-old tactics of misappropriation to deprive us of much of our property. Yet about half of it remained while we were growing up in Raipur.

The responsibility of bringing us up was shouldered by our loyal *ayah*, Peeran Bi, who was generally known as Bari Bi. Beheshti Mian, another old servant, looked after outdoor household chores. When the relatives from my mother's side of the family appropriated our property, my father broke off relations with them, and instructed us two brothers to stay away from them. Consequently, we remained unfamiliar with the environment that is known as 'family life', and we learned to know life not as it is lived inside a home, but outside it.

Awareness came to me at the age of four, when Father went to Patna on long leave, and took us with him. Our ancestral home was beyond Patna, near the Begumpur railway station. It was an old-fashioned, two-storied house, built on a hillock. On one side of it flowed a stream that joined the gushing waters of the Ganges, a few miles away. On the other side of the stream was a long line of mango orchards, some of which belonged to us. In front of the house were rice fields, dotted with toddy-palm trees. My grandmother lived with her maidservant in the house, while a male servant called Pooran looked after the fields and the orchards.

A boat used to be tied in the backyard of our house, and unknown to my grandmother, we would sneak out with Pooran once or twice a day for a boat ride on the stream. It was, in short, an altogether enchanting environment. And then when the monsoons came, land and water became as one. People began to say that the Ganges was going to flood, and the neighbours began to collect and store rations and fuel. Sleeping in an upper storey bedroom, it seemed to me that a gigantic animal was creeping toward me in the dark. When I woke up the next morning and looked out of the window, I saw the water from the Ganges spread everywhere, as though a boundless sheet of water had covered the earth. Since our house was built on high ground, the water could not enter it, but in many other houses the water had free passage. For about two months, every house looked like an island, and people used their boats for transport. Even shopkeepers laid out their merchandise in boats and floated from door to door calling out their wares.

What could be a more absorbing spectacle for a child? But I found the atmosphere in the sitting room more enjoyable, where Father used to either play chess with his friends all day long, or discuss with them the events of the First World War, which was then (1916–1917) raging. Meanwhile, a boy called Sadroo would grill kebabs on skewers, roast jackfruit seeds, or pour tea into cups from the samovar, and offer these to the gathering.

Almost a year later, on our return to Raipur, the thought of educating us occurred to Father. In line with tradition, I was first admitted to a *maktab*, whose administrator was Maulvi Mohammad Yaseen. After the *Baghdadi Qa'idah* had been taught to me, lessons in the Quran were commenced. A few days later I suggested to Maulvi Sahib that he should tell me the meaning of the Arabic text as I had not understood anything. This enraged Maulvi Yaseen who replied, 'People far greater than you have not understood the Word of God, how can you expect to comprehend it?' His answer did not satisfy me. My nature is such that I cannot accept a claim unless I understand it. Therefore I refused to go to the *maktab*. This episode became the talk of the town, and people said that because Akbar Husain had studied at Aligarh, he was emulating Syed Ahmed's 'nature' philosophy, and his son was following in his footsteps. My father parried these accusations by saying that his son would learn about religion when he grew up. And he was right.

Reacting to these events, my father put me in a primary school where the medium of instruction was not Urdu, but Hindi. The reason he gave for this was, if Hindus were willing to learn Urdu and Persian, why should Muslims hesitate to learn Hindi or Sanskrit? Subsequently, my instruction in Urdu and Persian came not from a school, but from my brother.

The method used in the education of those days was so effective that I still remember everything that I studied then. Primary schooling comprised the first five years of school. The teaching of English began in the fifth year, because in the six years of high school all instruction was in English. As soon as I became proficient enough in Hindi, the love of reading took hold of me like lunacy, and I became possessed by the need to look for books to read. My father was usually away on official tours, so I occupied his empty room, and browsed through his books. His books were mostly in Urdu and beyond my grasp at the time. However the thick English tomes had some attraction for me. I could not read them, but found their pictures beautiful. The colourful maps in the atlas especially, delighted me. I would look through its pages for hours, wandering all over the world in my childish imagination. I had no inkling then that much of my adult life would be spent in travelling. The incomprehensible text of the dictionary too was interesting because of the many pictures that were scattered on its pages.

I used to spend all of my pocket money in the only bookshop that stocked Hindi books. Its owner was an ironsmith, who for some unknown reason had accumulated piles of books, which lay next to piles of implements of all sorts. All the books had stories, poems, songs, and plays, printed on cheap paper. In no more than two to three years my mind had ingested all this material, and the ironsmith told me appreciatively, 'I have nothing more for you now. The library in the old temple is the only place in the town that can satisfy your passion for reading. The temple priest opens it every evening, and he alone can help you in this.' I lost no time in acting on the ironsmith's advice. My urge was such that I set off for the temple alone, late in the evening.

Situated near a pool at the end of the town, close to some lonely bushes which hid the ruins of an old fort, the temple was glittering in the light of many lamps. Inside it were statues of gods and goddesses with garlands of fresh flowers round their necks, who fixed me with their stony eyes. Screwing up all my courage, I entered the part of the building on which a sign indicated that it was the library.

I had never before seen such a large collection of books. They were all arranged neatly in cupboards, and seemed to beckon to me. I immediately recognized the priest because he sported the *tilak* on his forehead, and was sitting on a chair, writing something in a register. When I went and stood by him he looked at me questioningly.

He showed his appreciation of my habit of reading by saying that a child as young as I had never been there before, and then when he heard the name of my maternal grandfather, a well-known lawyer of his day, he commented that I had inherited from him my zest for reading. The priest allowed me to borrow one book at a time from the temple library, a privilege that gave me the feeling that I had discovered a treasure.

I rarely played with my friends after school. More often I would sit on the rim of the well and talk of things I had read about, to a rapt audience of playmates. The sessions ended when their elders came looking for them. I would then hasten to the library, preoccupied with the idea of finding my next book. Naturally, most of the books I read were about magic, or feats of detection. But some had to do with history, and these were my special favourites. During this period I read Napoleon Bonaparte's biography. I was so impressed by Napoleon's determination and courage that I read the book again and again, yet was not satisfied. The fact is that until that time the scope of Hindi literature was limited and it did not offer enough material to suit a serious taste.

About this time, a certain incident changed the direction of my reading. I was twelve years old and in the seventh grade. Our school had a decent library, which contained books in English, Hindi as well as Urdu. Pupils who liked reading would by turns help the teacher organize the library. When it was my turn, a parcel of Urdu books happened to arrive, and the teacher, who was a Bengali Hindu, and thought that I might be able to read them, told me to copy their titles in the register. The task unnerved me, because I had lost touch with Urdu after I had finished with the *Baghdadi Qa'idah*. Fifteen or twenty books emerged from the parcel. Their calligraphy and printing were very clear, so much so that when I looked at their titles I was able to read them without difficulty. Words cannot describe my delight. I copied the titles in the register, and taking the books home with me, I threw my schoolbag on the floor and sat down to read the books. The writing was so clear that I read it effortlessly. My happiness at this success was like that of a victory on the battleground. My brother was astonished at this feat, and said, 'You can read Urdu. You should now pay more attention to it.'

My interest in Urdu grew strong because there existed a much greater body of literature in Urdu than there was in Hindi. By the time I was doing my Matriculation, my Hindi was so strong that my articles were accepted for publication in magazines. In 1928, my first short story, 'Parajit' (defeated, vanquished), concerning Nawab Sirajuddaula, was published in the renowned Hindi magazine, *Madhuri*, which was published in Lucknow. A successor of Munshi Naval Kishore had published this magazine after his death. He was the same person who persuaded Munshi Premchand to start writing in Hindi.

By now my command of Urdu also had become so strong that I was caught for helping my fellow students in answering the Urdu paper during the annual examination. However, I escaped punishment because I was a student of Hindi and Sanskrit.

The standard of English in our school was high. The Anglo-Indian headmaster, Mr Tombay had graduated from Cambridge. The school comprised eleven grades, of which he supervised the teaching of English in the last three years. The course included two of Shakespeare's plays, one of which, I later discovered, was part of the college curriculum in Calcutta. In the last three years of school the national and classical languages were relegated to a secondary position, and English acquired the central and most important role. Consequently I was drawn to English, and my fascination with the language grew as I discovered that here was a language that held within its ambit the whole world of knowledge and literature. And so when in 1928, at the age of sixteen, I passed my Matric examination with distinction, I had a good command of English, Urdu, and Hindi.

When the First World War ended and peace was announced in 1919, authorized celebrations of Britain's victory were held all over India. Rewards were rained over the loyal servants of the Raj, prisoners were released, and cities and towns were illuminated. Lines of schoolchildren congregated in parks, where sweets were distributed among them. An airplane began to circle in the sky above the town, and because nobody had ever seen such a spectacle before, men and women left their houses and came out to gaze at the sky. Old people were saying, 'It's the flying carpet, mentioned in ancient stories'. They were not prepared to believe that the plane was a modern invention because they were convinced that there was far more learning and civilization in the olden days compared to modern times, and that in those bygone days men knew all there was to be known. The caretaker who worked for the English Deputy Commissioner of the town did not believe that the telephone in his employer's room was merely an instrument for transmitting the human voice. He insisted that Sahib was given to talking to himself under the influence of drink, while sitting in his room.

Nobody could have imagined that from this darkness of mental backwardness would rise a wave of political awareness that would shake the foundation of the British government. But on the one hand the Congress initiated the Non Co-operation movement under the leadership of Gandhi, and on the other hand, led by the Ali brothers, Muslims rose to protect the Caliphate. In no time the two movements had mingled, and for some time Muslims and Hindus attained a unity that they were never able to achieve later. From one end of the country to the other, people could be seen waving flags and heading towards meetings or processions. Newspapers, magazines, pamphlets, and posters, produced in heaps, began to sing praises of nationhood, and versifiers and speechmakers created such a turmoil that the British lost their nerve. A new word, 'boycott' entered the dictionary. Along with foreign goods, the 'boycott' of offices and educational institutions became common. The tumult was such that even our sleepy little town was jolted. The 'national volunteers' type of individuals began to frequent the railway station on the off chance of glimpsing one of the leaders in a passing train. Women brought out and cleaned old spinning wheels, and in compliance with Gandhiji's instructions, began to spin yarn. Wayfarers began to carry spindles instead of sticks, and in social or cultural gatherings, love poetry was replaced by patriotic songs. I too joined a group of students who demonstrated feats of callisthenics regularly every morning after the *fajr* prayers. Public meetings were held in Gol Bazaar early in the afternoon. Ever so often I would give speeches there, under either the Congress or Khilafat Committee banner. Adult males could not enter a gathering where

purdah-observing ladies were present, so I was chosen to deliver the
messages of Home Rule and Khilafat, and collect contributions.
Meanwhile leaders of varying status would arrive in the town and were
treated with much hospitality. In proportion to their eminence, they
would be seated on an elephant, in a carriage, or a cart pulled by oxen.
On such occasions our throats would go hoarse shouting slogans. Like
everywhere else, the police would arrest the active workers and
conduct them to jail. Flowers were then rained on those workers as
though they were on their way to be wed. So, from a very early age I
acquired a taste for politics, which lasted a long time.

Despite his government job, my father was interested in politics. He
used to buy the journals, *Al Hilal* and *Comrade*, and subscribed
regularly to nationalist daily newspapers. He used to camp on the
banks of the Mahanadi, thirty or forty miles from the town, and would
come home once a week. After spending hours poring over the
newspapers, he would spend the evenings in discussions with his
friends. Our family had a long tradition of hating the British. My
ancestor, General Mir Madan, was martyred in the battle of Plassey, in
the year 1757. My grandfather, Syed Shujaat Husain was a young
man during the War of Independence in 1857. Fearing for his life, he
went into hiding for a few years, and when, contrary to his wishes, his
two sons opted for education in English, he never forgave them.
Therefore it is understandable that since he was barred from taking
part in active politics on account of his service under the British
government, my father was intellectually if not physically involved with
nationalist politics. News of his predilection used to reach the
establishment. So, in 1921 when he secretly attended a Congress
meeting in Nagpur, informants carried the news to the authorities, and
my father was interrogated. The matter dragged on and caused such
unpleasantness that my father's promotion was stopped. Shortly after,
my father opted for early retirement as a protest. What happened next
will be recounted further on.

For some years the country was caught in a storm. People in their
hundreds of thousands were sent to jail, and hundreds more were
martyred; yet no political movement can be sustained for long on
fervour and passion alone. Since the Turks themselves had bidden
farewell to the Caliphate, how could Indian Muslims save it from
termination? How was it possible for every individual in the country

to practice Gandhiji's philosophy of non-violence? So it came about that when, tired of the government's tyranny, people attacked a police station in a village called Chauri Chaura, Gandhiji suddenly stopped his movement. This started an era of political confusion, which not only destroyed Hindu Muslim unity, it also created confusion in the Congress for some time.

However, there is no doubt that Gandhiji's movement had a far-reaching effect, and it awakened a society that had been asleep for centuries. It began to be said and written that it was not just the landlords who had rights, but that the peasants too were entitled to them. The numerous untouchables of our province, who had always been crushed by those belonging to the higher castes, began to look for ways to free themselves from their oppressors. Word went round that in large cities like Calcutta and Bombay industrial workers were going on strike. There was the strange news that in Russia industrial workers had formed their own government. Educated young men in the town began to criticize Pandits and Maulvis. New issues were given expression in the literatures of the indigenous languages. In a word, old values, that had been considered eternal, began to be gradually denuded. About this time I happened to read Bertrand Russell's and Ingersol's writings, in which they had denied the existence of God. When I told my father about this, he explained to me that these were matters that could not be borne out by logic. The real issue was to find the best course for humanity to follow, and true knowledge concerned the discovery of this course.

I was now almost fifteen years old. Unconsciously I felt that the environment I was in did not have an answer to my doubts. I would lie on the charpoy long before it was night, and gazing at the sky for hours I would ask myself questions such as when the universe had come into existence, and what was the purpose of life. I did not know at the time that these questions had exercised men from the very first, and perhaps they would never find their answers. However man could, if he so wished, find a purpose for his own life.

The town had no cinema or theatre, but now and then an itinerant group of entertainers would arrive and put up their show in a tent. Sometimes an American comedy or thriller was presented, accompanied by a storyteller who loudly narrated the story of the film as it was shown, adding to it vivid and dramatic dimensions of his own. The era of the talkies had not yet begun.

About the same time, the Indian movie, *Alam Ara* was made. It became such a rage that the whole town went to see it.

As the popularity of movies grew, old pastimes died out. People used to be fond of cockfighting and quail fighting. There were plenty of pigeon fanciers. Every neighbourhood had as a minimum one arena, where every boy was expected to spend at least some time. Teahouses and sweetmeat shops were frequented by carefree young souls, but the more colourful among them thronged the shops of the betel leaf vendors, accompanying their tall tales with rolls of betel leaf or puffs of *biri*. The storyteller, Shehbaz Khan, would sit among them and begin recounting the endless tale of Amir Hamza with such gusto that passers-by would stop to listen. I too would sometimes go there and laugh uproariously along with others at the exploits of Umro Ayyaar.

Muharram and Ramadan used to be celebrated with as much zest as the Hindu festivals of Holi and Diwali. On the special days of Ramadan, Muslim youths would sing special *sehri* songs, making their rounds with gas lamps in their hands. And every evening during *iftar*, the mosques would be full, and humming with activity. Muharram used to be observed in the Deccan tradition. Hindus would join the Muslims in lifting the *tazias*. They would also participate enthusiastically in the processions known as *savari* that would be streaming down, amidst a multitude of lights. Some caretaker of a shrine, in a state of religious ecstasy and holding a faceless image wrapped in silk and brocade, would head in the direction of the fire that had been lighted in the open ground outside the town, early in the evening. He would stride into the blazing fire, walking through it as though he were strolling on a cool street, while rapturous spectators raised deafening slogans of 'Husain, Husain'. During Muharram, many enterprising spirits dressed up as tigers, that is, they wore loincloths and painted their bodies to resemble the beast, and presented war dances at the beat of the drum. For ten days there was an atmosphere of festivals and entertainment alongside the mourning, which is difficult to imagine now.

Holi was an extraordinary festival. When Hindu men and women squirted coloured water at each other, rubbed one another with a red powder, and came out on the streets, the more serious Muslims would hide in their houses. But children of my age would take part in the fun uninhibitedly. When evening fell everybody would take their bath and collect at the crossroads, where the Hindu shopkeepers had arranged a dance show, and a feast to which everybody was invited. The intoxication of hemp enhanced the pleasure from the song and dance of Holi. The fact is that these pursuits of the past were far more innocent and attractive than the artificial amusements of the present era.

When I was in secondary school and my brother was a student of matric, the town's first *mushaira* was held. You could consider it an expression of the Muslim bent of mind that suddenly a number of poets materialized. Among them was my brother. He had written his first *ghazal* for the occasion, and chosen Shameem as his nom de plume. After this, poetry held him in thrall and he was lost to the rest of the world. The result was that he failed his examination, and Father sent him to one of his friends in Calcutta to study.

I have mentioned the reasons that persuaded Father to opt for an early retirement. I was so lost in the world of books and ideas that I did not realize the importance of this event. Nothing had changed in the house, but I missed my brother, and my father would spend many months with my stepmother, who lived with my grandmother in our ancestral home in Patna. Too late I came to know that Father had spent much of his pension funds and savings on obtaining a contract for a forest of cotton trees. He was a man of very simple temperament, and was utterly ignorant of the complexities of trade. Moreover he was credulous in the extreme and trusted people indiscriminately. For such weaknesses of his character we had to suffer the consequences, along with him. As he had handed over the management of the Patna property to a hired manager, so he entrusted the administration of our village also to an agent. He then followed the same pattern for the cotton forest, and as a result he sustained such losses for three years that he was left penniless.

After my brother Shameem had left for Calcutta, Father told me, 'You have never seen your village, Parasti. Such property is lucrative only if one lives on its precincts, but I was not able to live there. The income of a few hundred rupees that came from it has been spent on the two of you. However it is now time to collect the annual revenue, and since you have to manage the property yourself one day, you may as well go there now with a servant.' And so I set off unwillingly for the village, which was 25 miles from the town, travelling on a bullock cart and accompanied by Behishti.

Next morning we reached a small town, where Abdullah, an acquaintance of my father, lived. He used to manage our village as well as a few others. He welcomed me warmly and told me that the landlord should never arrive in his village before his tenants had been informed of his arrival. So he sent his messengers to the village to announce our arrival and accompanied me there in the afternoon. We stopped near a cluster of trees where he pointed to the ground and said, 'Your property begins here.' As far as one could see there were rows of huts, and lush, green fields spreading out in every direction. At a short distance from them was a pool of water, by which stood a small temple, hiding some idol in its lap. A group of impoverished peasants was waiting for us near the temple. When their headman or *mukhia* advanced towards us, Abdullah said in an authoritative voice, pointing to me 'This is your master'. When he heard this, the man bowed down at my feet, but I immediately raised him. However, my humility could not prevent the peasants from expressing their devotion in the traditional way, and they bowed low in front of me. The truth is that at that moment I was more ashamed of my elevated position than their misery and vulnerability. The *mukhia*, Mangal, then proceeded to deliver a speech, the gist of which was that my mother's death had orphaned her subjects, but they were happy to see that her successor, and their new protector, was now old enough to understand their problems. When he had finished his speech, Mangal went to the village pavilion and brought the sum of money that had been calculated for the revenue, and handed it to me. The peasants then began to tell me about themselves and their problems, in their dialect.

The dwelling where Grandmother or Mother used to stay when they came to the village was neglected and rundown. The peasants promised to repair it so that I could come and stay there.

It was after I went to Calcutta that I began to reflect on the troubles and tribulations that beset human beings. With that my empathy for my peasants grew. When they and Abdullah realized this, they began to evade making revenue payments to the government. Things came to such a pass that twice during my stay in Aligarh I had to pay the taxes to the government from my own pocket. You could call it negligence or impracticality, but the outcome was that the property became a pain in the neck for me.

My dearest friend was my classmate, Basant Kumar. When as a child he was orphaned, his grandfather had assumed the responsibility of bringing him up, and had left Bengal and begun to practice in our town. My friend and I used to seriously discuss issues that engaged mightier brains than ours, and believed in our naivety that we could find solutions for them.

Our matriculation exams were over and we were waiting for our results. My friend told me that about 150 miles north of the town there was a mountain known as Amar Kantak, from where the river Narbada emerged, and after a journey of eight hundred mile, flowed into the Arabian Sea. Thick forests covered the whole region, and scattered among them were the ashrams of many sadhus or Hindu holy men. Some of these sadhus were saintly and sagacious. It was Basant Kumar's suggestion that instead of remaining in the town during our two month long holidays, we should spend the time in the forest. If we liked it there, we would remain there, and if we did not, we could always come back. I liked the idea so much that the two of us boarded the train straightaway, and without informing anyone at home, set out for the forest.

We had heard that the forest started immediately after the station named Champa, and we could get information about the sadhus there. So we left our bags in an inn near the station, and went and sat in a sweetmeat shop. Rows of tall trees extended before us, as far as the eye could see, and the mountain peaks were visible despite the mist. The impression that this loveliness of nature created, sensitized me to natural beauty for the rest of my life.

The shopkeeper gathered from our conversation that we had come, like many others, on a pilgrimage to the sacred river Narbada. He therefore explained the way to us in detail, and informed us in the course of conversation that Swami Parbhoo had a camp on the banks of a certain lake, eight miles away; that along with his disciples, the Swami had been engaged in meditation for a long time, and that he had become famous for his miracles and marvels. The very day after we heard this piece of news, we set out in the direction indicated. After much exertion we found, under two mighty banyan trees, the abode of the old sadhu, who was sitting on his prayer mat, deep in meditation.

After greeting him we sat down on the grass nearby, overcome with fatigue. Stroking his white beard, the sadhu watched us attentively for some time. Then he said, 'If you wish to pay your respects to the deity Narbada, you will have to travel for two more days. If you like you can stay the night here.'

We replied, 'We have come to see you, and have no intentions of travelling further, at the moment'. We described our feelings to him and when he was convinced that we were students he gave us permission to stay at the ashram.

Whether or not we learned anything from the sadhu, the impression left by our few weeks' stay in the jungle stayed with me for the rest of my life. It was my first experience of lying on a mat, covered by a blanket. In the dead of the night, amidst the endless chirping of crickets and perpetual murmur of a waterfall, the screams and roars of wild beasts created an atmosphere that caused sleep to flee from our eyes despite our exhaustion. We used to spend most of the day wandering around in the jungle, and though we were but uninvited guests, we were assured of food, handed to us on banyan leaves, and in addition, we received wisdom and counsel from the sadhu.

One day, the sadhu told us that human life could be divided into four ages. 'The first age,' he said, 'is the time when one seeks knowledge. It is the age that you are passing through. The second age is when one gets involved in all the turmoil of matrimony. To deal with the responsibilities thus acquired, a man has to spend most of his life in worldly pursuits. Finally the time comes when his children grow up, and neither the world needs him, nor does he need the world. If he is wise, he can then say good-bye to everybody and head for the jungle, and spend the rest of his life in search of reality.'

'Does that mean that real knowledge can be achieved only after renouncing the world, and not while one is a part of it?' I enquired. When the sadhu confirmed this view, I said, 'What is the use of knowledge if it remains confined to an individual, and the rest of the world cannot benefit from it?' The sadhu replied, 'You are still at the first stage of acquiring knowledge, so you are not yet ready to give the world anything. When you do have something to pass on to the world, you can decide what you want to keep for yourself and what you want to share with others'. It was much later that I understood the meaning of what he said.

At full moon, a month later, the sadhu's disciples brought the news that there was going to be a fair near the railway station the next day. Shopkeepers and spectators would arrive there from far and wide. 'We should all go there to collect donations for our ashram,' they said. So the next day, early in the morning, Basant Kumar and I dressed ourselves as mendicants, and accompanied the others to the fair. The little hamlet had come to life with hundreds of marquees and tents that contained all kinds of wares for Hindu travellers and spectators. Singing devotional songs and holding begging bowls in our hands, we were walking in the direction of the police station in the company of eight or ten other youths, when somebody called out, 'Those two seem to be the boys who disappeared from Raipur and whose pictures were distributed everywhere'.

Hearing those words we panicked, but before we could make our escape, policemen gripped our arms. They brought out file pictures of us and identified us, and dismissed all our protests by saying that we had not yet come of age and therefore had no right to do anything that went against the wishes of our elders. And when we were conducted to our homes in the custody of the police, dressed as mendicants, the news spread, and for a long time after, it was the talk of the town.

This episode was the beginning of my literary life and search for truth. On many later occasions too I found godly people meditating in the solitude of forests and monasteries, on those arcane matters which the Creator has hidden behind myriad veils, and which none have so far been able to unravel.

The first university in the province had been established that very year, and the matriculation examination had been conducted under its management. When the results came out, I had passed, as expected, in the first division. I had been waiting eagerly for my result as I had decided to go to Calcutta for a college education. My brother Shameem had gone there already, and when he learned of Father's financial problems, he began to work for the daily, *Asr-e-Jadeed*.

The day on which I communicated the good news of my matriculation result to my father was a trying day for me. For months he had been sitting alone and silent in his room. I was so foolish and inexperienced that I comprehended neither his anxiety nor the reason for it. When I informed him of my result, he smiled at first, and then suddenly stopped smiling. Signs of anxiety appeared once more on his face, and he asked, 'What do you want to do next?' I was somewhat taken aback at this question, and answered, 'I have only climbed the first rung of my education; to study further I would have to go abroad.'

Sadly he said, 'That is what I had hoped too, but at present I am not in a position to help you. However, if you can manage the property that your mother has left for the two of you, the problem can yet be solved. So far I have guarded it for you, but to develop it is beyond my powers. I have no intentions of staying long in this town. Once you leave I have no bonds with anybody here. Muzaffar has the temperament of a poet, and he is not interested in these issues. So, it is now your duty to manage what is yours, and release me from this responsibility'.

Stunned, I stared at my father. Managing a property and shortage of money were concepts that could not have been further from my mind. So, I said to him in reply, 'Please let Abdullah continue to discharge this duty, as he has been doing, and allow me to go to Calcutta and try my fortune there. Father handed me two hundred rupees and said, 'Use this for the present. God willing I'll find some way of helping you in the future.' The very next day I left for Calcutta by train.

This happened on 26 June 1928. My father himself handed the full management of the property to the agent, Abdullah, and went to live permanently in Azimabad (Patna). Aware that it belonged to a couple of orphans, Abdullah wrecked our property so completely that it became a burden for us, and so in 1937, when I decided to go to Europe, I sold it off at a fraction of its value. The psychological impact of this episode was such that in Pakistan we never put forward a claim for the small piece of ancestral property in Patna, that belonged to Father.

2

Memories of Calcutta

A short street called Nawab Baduruddin Street branches off from Zakaria Street in Calcutta. On the third floor of a four-storey house in this street, three friends rented and occupied three adjacent rooms. The three young men were, Muzaffar Husain Shameem, Chiragh Hasan Hasrat, and Saleemullah Fehmi. I spread my bedding on the floor in my brother's room, and when I could not find a pillow among my bedclothes, I wrapped a towel round a dictionary and putting it under my head, was immediately lost in thought.

I had no idea that my life was taking a new turn. The quest for a livelihood was something I had never heard of, and the past was so close that I could touch it—not with my mind but with my hand. My past held few imprints of love and warmth, however the thought of Bari Bi often interrupted my reflections. I had left instructions with Abdullah to see that she did not lack a home, a maid to look after her, and an adequate supply of money. Now and then the laughter of some dear friends mingled with memories of temple bells, and shepherds playing the flute, to convince me that my world had changed forever.

As evening fell, my three elders arrived one by one in the house, bringing with them two others, one of whom I knew. The two newcomers were Mahfoozul Haq and Najeeb Ashraf Nadvi, who, after taking their Masters from Calcutta University, were engaged in research with their teacher, Sir Jadunath Sarkar. Later, both became famous professors. Najib Ashraf's father Dr Mubeen Ashraf used to practice in Raipur, and was my uncle Dr Asghar Husain's class fellow. On account of this connection, Najib Ashraf was fond of us two brothers. His younger brother, Ali Ashraf, was married to Maulana Suleman Nadvi's daughter. The Maulana had come to Raipur once or twice, and later, whenever I met him in Aligarh or Karachi, he treated me with much benevolence.

It was a good omen for me that on my very first day in Calcutta I met such lovers of art and literature. All of them treated me like a younger brother and guided me in the early days. By extension of the same relationship somebody requested me to make tea for the group, adding the promise that, 'We'll eat at the Rangoon Restaurant after tea'. Made nervous by the demand, I answered frankly that I had never made tea in my life. All of them laughed, and Fehmi Sahib showed me how to light the stove, boil the water, and add the right amount of tea leaves for each cup of tea.

Rangoon Restaurant on Zakaria Street had a standing similar to what the Arab Hotel in Lahore or the Coffee House in Bombay used to have. Its owner was an Iranian and the restaurant used to be thronged with poets and Urdu and Persian writers. On the same road was situated the Amjadya Hotel, in the upper storey of which the office of the Khilafat Committee bore witness to the fact that the Muslims of India were still suffering from the same weakness of memory that they had been demonstrating since the thirteenth century, when thirty years after Halaku had destroyed the Abbasid Caliphate, the Friday sermon was still being read in the name of Mutassim Billah in the mosques of Delhi. The President of the committee in those days was Huseyn Shaheed Suhrawardy. The office of the Committee as well as the rest of Amjadya Hotel used to be abuzz with political gossip. Later, whenever I needed to fill some leisure hours, I would head for the Rangoon Restaurant, where I enjoyed the company of the young Iranians who used to relate gory episodes of their country's unsuccessful revolutionary struggle. In the same place I became interested in Iran's culture and poetry. From the time of the East India Company, until then, a fairly large number of Iranians had been living in Calcutta, along with traders from other foreign countries. Many of them had literary and scholarly tastes. The most dominant figure among them was Mueedul Islam Jalaluddin, who was well known in the world of Islam as a friend of Jamaluddin Afghani and the editor of *Hablul Matin*. Although he was blind he was much respected for his political, as well as general acuity.

The serious type of Muslim intellectuals used to collect at the Muslim Institute. Now and then I listened to Maulana Wahshat, Salahuddin Khuda Bakhsh, and Nawab Nasir Husain Khayal speak there. However it was Maulana Azad's custom not to go anywhere, except for Eid prayers. Twice a year he used to lead prayers in the Chorangi Maidan. Agha Hashar Kashmiri too never went anywhere except to Mukhtar Begum's house. With the passage of time I somehow gained self-confidence, and began to seek out and meet these venerable gentlemen in the course of my pursuit of knowledge.

There was an extraordinary attraction in the environment of the Rangoon Restaurant, and now and then one met exceptional characters there, the like of whom I never again encountered. I remember Humayun Mirza well. He used to live in Matya Burj, and had seen the days of Wajid Ali Shah. His father had landed in Matya Burj with the last ruler of Oudh. Humayun Mirza was much advanced in age, but stronger than his faith in the purity of his lineage was his belief that the fairies of Caucasia had fallen in love with him. In the course of his opium-induced intoxication, he would tell such tales about the Lucknow court, and the old houses of Matya Burj, that Iranians and Indians, customers and employees alike would listen to him in hushed silence, and break out in spontaneous applause. It is said that before the First World War, when Maulana Mohammad Ali used to publish *Comrade* from Calcutta, and Hasan Imam practiced law in the same city, Humayun Mirza joined their circle of friends on the condition that they would vouchsafe him an income of 1000 rupees every month, so that he could maintain the style of life that he was accustomed to. However if he uttered something that was incorrect, he would have to pay a fine. His fine amounted to 900 rupees a month on an average, and after deducting this sum, he was paid 100 rupees a month, regularly. He was an admirer of the Lucknow school of poetry, and wrote excellent verses in that style. It is a pity that I acquired a taste for such things rather late, because at the time a good deal of material was available on Humayun Mirza and the ruined culture of Matya Burj. I remember just one couplet of Mirza Sahib:

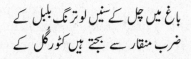

Let us go to the garden and listen to the chant of the nightingale
Struck by beaks, the flower-bowls tinkle

Matya Burj is now an industrial neighbourhood, but in those days, despite its decrepit state, it still retained a glimmer of old Lucknow. Here and there in the crumbling houses, miserable scions of wealthy families eked out a living on meagre stipends. Here it was that I sought out Prince Jawan Bakht's grandson, Mirza Bedar Bakht, and wrote an essay with the title of 'The last glimpse of the House of Tamerlaine'—a piece of writing that was translated into many languages of India. This happened in the year 1931.

There were some intellectuals among Maulana Azad's followers. Noteworthy among them were Maulana Abdur Razzaq Maleehabadi, Abdullah Misri, and Ishaq Amritsari. They brought out, first, the weekly, *Payam*, and then the *Roznama-e-Hind*, in line with his ideas. I used to meet these gentlemen, and in fact, still see Ishaq Amritsari in Karachi, and whenever we meet we talk about our old friends and the old times.

When I arrived in Calcutta, the *Al Hilal* had gone out of publication a second time. Abdur Razzaq Maleehabadi and Najib Ashraf Nadvi had been part of its editorial board. The magazine, *Aftaab*, in all its splendour, was published for two years under the editorship of Chiragh Hasan Hasrat, and then closed down. The only Urdu journal that remained was Maulana Shaiq Ahmed Usmani's daily, *Asr-e-Jadeed*, and Hasrat and Shameem were both associated with it. Chiragh Hasan Hasrat and Muzzaffar Husain Shameem's journalism hurt their poetry, and their interest in poetry hurt their journalism. If one thinks about it, while the literary flavour that typified Urdu newspapers may have increased their popularity, it also adversely influenced their standard. It even damaged masters of prose such as Maulana Azad, Qazi Abdul Ghaffar, and Maulana Zafar Ali Khan, for events cannot be analysed through the medium of emotions.

Everybody acknowledged Hasrat Sahib's liberal mindedness, boldness and superior wit and humour. I found him consistent in his characteristics from Calcutta to Karachi. His maxim was something like, 'If the environment is unpleasant, banish it from your mind.' In practice he expressed this conviction whenever he heard bad news, by drawing a deep puff on his cigarette, and shaking off the ash with his finger, as though he were getting rid of the malaise. He had a deep appreciation of Urdu and Persian literature. However his taste did not advance beyond romanticism and pleasure seeking. In his room were heaped the novels of Conan Doyle, Marie Corelli, and Rider Haggard, which he bestowed on me a year later, when at the behest of Zafar Ali Khan, he left for Lahore.

Calcutta was the political and cultural centre of India in those days. It took me some time to become aware of this. But what I did comprehend immediately on my arrival there was that it was the most wonderful of cities. Every day I would ride the tram, sometimes to the banks of the Hugli where for hours I would watch the life on the river, or to the Alipur zoo, where I took delight in the gambols of birds and beasts, or to the Victoria Memorial Museum and Art Gallery, where the work of man never ceased to astonish me.

When Calcutta became the capital of the East India Company in the eighteenth century, it became a haven for, first of all, Bengali hopefuls, then Marwari traders, as well as numerous foreign merchants, among whom were Englishmen, Iranians, Armenians, and others. Thanks to Tipu Sultan's progeny, and Wajid Ali Shah, who had been exiled there, education and culture were nurtured, and the elite accepted the responsibility of providing patronage for their culture. Thus, by the beginning of the twentieth century, this city was host to an unrivalled convergence of Eastern and Western cultures. Moreover it became not only the largest centre for publication in Bengali, but was also an important hub for publishing in English, Hindi and Urdu.

I was so engrossed in all that I saw and all the novels that I was reading, that for weeks I was lost to all but their world. My brother did not feel the need to talk to me about this, but one day Najib Ashraf Nadvi told me that one has to be selective in reading. It was not good enough to read anything that fell into one's hands. 'I'll take you to the reading room at the Imperial Library, and introduce you to its Administrator. You can read English effortlessly, so let him help you in selecting the right books. You should now start reading seriously and in a more organized way.'

This library is now the national library of India, and stocks some 1.5 million books. In those days it had 300,000 books, and was even then, the largest library in the country. The discovery of this treasure house of books brought about a dramatic change in my intellectual level, and for years after, I used to do everything in my power to be able to go there everyday. Its Chief Administrator, Khalifa Asadullah, encouraged me greatly. Were it not for the attention that he bestowed on me, I would not, as a student, have gained access to some of the most eminent scholars of the day.

I spent my first few months in Calcutta with the unconcern of one who had no responsibility, and no duty, except to read, and enjoy the sights and sounds of the city. However one day, my brother explained to me that like him, I too would have to look for ways to earn a livelihood. He told me not to expect any help either from Father or from Abdullah. 'Many Hindi newspapers are published in Calcutta,' he told me, 'Go and make contact with them. You have already published some articles in Hindi. If you continue to write, you will be paid for your work, and one of the magazines may even offer you a job. If that happens you may be able to seek admission in one of the colleges next year.'

My brother had a meagre income, and the money that Father had given me could hardly last long. So I began to frequent the offices of Hindi newspapers and magazines. Muslims had been disassociated with Hindi for a long time. A few poets in the past had worked in the language, but in contemporary times none had given any importance to its prose. As a result, when I arrived with cuttings from my published articles, and the manuscripts of unpublished ones, everybody welcomed me. Equipped with a sharp mind and a confident pen, I was able to effortlessly dash off several articles in a month, and leave them with various publications, earning a name for myself in the process.

The most popular Hindi daily, *Vishwamitr*, and the most prominent magazine, *Vishal Bharat*, were both published from Calcutta. The magazine was owned by Ram Anand Chatterji who was renowned as the editor of the English monthly, *Modern Review*, and the Bengali magazine, *Parwasi*. For a long time these magazines in the three languages were admired for their content as well as their extrinsic qualities. Pandit Banarsi Das Chaturvedi, who was a sincere supporter of Hindu Muslim unity, and an experienced journalist, used to live in the rear portion of a building in Circular Road, which housed the offices of these magazines. Munshi Premchand and Pandit Sundar Lal used to stay with him whenever they were in Calcutta. The bonds that I formed with these venerable people never weakened, and their memory is still dear to me. Pandit Sundar Lal brought out a magazine called *Vishwani* from Allahabad, and when he was imprisoned in the political movement of 1942, I was its honorary editor for three years, during the course of my employment at the Amritsar College. The diligence with which I discharged this moral duty, despite financial constraints and the ire of the government, illuminates that chapter of my life.

My association with this institution opened new vistas of knowledge for me. Tagore's works were published there, and the publications of the Greater India Society were also printed there. The most eminent Bengali writers used to be gathered there, few of whom were Muslim. However Jasimuddin and Ghulam Mustafa Kawi's poems did appear in *Parwasi*. It was the time when Qazi Nazarul Islam's fame was at its height. But this group did not favour him.

The Greater India Society had been initiated for the purpose of researching ancient India's circle of influence. It tried to prove in its publications that in the ancient times, Hindu civilization extended all along the Indian Ocean. Pandit Nehru accepted this concept enthusiastically, as is apparent from his book, *The Discovery of India*. After Partition, this same concept became the basis of the Indian foreign policy. I have debated this idea at length in my article, 'The Concept of Greater India', which was published in the English language magazine, *Tempo*.

I have met few people as honourable and liberal minded as Pandit Chaturvedi. He subscribed to the idea of anarchism, and used to propagate the teachings of Bakunin and Kropotkin. Moreover he had no hesitation in condemning every instance of injustice in his writing. He was a supporter of national unity as well. I was so impressed by his human and moral values that I began to visit him frequently. After he had met me a few times, he said to me, 'You write Hindi well, but be sure to stay close to Urdu, and not to Sanskrit. And don't write articles just for the sake of writing them. It is when your work demonstrates that you have studied and observed what you are writing about, that it will be of some value. If you make a little effort, you can learn Bengali as well. It will benefit you to know the language because it has the richest literature among all the languages of India.'

I took his advice so seriously that for almost two years I read diligently, and carefully observed my environment. Nor did I wield my pen needlessly during this period. Later I wrote 'The last glimpse of the Timur Family', 'The poetry of Azmatullah Khan', 'The characterization of the Englishman in Bernard Shaw's plays', 'Oscar

Wilde's socialism, etc. for *Vishal Bharat*. These articles were acclaimed by readers of Hindi. Soon I began to be considered a stylist among prose writers. One of Pandit Banarsi Das's books contains an article on my personality and my prose style.

In the month of November, I was told that there was a vacancy for a junior sub editor's post in the newspaper, *Vishwamitr*. Its proprietor, Babu Molchand Agarwal was held in high esteem in the newspaper world of India. Three editions of his daily paper were published simultaneously from Calcutta, Kanpur, and Bombay, in addition to a weekly and a monthly edition. Later, he bought the English daily, *Advance* as well. During the period of the First World War, his status was that of a multimillionaire. He was a supporter of the Congress policy, and the spokesman for the Marwari capitalist class. Few people had a better understanding of the newspaper business, and everybody admired his acumen and flair for organization. A large mansion on Harrison Road accommodated a printing press on its ground floor, administrative offices on the first floor, and editorial offices on the second floor. Agarwal himself lived on the third and highest floor. The proximity of his living quarters to his office allowed him to keep an eye on every employee and every matter pertaining to his business.

One day, I plucked up the courage to go to his office, and sent up my name on a piece of paper, with the peon. When I was summoned I found myself facing a big, heavy man, who with a pleasant smile indicated that I should take the chair opposite him. He then addressed me, saying, 'I had heard of you, but did not realize that you are so young.'

When I stated the purpose for which I had come, he was startled. It was unheard of for a Muslim to be associated with the editorial section of any Hindu newspaper, let alone a Hindi paper. So, what explanation did I have for making such an application? At first he made some polite enquiries. Then he asked me if I could do a spontaneous translation from English into Hindi. When I replied confidently in the affirmative, he marked three or four local and foreign news items in some morning newspapers, and told me to sit at the corner table and translate them. This was a test that I could pass easily, and I finished it in no time. My handwriting was so clear and well formed, and the text was so correct that Babu Molchand looked at my face and then at what I had written, with astonishment. He then handed me an editorial from some newspaper, and asking me to translate it, said, 'Take the dictionary if you need it.' But I did not need the dictionary and managed to render the piece from one language into another, quite effortlessly. Babu Molchand no longer doubted my ability and he asked me to give him some time to decide.

Later I came to know that Babu Molchand's decision to engage me had been taken against the wishes of the newspaper's editor, Pandit Maya Sevak Patekh. Patekh was strictly Arya Samaj, and it took him some time to accept me. His attitude was not surprising because it must have been difficult to accommodate an individual from one sect into a newspaper belonging to another sect, at a time when newspapers were freely and openly propagating sectarianism. For example, in 1935, when I heard in Aligarh that the newspaper *Hindustan Times*, published in Delhi, needed a subeditor who could write a daily column based on an analysis of the Hindi and Urdu Press, I applied for the post. A few of my articles had already been published in the newspaper, and when Dr Zakir Husain passed on my application to its managing editor, Devdas Gandhi who was Mahatma Gandhi's son and was already acquainted with me, the latter was pleased, and said that he knew of no one who was more suitable for the post. But the proprietor, Seth Birla rejected me on the grounds that he did not like the idea of hiring a Muslim for his paper.

زاہد تنگ نظر نے مجھے کافر جانا
اور کافر یہ سمجھتا ہے مسلمان ہوں میں

The narrow minded ascetic thought I was an infidel.
The infidel thinks I am a Muslim

Iqbal

And so when I was informed, unexpectedly, that I had been hired by *Vishwamitr*, with effect from 1 December, I was afforded at least the distinction of becoming their youngest journalist.

There are two people to whom I am especially indebted for their salutary influence on my life. Babu Molchand, trained me to be organized in my work, while Maulvi Abdul Huq taught me to be methodical in my life.

For a week I was given basic lessons in the principles of printing and proofreading. All of the next week I went through the file that contained the newspaper's back issues for the previous year, and memorized technical terms, for which Hindi did not yet have a dictionary. Now and then I was given practice in writing headlines for some news items.

By then the date for the annual meeting of the Congress in Calcutta, in which the Nehru Report was to be presented, was at hand. At about the same time was scheduled a convention of the different political parties of India The yearly gatherings of the Liberal Federation, the Muslim League etc, too, used to be held during the same period. Babu Molchand, who wished to train me, gave me a press card, and a sash attached to a kurta of homespun cotton, with the name of his newspaper printed on it, and directed me to attend the political gatherings every day for two weeks and report on them orally every morning, either to him or the editor, so that they could form an idea of what I had gleaned from all that I saw and heard.

This was the beginning of my political education.

From the political point of view, this was a period of great mental confusion and discord in India. After the First World War, both Hindus and Muslims had gathered under the leadership of Gandhi and the Ali brothers, and the banners of Congress and the Khilafat Conference. Slogans of national independence and national unity were on every tongue. The movements for non co-operation with the British government and defense of the Caliphate had gathered such strength within a few years that the colonial power had weakened. Like all other areas of life, literature was deeply affected by these developments. But when Ataturk put an end to the caliphate in Turkey, and when the Indian public began to show signs of going out of control, Gandhi suddenly abandoned the non-cooperation movement, unleashing first, a flood of confusion and a sense of disorientation, and then a great shattering of Hindu–Muslim unity. Arya Samaj and Hindu Maha Sabha talked of greater Hindu influence and absorption of the Muslim minority, and Muslims retaliated with calls for discipline within their ranks, and with proselytizing. Hindus played music in front of mosques, provoking Muslims to shed blood. Swords flashed when Muslims slaughtered cows. The same journalists and poets who were encouraging harmony between Hindus and Muslims, now began to fan the fires of hatred. Muslim politics fell into the hands of members of the Khilafat committee still obsessed with the caliphate, while there was so much confusion in the Muslim League that it split into two factions: one led by Mr Jinnah and the other headed by an admirer of the British, Mian Mohammad Shafi. Vexed with Congress, Gandhi shut himself in at the ashram in Ahmedabad. The famous Bengali leader, Chitta Ranjan (C.R.) Das, and Motilal Nehru took over Congress, and demanded seats in the legislative council and constitutional reforms, provoking Pandit Sunder Lal to resign from his post as the General Secretary of the Congress. C.R. Das then died suddenly, leaving Motilal Nehru in sole charge of the Congress.

Britain found this atmosphere so salutary to its own interests that in 1937 it established a commission headed by Sir John Simon, whose task it was to find out how much independence India deserved. Since there were no Indians among its members, the Commission was generally boycotted. The Anglo–Indian headmaster of our school chided me severely for participating in the protest that was organized in Raipur.

After its tour, when the Commission returned to England to frame its recommendations, Congress decided to frame its own constitutional demands, and to this end a committee was established with Pandit Motilal Nehru as its Chairman. Its Secretary was Shoaib Quraishi. Its report was to be studied in the full party convention held in Calcutta.

The two nation theory was yet to be born, and the political debate was conducted on the basis of a Hindu majority and a Muslim minority. It was disappointing that despite his social and cultural bonds with the Muslims, Pandit Motilal Nehru showed no political open-mindedness, and rejected even the legitimate demands of the Muslim delegates. In the session of the convention presided over by his ally, Dr Ansari, the same attitude was reflected. Maulana Mohammad Ali, Shoaib Quraishi and others therefore announced their severance with the Congress right away. The fiery speech that Maulana Mohammad Ali gave on that occasion established him as a great orator. Nobody was a better speaker in English than he, while in Urdu, it was Maulana Azad who possessed that distinction.

It is an irony of history that the possibility of a constitutional adjustment between Hindus and Muslims, which was severely damaged by Motilal Nehru was eventually shattered by his son Jawaharlal Nehru when he smoothened the way for Partition by rejecting the Cabinet Mission formula for compromise. This is a bitter but irrefutable fact.

My immature mind was at the time incapable of comprehending these constitutional points. What left a lasting impression on me was the personality of Subhash Chandra Bose, who, despite his youth, dominated the political horizon. When the Nehru Report was presented for approval at the Congress session, there was a statement in its preface to the effect that the object of the Congress was that India should achieve dominion status in the British empire. Subhash Chandra Bose proposed that this be amended to read that the objective was complete independence. He then lambasted the oppression and tyranny perpetuated by the British so forcefully in his speech, that everybody was aghast. Delighted with his eloquence, Maulana Mohammad Ali kissed the young man on his forehead. Jawaharlal Nehru discreetly put on a façade of detachment. When balloting started, he was allocated the task of counting the votes. At this transformation he was publicly humiliated, and was overheard complaining to the chairman of the meeting (his father) that some people had been badmouthing him. However, the Nehru Report was approved, and Congress split into right and left wings. Afterward, thanks to Jawaharlal Nehru's wavering, Subhash Chandra Bose's departure from the Congress was followed by a strengthening of Gandhi and Patel's conservative hold on the party. C.R. Das, Subhash Chandra Bose, and Chakravarthi Rajagopalachari were the three leaders who were open minded and farsighted enough to have found a way to compromise with the Muslims, but the sudden death of C.R. Das, and the departure of the other two from the party, destroyed any such possibility.

A session of the Muslim League was held in Albert Hall, with Mr Jinnah in the chair. The League was not yet a party with extensive public support, and had been further weakened by the disruption created by Mian Mohammad Shafi. Dr Saifuddin Kitchlew was its Secretary. During my stay in Amritsar I met him frequently, and was deeply impressed by his sincerity. He had by then, rejoined Congress, but Nehru never forgave him for his brief involvement with the Muslim League. After Partition therefore, I found him in poor health and living a life of hardship in Delhi. But despite his adversity, his magnanimity was such that when he received the 100,000 rupee Lenin Peace Prize award from Russia, he gave away the whole amount in charity.

Although Calcutta was always besotted with politics, the mood in those days had intensified into that of feverish excitement. Every individual was carrying a flag and was part of a meeting or procession, while the air seemed to be trembling with the sound of loud slogan chanting. Such was the state of fervour that one day I saw Chiragh Hasan Hasrat on the thoroughfare, crying out,

'There lies the road to freedom, move forward, move forward.'

Gazing intently at something overhead, with his large red eyes, and pointing his finger at it, he was repeating this line so loudly, that for a moment I thought that a woman called Huriyat [freedom] was sitting on the wall! But I understood the real meaning of the word *hurriyat* when I happened to stroll towards the Albert Hall. A meeting of the Mazdoor Kissan Party was in progress there. In those days it was a crime even to mention communism; to organize a communist party was unthinkable. Many Indian youths had gone to Soviet Russia after the revolution, and some of them had returned in order to spread the message of the Soviets. Four of them, viz. Dange, Nimbakar, Muzaffar Ahmed and Shaukat Usmani, had been arrested on the charge of trying to organize a communist party, and had been sentenced to three years' imprisonment in Kanpur, in the year 1934. When they were released from prison, they, along with others of the same mind, organized the Mazdoor Kissan Party, and held its meeting in Calcutta. The explanation of socialism that I heard here, set me on a new path of thought and study. On this occasion I was introduced to Syed Jamal Bukhari, who has been living in seclusion in Larkana for a long time. Last year he came to see me on hearing of my illness. I was very happy to see that despite his eighty years, he had not lost the brightness of his eyes and the crispness of his voice. The hymn to *huriyat* that he sang, along with his friends, went like this:

نقارے پر ڈنکا لگا، تو کدال اپنی اٹھا

شروع ہوگئی ہے حریت کی جنگ تو تلوار اپنی سنبھال

Beat the drum, pick up your spade
The battle for freedom is on, take up your sword

I reflected that their 'freedom' was different from Hasrat's. Theirs had to do with iron weapons such as the spade and the sword.

I now started working in the office every day, from morning to evening. There was no telex in those days, so agents of news agencies would arrive every now and then, bringing envelopes that contained the latest news in English. The senior sub-editor would select some of the items and hand them to me, and I would translate them quickly. I would then turn my attention to the bundles of proofs. It would be no exaggeration to say that my speed of work was so fast that the staff was astonished, and in a few months even Pandit Patekh was praising my work. And then, they readily handed over to me the responsibility of choosing the news stories for the paper, devising headlines and organizing the pages.

At the end of the summer vacations, when college admissions opened, I had myself enrolled at the Vidya Sagar College, since it was close to the newspaper office. Usually people avoided the night shift, but I preferred it because it allowed me to spend time at the Imperial Library. It became my practice to work at the office from eight at night to two or three in the morning. I would then walk the half mile to my house and sleep. By about ten or eleven the next morning I would arrive at the Rangoon Restaurant which was close to where I lived. I would eat there and then take the tram to the library, where I studied seriously and made notes until four in the evening. I would then leave the library, and stroll off in a leisurely fashion in the direction of the college. I put in a cursory appearance at the college, and then headed for the newspaper office. I attended the college only to fulfil the requirement, because I never gained anything from attending classes either there or at Aligarh. I was always intellectually far ahead of others in any class in which I was enrolled. All I gained from any educational institution was the love of a few teachers, and beyond that—nothing.

The next year Hasrat Sahib left for Lahore. Saleemullah Fehmi was selected for the Bengal Civil Service, and Najib Ashraf Nadvi was appointed Professor of History at the Andheri College at Bombay. The following year, my brother Shameem too pushed off to Lahore at the invitation of the newspaper *Inqilab*, leaving me alone in Calcutta. However, I was too busy, and too preoccupied by my thoughts to be troubled by the state of affairs. Such was my unconcern that in more than two years I had not found the time to buy myself a pillow, and had been making do with a dictionary under my head, until my brother pulled it away when he was leaving. Perhaps that was the reason why I was involved with lexicography on many subsequent occasions in my life.

In 1929, the government made the foolish mistake of arresting several individuals with communist leanings. This case became famous as the Meerut Conspiracy, and went on for several years, during which time newspapers published the statements given by the defendants, and through these socialism was propagated in the country for the first time. Socialist literature in English, though not in the indigenous languages, became available clandestinely. Most of it was secretly imported from foreign countries, and some was published locally. My reading, which now extended to Bertrand Russell and Bernard Shaw, was, as a result, diverted in this new direction.

I began to see that the problem of sectarianism was not as superficial as I had always thought. It was rooted at the bottom of a thousand-year history, and it held within it many strands of unity and discord. But the British government promoted discord to such an extent, and encouraged the greed for power so much in its protégé, the nouveau riche class, that Hindus and Muslims began to destroy the common values which it had taken centuries to nurture. Hindu society was responsible for this to a large extent, for not only did Hindus form the majority in the country, they were also locked behind confining walls that hid them from the view of even the closest neighbours. Not just their rejection of ties with outsiders through marriage, but also their belief in contamination, and the caste system, prohibited communal intermingling. But despite these factors, the need of the times was to preserve national unity for the sake of national freedom.

Then, a new side of the picture came into view. Although on the surface it seemed that the root of the conflict lay in differences of religion, culture and language, I arrived at the conclusion that there was yet another fundamental cause for conflict, which had to do with economics. When I compared the residents of tall mansions with the stifled humanity that occupied hutments and footpaths, it seemed to me that they were diametrically opposed to one another. From the socialist point of view this conflict was between masters and slaves, but later I found Albert Camus's explanation that humanity was divided into three groups: masters, slaves, and rebels, more convincing.

I decided to devote my pen to working for human values.

In 1931, Gandhiji once again jumped into the fray of practical politics. Directed by him, Congress began the movement for Civil Disobedience, aimed at forcing Britain into granting constitutional concessions. As a result, the Round Table Conference was held in London, and in 1935 Parliament approved the Government of India Act, under which legal sanctions not only for Independence in 1947, but also for the running of post Independence government in Pakistan were put in place. Hundreds of thousands of Gandhi's followers went to jail, and the government issued an ordinance to curb the heated language used in the press. In protest, the newspapers stopped publication for an unspecified period. As a result Babu Molchand gave all his employees, including myself, a cheque for two months' salary and sent us home.

What happened to me next is an episode worth narrating. In the afternoon of the following day I went to the Allahabad Bank on Harrison Road, to cash the cheque. I put the 150 rupees that I received, in an old envelope, and shoved it into the pocket of my *kurta*. Then I left the bank and started walking down the road. Suddenly somebody pushed me, and before I could recover myself, the envelope had disappeared from my pocket, and the pickpocket was running down the narrow street nearby. I ran after him, shouting, 'thief, thief!' but he had vanished. Several passers-by stopped to admonish me, 'Don't you know that pickpockets lie in wait outside banks?' they said. 'Putting money in your pocket publicly could only lead to this.'

In a short space of time I had become both jobless and penniless. I didn't know what to do, so kept walking, burdened with my new anxiety. At the turning of Chitpur Road was a fruit shop, where Syed Buzurg Shah was present, wrapped in his usual panache. This venerable gentleman was a covert spiritual mentor of criminal gangs, but ostensibly he was a sympathizer of political workers and newspaper journalists. I was acquainted with him. When I told him the details of what had befallen me, he laughed, and said, 'Don't worry. The leader of the pickpocket gang, Chaudhry Panna Sardar, is an acquaintance of mine. I'll take you to see him this evening, and God willing, the money will be returned to you.' So, that evening I accompanied Shah Sahib to Machwa Bazaar on a rickshaw. We left the road to walk through the twists and turns of a network of streets, until we arrived at a mysterious looking house. Shah Sahib whispered something into the caretaker's ear and the latter went into the house and fetched another person. This person led us very respectfully into the house where an imposing person in a *lungi,* with his head covered by a turban, was sitting on the floor, speaking to his followers. He greeted Shah Sahib, and for some time conversed with him in low tones. He then turned to me and inquired at what time and where the incident had taken place, and whether I recalled the face of the pickpocket. While I was telling him the details, I remembered that the thief had whiskers. Panna Sardar ordered someone to find out who he was and whether he had returned from his post; also, whether he had left my envelope, with the money that he had deposited with the treasurer. I was listening in amazement to this exchange, when a short and pitch black person, who was possibly the treasurer, arrived with my property, and placed the envelope before Panna Sardar. The latter then returned the envelope to me, through the good offices of Shah Sahib, saying, 'Babuji, count your money, and don't think that Panna Sardar's men are swindlers.' I was overwhelmed with joy, and lavishly praised the dexterity and honesty of his followers. On our way back, Shah Sahib gave me such an account of their organization that I was astounded. When I expressed a million thanks for the help he had given me, he told me to be careful in future, and never to mention what had taken place to anybody.

An acquaintance of mine, Mirza Hatim Beg, who was a jeweller from Delhi, had been working in Calcutta for a long time. When he heard that I was unemployed, he kindly offered me a job, saying, 'Your troubles will be over if you work with me. I speak no English so I don't take my merchandise to the English jewellers' shops. If you learn some basic facts about gems, and accompany me to those shops, we can make a tidy profit between us'. Consequently, I spent some time with Mirza Hatim Beg, learning gemmology; and still retain the skill I acquired in telling apart real gems from fake ones.

Meanwhile the newspaper office notified me that the government had repealed the press ordinance, and that the publication of the paper was to be resumed. I was directed to rejoin my work immediately. I therefore abandoned the gem business and returned once again to the pen and paper industry.

In the course of describing Matya Burj I mentioned Mirza Bedar Bakht, who was the grandson of Prince Jawan Bakht. Shortly after meeting him I wrote a Hindi article entitled The Last Glimpse of the House of Timur, which was much acclaimed. Up to that point, I had written nothing in Urdu, but at the insistence of friends I translated this article into Urdu, and sent it off for publication to the Delhi weekly, *Riasat*. When the article was published, Sardar Diwan Singh Maftoon, the editor of *Riasat*, offered me, as a token of appreciation, the place of Associate Editor, at a salary of 150 rupees. My salary doubled at a stroke, and this combined with my wanderlust, sent me unhesitatingly to Delhi. However I did not resign from the newspaper, and instead, took a month's leave without pay, so that if all did not go well at my new job, I could return to the first.

Riasat was in those days a much-esteemed newspaper. And there is no doubt that Diwan Singh Maftoon will always be remembered with deference in the history of Urdu journalism. His deputy, Sardar Ali Sabri, was an amiable and noble man, but I lacked the forbearance and patience that are needed for coping with the office environment. Therefore, having made a muddle of accounts and other matters, I wandered off to see the archaeological relics of Delhi, and then, with nothing gained from my exercise in changing jobs, I returned to the newspaper in Calcutta, and sat down in my old place. Agarwal laughed and said, 'You have a mercurial temperament. You will be wandering around all your life, but there will always be a place for you in my organization.'

One day, during some casual conversation with a friend, I discovered that Qazi Nazrul Islam used to visit his home. I have a natural flair for languages, and was by then so conversant with Bengali that I could read Bengali literature without any trouble. When I saw Qazi Nazrul Islam I found his personality so attractive that I felt I would like to see his poetry introduced in Urdu. Between 1931 and 1936, I translated selections from his poetical works, which were then published in *Nigar, Saqi, Urdu*, etc. Later they were collected in a single volume known as *Piyam-e-Shabab*, which went into several editions. The effect these translations had on Urdu poetry of the day is an open reality, and can be witnessed in the works of Josh, Majaz, and Makhdoom.

In this way I came closer to Urdu, and my stay in Aligarh and Hyderabad strengthened the tie. Nonetheless, my link with Hindi continued under some guise or the other, until the partition of India.

However, Urdu should be considered the real axis of my literary services.

The movement for Civil Disobedience was still echoing in the atmosphere, and the bugle of socialism was sounding from Meerut, when Bhagat Singh and his companions were tried for terrorism in Lahore. The spinning wheel, the spade, and the thunder of bombs together mesmerized me to such a degree that I was driven to either hang around the office of the Kissan Mazdoor Party in Dacca House, or discuss terrorism with Bengali friends in the college tearooms. Later, I would stick terrifying headlines on news stories in the *Vishwamitr*.

I was totally ignorant of the fact that Kundan Laal, a companion of Bhagat Singh, and a fugitive, was working with me under a pseudonym. Babu Molchand used to secretly help such people. After working for a few months, he suddenly disappeared, leaving me with a sense of his reticence, gravity, and patriotism. Later, when he was arrested in the suburbs of Delhi, an investigation was started in Calcutta. Since the police were already wary of me on account of my passionate speech and indiscriminate company, and since political workers were being apprehended under the Bengal Ordinance, my well wishers as well as Babu Molchand advised me to leave Calcutta for a while.

This happened in September 1932, when I was already in my first year of Bachelor of Arts. So I left Calcutta reluctantly, and joined the university at Aligarh. Babu Molchand was so kind to me that I could still write regularly for his weekly paper and earn forty rupees a month, a sum that was sufficient for my educational expenses. In addition, I used to go to Calcutta during the summer vacations, and work there for three months for weekly or monthly publications.

Although I had arrived in Aligarh, I never forgot Calcutta. It was hard for me to estimate the value of its contribution to the vulnerable and friendless student that I was. The foundations of my intellectual and working life had been laid on the right lines. Who could predict the kind of edifice that would be erected on them?

3

Intellectual and Literary Directions

The atmosphere of Aligarh was very different from the environment I was used to. Not only were the restraints imposed in the students' hostel a torture, there was also the stagnation that prevailed over the whole institution that was exasperating. There was no dearth of able teachers and intelligent students, but their talents were so crushed into a shell of complacency, that no scientific, cultural, or literary activity worth its name was ever conducted. All everybody thought about was sports, the annual *mushaira*, and the elections for the college Union. Joviality, a facile tongue, and keeping up appearances were considered the essence of culture.

Great Muslims of India had twice lit the lamp of enlightenment. Once when in the reign of the emperor Akbar, the movement for religious tolerance known as Deen-e-Ilahi was launched. The second time was when Sir Syed tried to interpret Islam rationally in the light of the Mutazilites. The goal of both these attempts was to harmonize the eternal values of religion with the demands of the times. It cannot be said that Sir Syed was altogether unsuccessful in his efforts, yet it is true that his objectives were no longer perceptible in the environment of Aligarh University. Education had come to mean no more than obtaining a degree, which could ensure a government job.

Fortuitously, there had gathered in the Aftab Hostel, several independent thinking newcomers, who did not approve of the prevailing situation. So, immediately after our admission into the college, we brought out a weekly newspaper with the title of *Payam*. Since the Calcutta paper of the same name had closed down, I had no compunction in suggesting this name for our paper. On the editorial board were Hayatullah Ansari, Sibte Hasan, Iltafat Maleehabadi, and I. The paper was soon closed down, but not before it had had an impact similar to a stone hurled into a still pool of water. The period of awakening awareness in Aligarh that followed, persisted, although it took different and disparate routes of thought and practice. What we wrote in our youthful enthusiasm I can no longer remember, but the fact is that we did not propagate any one political view or philosophy. All we wanted was that self analysis and freedom of thought should become desirable ideas in the university, and to that extent our objective was achieved. It was not surprising that the penalty we paid for our activities was that we became the target of abuse, but, as the poet has said,

دشنامِ یار طبعِ حزیں پر گراں نہیں

The abuse of the beloved does not weigh down the grieving heart.

However the truth is that the Vice Chancellor of the university, Sir Ross Masood, displayed much magnanimity, and did not castigate us on any count. Perhaps he felt in his heart that no centre of learning could make progress in research and critical thinking without freedom of thought.

Among my circle of friends was Asrarul Haq Majaz. My friendship with him, which began immediately after my arrival in Aligarh, lasted for the rest of our lives.

The Beginning of Majaz's Poetry and his Drinking

When Majaz introduced himself as the pupil of Maulana Ahsan Marharvi, and read out two or three trite poems to me, I expressed my disgust quite openly. I did not try to criticize the language or content of the poems, but said merely that if a poet did not possess the ability to understand and express human concerns, then he did not have the right to address human beings. My forthrightness was unusual for the times, and it startled Majaz. I still remember the expression of dawning comprehension in his astonished eyes. After that he frequently came to see me at the Aftab Hostel.

The two of us would often stroll in the direction of the old fort or the railway station, and I would divulge to him whatever limited knowledge I had acquired (which though it was unsubstantial, was regarded by him as worthy of attention). These conversations lasted over a period of one year. By the end of it Majaz had abandoned the conservative style of *ghazal*. I understood that his creative talent was searching for a new channel of expression. My own creative bent was turning towards Urdu literature at about the same time, and my first short story, *The Tongue of Speechlessness*, had been published in *Nigar*, and earned the approbation of many discerning readers.

Once when the two of us arrived at the station at about sundown, we stopped short in front of a third class compartment. Inside it was an adolescent beauty of the Gujjar caste. Wearing a necklace of silver beads, and brass earrings, and clad in rags, she sat there with such splendid elegance that onlookers were spellbound and the usually raucous vendors were dumbstruck. As the train began to move she threw us an arch parting look, which sent us reeling, and we retraced our steps reciting prayers of benediction. I said to Majaz, 'That was a real princess in rags. Why don't you write a poem about her?' He replied that he had never written a *nazam*, but that he would try to write one.

A few weeks later he showed me the draft of his famous poem *Raat aur Rail* (Night and the Train), which though it did not encapsulate the scene we had witnessed, was definitely influenced by it. That was the true beginning of Majaz's poetry.

About the same time, I met Saghar Nizami somewhere in Aligarh. He used to come frequently from Meerut, and whenever he came, he would search me out.

It was a summer evening in 1933, about to stretch out into a full–moon night. I was strolling with Majaz and Ali Athar in the hostel compound, when a one-horse cart stopped at the gate and disgorged Saghar Nizami. When I had introduced him to Majaz and Ali Athar, he said, 'I have organized a dinner for all of you. There are kebabs, parathas, chicken, and much more. Let's go to the fort and revel.' We welcomed this invitation warmly and left for the fort on the horse cart. At the fort we ensconced ourselves in a secluded spot. Saghar had brought, in addition to many kinds of food, a large slab of ice with beer bottles in it.

I had had beer a few times but did not like the taste of it, either then or afterwards. Neither the taste nor the smell of it ever appealed to me.

But Majaz was unacquainted with its secret. So, when the moonlight spread, Saghar and he began to recite their poetry with abandon, and the beer drinking session began. Beer is only mildly intoxicating, but it is all a question of tolerance for alcohol, and the occasion. Therefore, when at midnight we got up to leave, Majaz was quite drunk, and we had to practically carry him to the carriage and haul him in. Meanwhile, despite our warning, he continued to croon his verses heedlessly. Finally we were at the Aftab Hostel, and Saghar departed. It was decided that Majaz should spend the night in Ali Athar's room, as he was in no condition to face his family at home.

We spent the night in trepidation, for had the hostel administration got wind of Majaz's drunkenness, they would have expelled the lot of us. Finally the next morning Majaz reached home safe and sound. Subsequently the infamy that alcohol brought Majaz, and that Majaz brought to drinking alcohol, became common knowledge. The trembling of his hands and the unsteadiness of his feet would begin with his first cup, and remained to the end of the session.

Majaz has written better poems than *Raat aur Rail*. But the magnitude and shape of his talent became visible in it for the first time. It contains the tinkle of harmony and music that made his work so much the rage. Although it was later that he kept company with Josh Maleehabadi, the influence of Josh's *Jungle ki Shezadi* (The Jungle Princess) on *Raat aur Rail* is quite apparent. However, in later years, despite their physical closeness, Majaz's personality and poetry were not as influenced by Josh as is commonly believed. To put it in Majaz's words, 'Maleehabad could not impair Lucknow.'

Majaz was not on intimate terms with Akhter Shirani, but people like me who knew both well, would bear out that not only in their poetry, but also in their personalities, they were astonishingly similar. Among contemporary poets it was impossible to find any who looked more innocent and deprived than those two. Always in a state of inebriation, both remained in search of some real or imaginary beloved, and when the intoxication of youth was over, the goblet of clay fell from their hands and broke into a thousand pieces. Urdu poetry resounded for a long time with the echo of that shattered goblet.

Some Prominent Personalities

During my stay in Aligarh the teachers whose influence over me lasted a long time, were Professor Mohammad Habib and Professor Rashid

Ahmed Siddiqui. One taught me to appreciate history and the other bestowed on me the correct understanding of classical Urdu literature. Both of them corrected my unruliness with such tact that I never became aware of it.

Professor Habib represented the generation that had absorbed the finest qualities of the oriental and occidental civilizations. Later, I observed the harmony of this cultural merger in Sir Abdul Qadir, Dr Syed Husain, Dr Kitchlew, Dr Tarachand, and some others. Their special characteristics were elegance and liberal mindedness, which allowed for enlightened thought and the freedom to disagree. It was Habib Sahib who was responsible for turning the attention of historians to the pre-Mughal regimes of Delhi. It was at his instigation that the History department of Aligarh University began the organized research into this forgotten period, which continues to this day. His detailed introduction to the new edition of Elliot and Dawson's comprehensive history of the Middle Ages is his masterpiece, and adopts the viewpoint of modern history, which focuses on the life of the common people rather than on those of the wealthy and the powerful.

I was proud of being Professor Rashid Ahmed Siddiqui's pupil during my stay in Aligarh. He was so hospitable that Muslim intellectuals and poets, coming from abroad, used to stay at his house. On such occasions Siddiqui Sahib was sure to send for me. I was already an advocate of socialism, and to put it in the words of Abul Fazl, 'was strolling in the garden of disbelief.' Therefore I did not kowtow to anyone, and did not in the least hesitate to talk on equal terms with Siddiqui Sahib's important guests. They too would enjoy conversing with me because they thought my views fresh. At first, under the influence of the Marxist view, I considered atheism to be an integral part of socialism. But later it became apparent that this was because reactionary trends of the Church had been confused with religion. Besides, Marx was unfamiliar with the revolutionary traditions of early Islam, and the materialist science of the nineteenth century kept him ignorant of the values and realities that have been recognized by modern science.

There was an unrivaled blend of intelligence, nobility, and self-discipline in the personality of Dr Zakir Husain. The combination of his will power and humility were immensely attractive. I have observed only Maulana Abul Kalam Azad and Maulvi Abdul Haq to be guarded in his presence. He breathed new life into the dying Jamia Millia, and took a firm stand in protecting Aligarh University at the time of Partition, both of which deeds are important facts in the annals of our educational history. His regard for me, which began in Aligarh, lasted even while he was the Vice President of India. Whether it was Delhi or Paris, he visited me at home without any formality and continued to calm my spiritual restlessness.

It was Maulana Shibli who laid the foundations of Darul Mussanifeen and Anjuman Tarraqui Urdu, but Syed Sulaiman Nadvi and Maulvi Abdul Haq respectively were responsible for the development of these two institutions. I have mentioned Syed Sahib above, and will recount the time I spent in the company of Maulvi Sahib later in this narrative.

Among the poets, I never found anyone as modest, cultured and sober as Asghar Gondvi. Now and then he would attempt to explain to me complex issues of Sufism, but I would evade such matters with the logic of 'bread, clothing, and shelter,' the socialist dictum to which I was devoted. In my opinion, Asghar Gondvi occupies an eminent position in Urdu Sufi poetry, second only to Khwaja Mir Dard and Shad Azimabadi, and is unrivaled by any of his contemporaries in the culture of *ghazal*.

Very appropriately, Jigar considered Asghar his spiritual mentor. Towards the end of his life Jigar even started to resemble Asghar physically. Whenever Jigar arrived in Aligarh for the annual *mushaira*, and Siddiqui Sahib wanted to show him special consideration, he would send for a bottle or two of alcohol from the market, so that the poet would not absent himself from the *mushaira* with the excuse of quenching his thirst. Once he entrusted the bottle to me with strict instructions that I should let him have enough of its contents to keep him animated, but not to let him get drunk. However it was not possible to restrain Jigar; as a result he emptied the bottle, and disrupted the mushaira.

After Partition, whenever he came to Karachi, he never failed to visit me. I have never seen anyone blossom as he did, once he had given up alcohol, nor have I seen an ugly face turn so attractive. Once, at his desire, I entertained him on a boat. The arrangements I made for a poetry recital on that occasion were such that he never forgot the event.

Just as the classical period of Urdu *ghazal* ended with Dagh Dehlavi, the renaissance of Urdu *ghazal* in the twentieth century came to an end with Jigar.

My three harsh years in Aligarh passed, as I spent the long summer vacation in Calcutta, and in between whenever I had the opportunity, set off for Delhi, Lahore and other places.

One summer evening in 1933, when I was on my way to some place, a car came and stopped near me, and Agha Hashar Kashmiri stepped out. This was a purely fortuitous meeting. When I advanced to greet him, he embraced me, complaining, 'How unfaithful you have turned out to be! Ever since Shameem left for Lahore, you have not set foot in my house.' When I had informed him that I had taken up residence in Aligarh (and did not live in Calcutta any longer), he accepted my apology and demanded that I visit him frequently. I not only complied with his wishes in this matter, but also revised the manuscript of a Hindi screenplay called *Sita*, which he had dictated to his *munshi*.

Heavy drinking had damaged Agha Sahib's liver. He would remain stretched out on his bed, cursing the doctors who obliged him to diet. In the literary splendour that he displayed in his wit and obscenities, he was matched only by Sauda and Inshaullah Khan. But when he was in the mood to speak with suavity, the most sophisticated of listeners would be struck dumb with admiration. Once when Jamil Mazhari mentioned Anees, Agha Sahib recited hundreds of couplets of elegiac poetry in Urdu and Persian, confounding all his listeners.

Agha Sahib used to live in a house that was located near Sialdah railway station, on Panchoo Khansama Lane (Panchoo the Chef Lane). One day his pupil, Inayat Dehlavi, had the ill luck to say impulsively, 'The Corporation people are so ignorant! They should have named this lane, "Agha Hashar Lane"'. Agha Sahib was so enraged at this that he pounced on the man, with, 'It's you who is ignorant! Do you think I am a successor of Panchoo the Chef? Why didn't it occur to you that thoroughfares such as the Circular Road, or Dharamtala Street should be named after me? Make yourself scarce, this instant!'

A similar incident occurred in Lahore in 1934, when Agha Sahib was the guest of his dear friend Hakim Faqir Mohammad Chishti, on an occasion when I, along with others, was listening raptly to his conversation. Introducing veteran novelist, M. Aslam, a journalist said,

'He is the son of a *malzada** in Lahore.' Agha Sahib swooped down on the journalist with, 'Maybe you are the son of a 'panderer'; as for him, he comes from 'a wealthy family'.

The second phase of Agha Hashar's playwriting is more significant from a literary point of view. This phase was influenced by the Non-Cooperation Movement. One should remember that Agha Sahib felt deeply for his people, an emotional state that he expressed openly in his famous poem, *Shukria Europe* (Thank you Europe). During the same period he wrote plays like *Ghulam Hindustan, Ankh ka Nasha, Rustam o Sohrab*, and *Dil ki Pyas*. According to him their texts had to be amended to fulfill the requirements of the stage, and in view of censor restrictions. They would be accorded the place they deserved in Urdu literature when they could be published in their original form.

After the death of Agha Sahib, these manuscripts remained with his younger brother, Agha Mahmood, who was a fine actor but was not interested in poetry and literature. After he too had passed away, I met a man in Delhi, in the year 1960, who told me that he was the secretary of Agha Hashar Academy in Benaras, and was arranging the publication of Hashar's manuscripts. God alone knows whether there was anything in his claim.

Nawab Nasir Khan Kheyal worked hard on *Dastaan-e-Urdu* (*The Story of Urdu*), but unfortunately this manuscript too was lost. A part of it was published under the title of *Mughal aur Urdu*, and discerning critics hailed him as the heir to Mohammad Husain Azad's prose style. He had a rare, unrivalled understanding of the genre of elegy, an example of which is his essay, 'Anees aur Firdausi.' In 1932, just when Sir Ross Masood had decided to make him the head of the Urdu Department at the Aligarh University, Nawab Kheyal suddenly died. The manuscript of *Dastaan-e-Urdu* remained with his son, Hasan Nawab, in Patna. At my suggestion Maulvi Abdul Haq was ready to publish it, but Hasan Nawab for some reason did not fall in with the proposal, and consequently, Urdu was deprived of a valuable book during the upheaval of 1947.

---

*Literally, 'son of wealth' or a 'rich man', but can also be interpreted as 'pimp' or "panderer".

The collection of Nawab Kheyal's uncle Shad Azimabadi's poetry met with the same fate, when most of it was lost as a result of his son's carelessness.

During the vacations in 1932, I stopped in Benaras on my way to Calcutta, to take the examination for the *Sahitya Alankar* qualification in Sanskrit. On learning of my arrival in Benaras, Munshi Premchand insisted that I stay with him, and had my luggage moved to his house. Premchand's personality was as great as his talent. Having witnessed the celebrated 'nights of Malawa', and 'evenings of Lucknow' his gaze was now taking in the spectacle of the 'dawn in Benaras'. It is the city which a man as arrogant as Hazeen loved so much that he never left it, a city whose praises Ghalib sang in his poem *Chiragh-e-Dair*.

How Jawaharlal Nehru came to Aligarh

This period of modern history was important because in the course of it the dictatorships of Hitler over Germany and Stalin over Russia were established. They inflicted unparalleled oppression, the one in the name of racial superiority and the other in the name of socialism. In order to end the reactionary movement of fascism, the Progressives ignored the tyrannies of Stalin, but such self-deception did immeasurable damage to socialism. The contradiction that lies between the assertions and actions of human beings, and between the views and behaviour of society became very apparent on this occasion. Although I became deeply conscious of this, I was neither oblivious to the importance of the Russian revolution in shaping an age, nor did I disagree with the basic doctrine of socialism. Jean Paul Sartre has said aptly, 'One must never forget the difference between philosophy and the police.'

Jawaharlal Nehru took the initiative in familiarizing the political Indian mind with international issues. In 1933, after his release from the Dehradun jail, he was waging a crusade against fascism. I already shared his views; and now I became eager to see him. It was early 1934 when newspapers published his itinerary, according to which at the end of his stay in Delhi, he would travel to Allahabad via Aligarh. The Aligarh University was controlled by the Government of India, so there was no question of the Pandit visiting it. I therefore decided to go to Delhi myself and request Pandit Nehru to stop on the way at the house of Makhan Singh, the President of the Aligarh Congress Committee, and to speak to us at Professor Habib's house after dinner. This suggestion could only be considered childish bravado, but Habib Sahib, who was the greatest admirer of the Pandit, supported it enthusiastically.

With this plan in mind I left for Delhi with Sibte Hasan, and found the Pandit, who was staying at Dr Ansari's house. We introduced ourselves very simply, saying, 'We are students of Aligarh University, and request you to stop for the night in Aligarh, so that our class can benefit from meeting you.' Pandit Nehru and Dr Syed Mahmood met us in a friendly way, consulted together, and agreed to our proposal. We therefore informed Makhan Singh and Habib Sahib on the phone. However, when Dr Ansari phoned the Vice Chancellor and told him about it, the astonishment of the latter can be guessed. Yet, such was the magnanimity of Sir Ross Masood's temperament, that he did not let on his ignorance of the matter. Meanwhile we knew nothing of the communication between Dr Ansari and Sir Ross Masood, so that when the train pulled in at the Aligarh railway station and we saw a throng of students instead of Congress volunteers, and instead of the gaunt frame of Makhan Singh, the corpulent one of Sir Ross Masood emerged to welcome Pandit Nehru, we lost our nerve, and I disappeared into the crowd as though I had never been the fellow passenger of the honoured guest. In no time Sir Ross Masood and his lady seated Pandit Nehru and Dr Mahmood in their car and whisked them off to their own home. While I was still nursing my disappointment, it was announced that a meeting would be held that night in the Strachey Hall, at 9 p.m.

Well in advance of the appointed time I dug in with my friends behind the presidential chair in Strachey Hall, wondering if I would be able to catch Pandit Nehru's eye, and what punishment the university officials held in store for me.

It was Pandit Nehru's first visit to Aligarh, and so, despite the cold, the Hall was packed with his admirers, while hundreds more were shouting slogans outside it. Sir Ross Masood presided over the meeting, and Nehru spoke to everyone as the occasion demanded and brought the meeting to a close. When the President moved ahead to make way for him, I grabbed the chance to say to Pandit Nehru, 'There is a big rush in front. It would be best to leave by the backdoor.' He concurred, and climbing through the hall window we found ourselves in the dark veranda of Sir Syed Hostel. My heart missed a beat, but luckily I noticed a car parked alongside, with a man in an overcoat standing close by. Promptly and boldly I got into the car with Panditji. The man in the overcoat inquired, 'Where would you like to go?' 'To Professor Habib's house,' I replied. When the car left behind the dark yard of the hostel and hit the road, I saw the driver's face under the streetlight, and recognized him. I almost had a fit, for the 'driver' was Professor Sharif (Mian Iftikharudin's father-in-law), a well-known figure at the University. All the way to Professor Habib's house I regretted having invited Pandit Nehru, and wondered what I had gained by it. I did not want to reveal my discomfiture to him and so I refrained from apologizing to the Professor.

In a little while, when we arrived at Professor Habib's house, we found him waiting for us along with a few others. For a long time we discussed world politics. After Pandit Nehru left, Habib Sahib embraced me and said, 'You were true to your word. Nobody could have dreamt that Jawaharlal would visit the University in this fashion.'

For me and my friends the whole episode was a joke, but it was Sir Ross Masood who had to suffer the consequences. In 1935, when his term of office came to an end, and he stood for re-election, the British government of India did their best to prevent his success. After he lost the election he left for Bhopal, where he became the state's Education Minister. He died in Bhopal a few years later.

I met Pandit Nehru several times afterwards, of which more later. Each time he would recount in detail, and with great relish, his visit to Aligarh.

Meeting Allama Iqbal

Around the same time, Rafeeq Bey, an old comrade of Ataturk, came to India on the invitation of Jamia Millia. To hear him speak, I went to Delhi along with Ashraf, and stayed at Ahmed Ali's house in Koochai Pandit. Allama Iqbal presided over the meeting, and spoke so pertinently and well that everybody acknowledged his acuity. Neither Ahmed Ali, Ashraf nor I had met Iqbal until then, and so we decided to meet him at Dr Ansari's residence at an appointed time. The next day, when I phoned to make the appointment, I was told that Iqbal met everybody who went to see him in the evening, and we too could visit him there without the formality of an appointment. At the last minute Ashraf and Ahmed Ali went off to some other place, but I in my enthusiasm set out for Darya Ganj. The house that Dr Ansari used to occupy is associated with Dara Shikoh, and despite the ravages of time, still retains its grandeur. Later, after Dr Ansari had died, Maulvi Abdul Haq made it his temporary abode where he stayed for short periods when he had moved to Hyderabad. During Dr Ansari's lifetime it was a national guesthouse, in which great political battles were fought, and Urdu staked its life on the political power of Muslims.

When, at a sign from a servant, I entered a room, I found Iqbal stretched out on a bed. I greeted him with a *salam alaikum* and sat down in a corner of the room. He was alone, and turned to me readily. When he heard from me that I had been to see the peasants' uprising in Mewat, and had stopped in Delhi to see him, he said with a smile, 'It looks like you do not devote much time to your studies, because if you did, you would not be able to indulge in these other activities.'

I replied, 'I am at that stage of my quest when formal education seems like an idle pursuit. I am a seeker of truth, which I consider to be the essence of education. How can an educational institution give me what I can gain from people like you?'

My answer pleased Iqbal, who now sat up on his bed, and asked me, 'How do you perceive truth?'

I replied, 'I have not yet been able to think further than the question of livelihood, and knowing that the destiny of man lies beyond seeking satisfaction of hunger and sex, I am still caught up in finding a fulfillment of these basic needs so that one can concentrate on developing one's latent capabilities.'

Iqbal looked at me attentively for some time, and then said, 'Hunger and sex are common to man and animals. The value that distinguishes the human from the non-human living forms is what is known in the language of philosophy as 'idea'. This is the strong innate feeling that appears in the various forms, of faith, conscience, conduct, etc. Reflect that nobody ever forced the people who suffered hardships for the sake of human progress to make the sacrifices that they did. It was some radiance of faith that inspired them in their endeavour. It is this same feeling that is the essence of humanness and assures its exaltation.'

So, for a long time I continued to badger Iqbal, but he did not lose interest, and when I was taking my leave he urged me to visit him in Lahore whenever I happened to be in that city. I therefore visited him in Lahore several times subsequently. The last time I met him was in 1936 in Panipat, at the famous meeting arranged on the centenary of Maulana Hali's birth. He had by then read my essay, 'Literature and Life'. When somebody introduced me to him with the words, 'He has written impudent things about you,' Iqbal responded magnanimously with, 'I appreciate such sincere young men. I prefer the disagreement of lively people to the concurrence of lifeless ones.'

At the time I had read his work only briefly. Now that I am better acquainted with it, it is only fair that I acknowledge the greatness of his personality and his poetry. No twentieth century poet ever wrote a lament for his age in such elegiac work, nor did any sing such odes to the greatness of humanity.

Tagore in Lahore

I first saw Tagore in Calcutta, in mid 1934. Whenever he used to return to Calcutta from Shantiniketan, he used to stay in his ancestral home, Tagore Palace, in Shyam Bazaar. I was acquainted with one of his younger relatives, who had recently returned from Europe and was residing in the same place. Once when I went to visit him at Tagore Palace I discovered that Tagore himself was present there. Despite his advanced age, he could be taken for the god of art. In the beginning of 1935, Tagore was on a tour with a troupe of singers and dancers, collecting funds for Shantiniketan. He arrived in Lahore at a time when I had come there from Aligarh to collect material for 'Literature and Life'. The reception committee for Tagore in Lahore included well-known Hindu personalities such as Gokal Chand Narang, Sir Shadi Laal, and Manohar Laal Zutshi. But it was a wealthy shoemaker called Bhala, whose shoes were worn all over Punjab, who donated the largest sum of money. Handing the bag which contained ten thousand rupees, to the committee, he laid down the condition that Tagore would stay at his house, declaring that since his mansion was not smaller than any other, and his furnishings not inferior to anybody else's, there was no reason why Tagore should not be comfortable there. Since no one could explain to him that his home lacked the fine something that used to be called civilization, and is now known as culture, poor Tagore had to suffer Bhala's hospitality. That magnificent house had everything that is usually present in a seth's household. Bhala had partitioned the spacious hall with a curtain, and furnished a study for Tagore in its rear. Whenever somebody came to see Tagore, he would personally part the curtain and announce loudly, 'There sits Guru Dev.' Instead of lightening up, I saw the expression on the sensitive poet's face betray signs of annoyance, and he returned our greetings dryly. But to top it all, when Bhala heard that Tagore was in the habit of listening to devotional songs early in the morning, he sent for Sikh vocalists from the gurdwara, who were the last straw to the poet's sensibilities.

And so, after about a week or ten days of suffering, when Tagore prepared to leave, Bhala arranged a lavish tea party for him on his lawn. I was present on the occasion with my brother and Hasrat. Somebody had counseled Bhala that as the host he ought to make a speech, but that it would be even more seemly to recite a valedictory prose poem in the style of Tagore himself. His advisor then wrote out the poem for him, which was somewhat as follows:

O traveller, will you go away?
The birds are preparing to fly,
The cows are heading for their pastures,
The train is giving off clouds of smoke
O traveller, will you go away?
The magic of Bengal is well known,
But the people of Punjab remember its spells very well,
O traveller, will you go away?
Etc.

All of us applauded the recital with laughter and clapping, and the tired traveller returned to where he had come from.

Among the venerable personalities whose names I had heard mentioned respectfully by educated people, ever since my childhood, was Maulvi Abdul Haq. In Aligarh, when it became apparent to me that in addition to his contribution to scholarship he possessed the quality of being a supporter of progressive thought and was a guide to newcomers, my esteem for him deepened. I had just returned from Lahore when fortuitously he happened to visit Aligarh, and Rasheed Ahmed Siddiqui introduced me to him. Maulvi Sahib appreciated the translations of Qazi Nazar-ul-Islam's poems that I had contributed to *Nigar*, and insisted that I should translate some more poems for *Urdu*. Complying with his demand, I sent him the manuscript of my treatise, *Adab aur Zindagi* (Literature and Life) along with the translated poems. I was studying for a Masters degree at the time, and had resolved to move to Calcutta in the summer and work for the English daily, *Advance*, as sub editor. This post had been offered to me by Babu Molchand Agarwal.

On receiving the manuscripts, Maulvi Abdul Haq wrote me a long letter, which was accompanied with 150 rupees as payment for my work. In those days none but Maulvi Sahib had the courage to accept such explosive material for publication. In his letter he had expressed great appreciation of my work, and had asked me what my plans were for the future. When I wrote to him telling him of my intentions, he sent me a telegram to say that he was planning to come to Aligarh in the last week of April 1939, and would like to meet me then.

Whenever he was in Aligarh, Maulvi Abdul Haq used to stay at Abdullah Lodge, which was the home of his old classmate, Khan Bahadur Shaikh Abdullah. When I heard of his arrival, I went to visit him in the company of Professor Rashid Ahmed Siddiqui. I will never forget the warmth and kindness with which he greeted me. After some formal conversation he said to me, 'I had some reservations when I heard that you were planning to go back to Calcutta and return to journalism. Actually your field is literature and scholarship, and that in Urdu. The dictionary that the Anjuman has compiled is being published. Now, I want its English-Hindi version to be prepared. One reason for this is that there is no good dictionary in Hindi at the moment. The other reason is that in this way many Urdu words will find their way into Hindi. Pandit Wanshi Dhar is working on it under my guidance, but he is unfamiliar with Urdu. In addition, I need a helper like you to assist me with the journal, *Urdu*.'

Siddiqui Sahib had much to say in support of Maulvi Sahib, and I found myself in a dilemma. I made the excuse that I had become so used to freedom of expression both in speech and writing that I would not be able to adjust to state controls. In reply, Maulvi Sahib assured me that there would be no restrictions on me as long as I did not take part in active politics. When I rejected his offer despite this assurance, Maulvi Sahib told me that he had decided to move the Anjuman to Delhi in two or three years, and in fact he was consulting Shaikh Abdullah on how to move the Anjuman to Delhi by giving it the form of a limited company. However, this strategy became unnecessary because by starting the Hindi Urdu controversy, Gandhiji created a situation where four years later the work of the Anjuman was transferred from Aurangabad to Delhi with the approval of the government of Hyderabad.

Partly because of my deference for Maulvi Sahib, partly because of my newly found enthusiasm for Urdu literature, and also in part for my natural proclivity for swift action, I accepted the offer, and left for Aurangabad in early May, having first looked for an omen in *Diwan-e-Hafiz*, and found the following:

منم که گوشنه ے خانه خانقاه من است

دعائے پیر مغاں ورد صبح گاه من است

As for me for whom the corner of the tavern is my monastery
The blessings of the tavern keeper is my morning prayer

4

The Anjuman in Hyderabad

I spent no more than just under two years working with Maulvi Abdul Haq in Hyderabad and Aurangabad. During this period I watched that venerable personality as attentively as the young Gorky observed the elderly Tolstoy. Those who saw Maulvi Sahib in Pakistan remained ignorant of many of his qualities, because it was the period of his decline. As a matter of fact I would say that even his stay in Delhi was a phase in which he was no longer his old self. In 1936, when Gandhiji challenged Urdu, Maulvi Sahib's life changed its course. He was a different person before that, and I witnessed the change closely.

In 1911, when his service with the department of Education brought him to Aurangabad, he decided to stay there. He found there the meeting of nature and history that he liked. Aurangabad is named after Aurangzeb Alamgir, who spent half of his long reign in annexing Muslim states and restraining the Marhattas, activities that caused the foundations of his dominions to wobble. Had he not insulted Shivaji publicly in his court, and desisted from destroying the tribute-paying Shia states of the south, he would not have invited the trouble that he did. Reminders of that period, the remains of broken down palaces are scattered between Aurangabad and Daulatabad. It is the same Daulatabad which Mohammed Tughlaq made his capital for some time, a few centuries ago. The people he left behind there on his return to Delhi, sowed the seeds of Deccani Urdu, and in the crispness of the faces and accents of their descendants, old Delhi left its stamp. Nearby are the caves of Ellora, from the veins of which a thousand years ago, some unknown wizards of art had created forms of beauty that no sculptor can conceive. At the same place the invincible fort of Deogari emerged from the lap of rocky cliffs, remembering the day when Deval Devi fled the hold of Malik Kafur, leaving behind her image in Amir Khusro's poetry.

On the outskirts of Aurangabad is the mausoleum of Aurangzeb's favourite queen, Rabia Zamani, which is known as the Taj of Deccan, because it has been built in the likeness of the Taj Mahal. Maulvi Sahib had chosen for his residence, the house meant for the warden of the mausoleum, and even after his transfer to Hyderabad he used to spend some time there every year, especially during the monsoons.

Two years before the First World War, *Anjuman-e-Taraqqi-e-Urdu* had arrived at his door in Aurangabad in a broken trunk, in the form of a few desultory looking pages. The story of how he tended this infant, which he nurtured with his own lifeblood, became a luminous chapter in the history of the Urdu language.

The office of the Anjuman remained here with the publishing house and the press, until it was shifted to Delhi in 1938. The truth is that Maulvi Sahib accorded Urdu the deference due to one's mother, and treated the Anjuman with the affection that is reserved for a daughter. Apart from his relationship with them he had no human bonds. He saw beauty only in nature and his vision was permeated with the landscapes of the subcontinent. He knew how to enjoy the weather, and though he ate little, he ate food of good quality. The tobacco for his hookah had to come from Ujjain, and his tea from Darjeeling. His cigarettes were always of the Abdullah brand. Living with him I too became spoilt. Whenever he illustrated the philosophy of his life with the following verse, I would repeat it with enthusiasm:

> *Whoever is straight with me,*
> *I too am straight with him*
> *But whoever acts crooked with me,*
> *I too act crooked with him*

Reciting the second couplet he would stand stiffly like a large, sturdy tree, and would brandish his walking stick as though preparing to attack an invisible enemy. But in accompaniment to the first couplet his body would bend in deference and submission.

It is not easy to achieve a balance between sovereignty and submission, and in old age the yardstick of balance is itself broken. Sadly, those who humiliated him in Pakistan were the very people who he had nurtured. It was for such instances that the Prophet [PBUH] has said, 'Be wary of those to whom you have done a good turn'.

Sitting in a room of the house next to the mausoleum I became engaged in lexicography, and became as absorbed in the search for words and their meanings as an alchemist seeking to prepare gold with the help of his herbs and roots. Early in the morning I used to accompany Maulvi Sahib into the hills for our daily walk, and in the evenings I would wander alone among archaeological remains where my unbridled imagination sought centuries old ghosts or buried treasures.

Whether in Aurangabad or in Hyderabad, Maulvi Sahib's home was like Rashid Ahmed Siddiqui's in Aligarh, where there was a constant coming and going of scholars and intellectuals. However, poets were deprived of his hospitality. With the exception of Iqbal, Maulvi Sahib did not approve of any of the modern Urdu poets. In Hyderabad I did hear Fani recite his poetry in Maulvi Sahib's drawing room, but after he left, Maulvi Sahib said with a grimace, 'The ache of sorrow is quite a different thing from mere tearfulness.'

Anyway, I was on the subject of Aurangabad, where Dr Lateef, Dr Abid Husain, Qazi Abdul Gaffar, etc. were staying in Maulvi Sahib's house. Maulvi Sahib was somewhat hard of hearing, so he used to speak in a loud voice. One day I heard him say of me, 'I have never seen a person so indifferent to his own interests. To begin with, he wouldn't agree to accept this post, and when he did, he never mentioned either his travel expenses or his salary'.

The truth is, there is such self-sufficiency in my temperament, that I find it difficult to talk of my interest whether to a loved one or a friend. I could never bring myself to ask anyone for anything. Whatever someone gave me gladly, I accepted. The result was that sometimes I was denied my rights and sometimes I incurred losses; yet my mind and heart were at peace, and that is something to be grateful for.

The rainy season is the most charming of all our seasons, and it can be enjoyed best not in the north, but in the south of India. In Aurangabad the hot weather exists in name only. However the trees and plants wither in the summer sunlight and the streams dry up. But when I was there, by mid-June, the clouds broke, and the rain came down with such force that land and water became one. I woke up in the morning to find a stream roaring down the side of the house. The air had become moist, and waterfalls were rushing down the neighbouring hills. The trees had shed their yellow leaves and were transformed into a verdant green. Maulvi Sahib was calling out, 'Put away your books and come and look at nature, which is the source of all knowledge.' His servants were preparing good things to eat in some picturesque spot, and all of us headed outside to join Maulvi Sahib on a walk.

One day, towards the end of July 1935, while we were preparing to leave for Hyderabad, Maulvi Sahib received a letter from his old friend Zafar Omar in Aligarh. Mr Omar was a senior officer in the Police, as well as the well-known author of detective novels like *Behram ki Giriftari* and *Neeli Chatri*. Before I left Aligarh I had written to him asking for the hand of his daughter Hameeda. My audacity at doing so had irked him, but nevertheless, he had left the decision to Maulvi Sahib. The latter therefore showed me the letter and asked me, 'Do you know this girl and want to marry her?' When I replied that I did, he was silent for a moment and then stated, 'You don't understand the responsibility of marriage. You are too young and too inexperienced to do so.'

In reply I said, 'Time will give me the experience of dealing with the responsibility. If you have faith in my sense of commitment, please recommend my case.'

A short while later I was married. As long as Hameeda remained in Hyderabad, Maulvi Sahib treated her like a daughter and entrusted her with the management of the household.

Hameeda is my wife, and though all my life I soared far away from her like a kite, she neither let go of the kite string, nor allowed anyone to sever it.

In Hyderabad Maulvi Sahib lived in a spacious bungalow known as Nadir Manzil. Pandit Kaifi and Dr Abid Husain were staying in one part of it, in connection with their work. In one room Maulvi Ehtishamuddin used to be busy compiling the Urdu dictionary. Maulvi Sahib would be sitting among the thousands of books and manuscripts in the library as though he were meditating. Only the sound of the gurgling hookah and the drone of him reciting Deccani's verses gave away his presence.

When my article, *Literature and Life* was published in the journal, *Urdu*, in July 1935, it caused quite a stir. On Maulvi Sahib's instructions

I was writing an article for every issue of the journal, and was also compiling important events of the literary world, and reviewing books under the pseudonym, Nakhuda. These activities continued for two years. Although the style of my writing was different from the rest of the journal, while Maulvi Sahib's was a pure classical, he never put restraints on my work, and did not heed anybody who objected to it. These articles were later published in two anthologies of my critical writing, *Adab aur Inqilab* (Literature and Revolution), and *Raushan Minar* (The Lighted Tower). The short stories I wrote during leisure hours were collected in *Mohabbat aur Nafrat* (Love and Hate).

At the same time, I was going through the initial stages of the English–Hindi dictionary, but an interesting episode halted this activity.

Zafar ul Mulk Alvi, the editor of the Lucknow-based magazine, *Al-Nazir*, used to make a trip to Hyderabad every year, and in addition to enlightening the rich on the subject of miracles, he also gave them lessons in yoga exercises. He taught Maulvi Sahib how to stand on his head, in order to effect a better flow of blood to the brain—an exercise known as *Shish Aasen*. Maulvi Sahib was then sixty-five years old, but sinewy and strong. However, his shoulder was dislocated when he stood on his head, and we placed him on his bed. He was never in the habit of screaming when in pain. Once when a scorpion had bitten him on the finger he had endured the agony in silence. So, this time too he suffered without a word, though continuing to abuse Zafar ul Mulk while he lay prone on his bed. Suddenly, in the middle of the massages and the medication, he remembered the piles of final proofs of the English–Urdu dictionary. He was in the habit of going over the final proofs himself. The Aurangabad press was printing away diligently, and he fretted that the proofs would not be ready in time for the press. So, he said to me, 'Go over the proofs carefully, then give me each page for a final scrutiny and send the lot to Aurangabad.'

I was capable of doing such work with attention to its minutest detail. Therefore, while going over the proofs with Maulvi Sahib for the final check, I pointed out other errors that had not been corrected in the previous proofs. Maulvi Sahib was very pleased, and told me to put away the Hindi dictionary for the time being, since there was no hurry for it, and concentrate on the work in hand. Subsequently I read the final proofs of the English–Urdu dictionary from the letter 'S' to the end of the alphabet. I also prepared the appendix and an abridged edition of the dictionary. I still have in my possession, the initial manuscript of the English–Hindi dictionary, the first copy of the first edition, and Maulvi Sahib's letters in connection with the dictionary.

If in the north of the India of those days, one experienced a feeling of excitement and turmoil, the south filled one with a sense of peace and quiet. In the rest of the world too, be it America or Europe, northern and southern regions seem to follow a similar pattern.

Madras was the centre of Hindu learning, while Hyderabad was the cradle of Indo-Islamic culture. After the seventh century, when Hindu civilization began to disintegrate in the north, it was revived in the south, where it has still retained its form. The rare beauty of Hindu music and dance is found in the south, which is home also to peerless scholars of Sanskrit or the Vedanta. One cannot make such claims about Islamic learning in the south. However, the Translation and Encyclopedia departments of the Usmania University, and the Anjuman Taraqqi Urdu, added a chapter to Islamic scholarship that was unmatched in the north of India. Hyderabad and Lahore were the two big centres of Urdu. When the Muslims of the north lost their sword in the eighteenth century, and their armour in the nineteenth century, one was retrieved by Mysore and the other came to rest in Hyderabad. Whether it is in the past or in the present, the civilization of no era is either entirely perfect or altogether defective. The same was true of the cultural traditions of Hyderabad, which grew out of the civilizations of Delhi and Lucknow. Although it is indisputable that the Hyderabadi culture was closely associated with the feudal system and showed signs of the same decadence, India's military action in Hyderabad was not the invasion of a superior economic system, rather it was the assault of Hindu nationalism, a gory account of which is preserved in the report of Pandit Sunderlal's inquiry. One should not forget that if under the feudal system a man was tied to the plough, in the industrial society he is bound to the machine. The man of today is the slave of the machine and yet rejoices in the fact that he is no longer stuck in the rut of cultivating the land.

Mrs Sarojni Naidu's Family

Mrs Sarojni Naidu's home in Hyderabad had the same panache that is associated with the salons of famous Parisian women who were patrons of art and learning.

Mrs Naidu wrote English poetry of such calibre, and was so well spoken that she was known as the 'Nightingale of India'. Although she was one of the principal leaders of the Congress, she was popular among the Muslims on account of her liberal mindedness. Few families could boast as many intelligent and accomplished people as there were in hers. Her father was a famous scientist of his day, and her husband was a well-known surgeon. One brother, Chattopadhyay completed his education in Europe and went to Russia after the Bolshevik Revolution. Like M.N. Roy, he became involved with the Communist International. Subsequently, when Stalin massacred the old revolutionaries, he was one of the victims. Had M.N. Roy not fled to India, he would have suffered the same fate.

Mrs Naidu's younger brother Hiren Chatterji is an incomparable actor, poet, and musician, but I have never seen a more restless individual. Mrs Naidu's older daughter, Miss Padmaja was Governor of West Bengal for a long time, and her younger daughter Lila Mani held a high post in the Ministry of Foreign Affairs. In short, the whole family was brilliant. I was acquainted with all of them, but it was Mrs Naidu's eldest son, Dr Jaisurya, known as Baba, who was my friend.

Baba had just returned from Germany after ten years, with an advanced degree in medicine, and as he was leaving Germany, he married and brought Eva with him. Both of them had taken part in the anti-Nazi movement, and so as soon as Hitler came to power, they left for India. The bond Hameeda and I formed with them proved to be lifelong. Baba was an unconventional socialist. I have rarely known another person with such originality of disposition as I found in him.

His company lit up many areas of my soul. My ears had been unacquainted with the charm of music. Baba and Eva introduced me to the esoterics of Western music, and during my stay in Europe I had ample opportunity to familiarize myself with the exquisite pleasure of it. Later, when we were in Amritsar, I acquired the taste for Indian music. These friends of mine loved animals, and in their little flat, birds and beasts lived in peace and harmony. I developed this interest too in the same period, and have described my first experience of it in Nadir Manzil, in an essay entitled 'Maulvi Abdul Haq's Zoo' (published in *Auraq*, Lahore 1969). For Hameeda and me their flat was our second home in Hyderabad, after Nadir Manzil.

By the beginning of 1936, there was a crisis in Europe and tumult in India. Fascism had become so powerful that Mussolini had the audacity to occupy Abyssinia, regardless of the violent protests and expressions of outrage from many parts of the world. This event made a deep impression on Maulvi Sahib, and he directed me to compile a book which contained essays by Qazi Abdul Ghaffar, Dr Hamidullah, Dr Yusuf Husain, etc. This anthology was published by the Anjuman under the title of *Habsha-o-Italia* (Abyssinia and Italy).

Immediately after Mussolini's invasion of Abyssinia, General Franco began a revolt against the democratic government of Spain with the support of Hitler and Mussolini. The civil war that ensued, and lasted for the following three years, shook the conscience of modern Europe. Capitalist interests in the Western countries deliberately encouraged fascism, but Stalin was deeply conscious of the danger from fascism, and on his directions, communists the world over were busy creating united fronts with anti-fascist elements. This movement was active in the fields of scholarship, art, and literature, besides politics, and attracted socialists and liberals as well. This was the background against which Sajjad Zaheer and others founded the Association of Progressive Writers in 1936.

National politics too, now found itself taking a new turn. In 1935 the British parliament had passed an Act for constitutional changes, which acknowledged the principle of provincial autarky. Based on this, preparations were being made for provincial elections. This act remained effective even after Partition, until the two countries had promulgated their own constitutions.

Congress was at the time a very well-organised party, and it had the support of the nationalist Muslim group and the Congress Socialist Party as well, owing to which the reactionary character of its leadership was well camouflaged. The majority of Muslims did not trust this leadership, but did not have the option of another party that was on par with the Congress, as Jinnah Sahib had just begun the reorganization of the Muslim League. It was clear that the Hindu nation and the Muslim nation were moving in different directions and that the movement for a united Indian nation was confined to a few well-meaning individuals. The left wing of Indian politics was weak and it feared the fascism in Europe more than British imperialism. And then it came under the spell of Jawaharlal Nehru, which did not leave it until Indira Gandhi's rule.

Such was the state of affairs in the month of April, when Maulvi Sahib was about to leave on his annual tour of the north. At this time we received Gandhiji's invitation, which stated that he had organized a meeting in Nagpur at the end of the month to review the role of the writers in the national struggle for independence. One hundred intellectuals and writers from all over India had been selected to attend. Besides Maulvi Sahib, I too was among the invitees. At the time, we paid no attention to the invitation, and got into the train for Delhi.

On the northern border of Hyderabad, there is a junction called Qazi Peeth, where the train changes tracks and proceeds in the direction of Delhi. I had got off to stroll on the platform there, when in the dusk I discerned the figure of the poet Jigar, who was charging around in what appeared to be great agitation. He was delighted to see me, and said, 'Please help me, my throat is parched. I understood the reason for his distress, and suggested that he ask the bearer to bring him a drink in his train compartment, or if he preferred, he could go to the station bar room and drink there. But Jigar did not take to either idea. His travelling companions in the inter class compartment were not likely to allow him to drink, and if he went to the bar the chances were that he would miss the train. When I told Maulvi Sahib about his quandary, the latter told me without further ado, 'Call Jigar here, and tell the bearer to bring him his drink.' I was astonished at his response, but then Maulvi Sahib disliked being judgmental. Consequently, Jigar entered our second class compartment, looking sheepish, and after rendering endless apologies and sitting down respectfully before Maulvi Sahib, proceeded to down glass after glass of alcohol. A little later, when his drink began to take effect, he recited his poetry with much gusto, while Maulvi Sahib responded with a nod or a grimace. After a long while, when the train stopped at some place, Jigar bid farewell to us cheerfully, and left for his own compartment.

When we arrived in Delhi, Majaz was waiting on the platform. I had informed him of my arrival. Maulvi Sahib was going to his ancestral home in Hapor for two days, to see his brother, Zia-ul-Haq, while I was headed for Aligarh. However Maulvi Sahib told me, 'Come to Hapor with me. You can go to Aligarh from there while I stop in Lahore, before I go to Delhi on [such and such date]. I'll see you at Dr Ansari's house, and we will return to Hyderabad the same night.' After this plan had been finalized we sat down in a restaurant, as there was still an hour and a half to kill before the train was due to leave. During this time he bantered with Majaz to the extent that he began to call the poor fellow 'chonch' (beak). Even afterward, whenever Majaz was mentioned, he referred to him as 'chonch'.

Maulvi Sahib's Older Brother, Zia-ul-Haq

Shaikh Zia-ul-Haq was many years older than Maulvi Sahib. Tall, broad-chested, wide mouthed, and of a fairly dark complexion, he had eyes that were tiny, sunken, and bright, and a booming voice. In short he was a man of such grandeur that at first sight one was awed by him. He was known as the 'pamphleteer' because he communicated his views not through books or articles, but through pamphlets. The anecdote that is linked to him will be related in detail in the coming pages.

At the beginning of this century, British imperialism appeared to be so strong that except for some lawyers and intellectuals nobody dared to criticize it. However some young nationalists chose the path of terrorism, and of the secret organizations that they created, two played a special role in the war for independence. One of them was the Yugantar Party of Bengal, and the other was the Ghadar Party belonging to exiled freedom fighters, which was nurtured in Canada and the US. Maulvi Barkat Ali Bhopali was an active member and has described it in detail in his autobiography.

The first objective of the Yugantar Party was to annul the partition of Bengal which had come into force in 1905. Many incidents of violence against the British were perpetrated in this connection, the most serious among which was known as the Alipur bomb case. A young man by the name of Khudi Ram Bose was condemned to the gallows for killing a British Sessions Judge in the courtroom. The young man gave such a stirring speech in his defence that the country was shaken awake from its state of somnambulism. Akbar Allahabadi wrote the following couplet on this occasion:

پروانہ کا حال اس محفل میں ہے قابلِ رشک اے اہلِ نظر
اک رات ہی میں پیدا بھی ہوا عاشق بھی ہوا مر بھی گیا

In this company, the fate of the moth is enviable
In one night he was born, loved, and died

Tagore wrote a poem for the same occasion that began with the following lines:

Never mind if nobody hearkens to your call
Walk alone, walk alone, walk alone

Countless firebrands took to the road of freedom and revolution, marching in time to the music of this poem.

When the two parts of Bengal were reunited, the Yugantar Party broke up and some of its members were scattered in the north of India. Among them a prominent name was Ras Bihari Bose, because when a bomb was thrown openly in Delhi on the Viceroy, Lord Harding, it was his group on which suspicion fell. Several of its members were caught while many others managed to flee. Ras Bihari Bose went to Japan and fought British imperialism for the rest of his life. Among those who fled were Zia-ul-Haq, Sardar Ajeet Singh (Bhagat Singh's paternal uncle), and Sufi Amba Prashad. Of these, Zia-ul-Haq later returned to India, but the other two remained abroad. Ajeet Singh settled in Brazil, and during the Second World War he served the 'Azad Hind Hakoomat' on the Italian radio.

Umba Prashad stayed in Shiraz, and became so involved in Sufism that he was known as the 'Hindi Sufi'. In 1959, when I went to Shiraz for the first time, somebody directed me to his grave, which was close to Khwaja Kirmani's tomb.

On his return to India, Shaikh Zia-ul-Haq made his peace with the British, but turned on the rajas and the native well-to-do, pelting them with such masses of pamphlets that they cried for protection. During this venture he formed a friendship with Divan Singh Muftoon, and clashed with Khwaja Hasan Nizami.

The two days that I spent in his company left me with three strong memories. He had such a passion for cleanliness that with the evanescent light that precedes daybreak he would light a lantern and call up his servants. The swishing of brooms and gushing of water that followed put an end to all sleep. When day broke I said to Maulvi Sahib, 'Let's go for a walk', but he replied, 'This is not the right time for it because hordes of monkeys will be entrenched everywhere, and will not budge until the townspeople are up and about.'

Zia-ul-Haq Sahib's second passion was cooking, and feeding people. I have never forgotten the taste of the delicious fare he served us.

Shaikh Zia-ul-Haq had an invaluable personal collection of Urdu newspapers and magazines, the like of which I have never seen. In his study there were thousands of well-organized files containing his collection, which dated from the nineteenth century to contemporary times. When the two brothers were busy discussing their personal affairs, I used to spend hours looking through those files. A year later Zia-ul-Haq Sahib had died and his collection remained in his house. I do not know in whose possession it is now.

The Meeting of the Sahitya Parishad, Nagpur

When I arrived at Dr Ansari's residence on the appointed date in the last week of April 1936, I found Maulvi Sahib present there. While describing his visit to Lahore, he suddenly said to me, 'Your brother is a very useful person. I was pleased to meet him and after consulting my friends in Lahore, have decided to ask him to work as the Anjuman's manager in Aurangabad.'

In truth the Anjuman's affairs were in a mess at the time. Some people were openly taking advantage of Maulvi Sahib's good nature and his absence, and so Maulvi Sahib had been on the look out for an honest manager. Shameem Sahib took up his assignment a few months later, and worked with dedication to put right the mismanagement. His efforts however went against the grain of expediency in the environment of the princely state. The result was that Shameem Sahib was disheartened, and two years later when the Anjuman was shifted to Delhi, he resigned and left for Bombay.

Our train was to leave for Hyderabad in the evening, so in order to pass the time, Maulvi Sahib decided to go to the Jamia Millia which in those days was lodged in some rented houses in Qarol Bagh. We went to Professor Mujib's house, and he informed Dr Zakir Husain and others. During the course of the conversation, Dr Zakir Husain said, 'Gandhiji is holding a meeting in Nagpur tomorrow. Why don't you stop there on your way?'

I can't say whether Maulvi Sahib remembered the invitation. I certainly did, but had refrained from mentioning it because up to that point while Maulvi Sahib approved of Gandhiji, I was quite mistrustful of him. Anyhow, Maulvi Sahib espoused Dr Zakir's suggestion, for it offered a good chance of meeting intellectuals from the different linguistic groups of India, and also the opportunity of talking informally with Gandhi.

Our train arrived at the Attarsi junction the next morning. The train from Allahabad had also arrived, and I saw Munshi Premchand and Acharya Narendra Dev emerge from it with Pandit Nehru. Premchand called out to me and after asking after my welfare, informed Pandit Nehru of my literary activities. The latter said with a laugh, 'I know this gentleman from another context.' And then he recounted with much relish his trip to Aligarh. In the end he said to me with a frown, 'You should be doing something else. Lexicography is an old man's occupation, and a princely state is no place for a free thinker.' Acharya Narendra Dev was the President of the Congress Socialist Party, and a famous educationist. We had arrived in Nagpur on the spur of the moment, so we had neither informed anybody of our arrival, nor had we made arrangements for our stay. We therefore lodged in the waiting room of the railway station.

The Pandora's box that Gandhiji opened during the Sahitya Parishad meeting is well-known, and Maulvi Sahib's account of it is a historical document. When Gandhiji digressed from literary issues to dwell upon the linguistic controversy for the whole day, and the atmosphere of the meeting took on an ugly aspect, I expressed my weariness to Pandit Nehru. The statement I prepared the next day at his suggestion, on the obligations of writers, is now the preface to my book, *Literature and Revolution*. The document has the signatures of Maulvi Abdul Haq, Pandit Nehru, Munshi Premchand, Acharya Narendra Dev, and myself. Gandhiji rejected our suggestion that it should be considered a

resolution passed by the meeting. However he permitted me to read it
out, and even spoke a word of praise for it.

The controversy that was born here, later took the form of linguistic
politics, and became the indispensable appendage of national politics.
Subsequently, the defense of Urdu became an important issue of
Muslim League politics, while the other side raised the slogan of
'Hindi, Hindu, Hindustan'.

At first it was unclear why Gandhiji had started the Urdu Hindi
controversy, and instead of tackling literary issues, had created enmity
over the two languages. Later the mystery was solved, and it became
apparent that though Gandhiji himself was a well informed politician,
his cultural and literary advisers were biased sectarian writers like
K.M. Munshi and Kaka Kaliker, one of whom wrote in Gujarati, while
the other was a well-known Marathi writer. These two persons
explained to Gandhi that modern ideas were fast entering literature,
and if writers were not immediately gathered under the Congress flag,
they would be enticed in other directions. On these grounds Gandhiji
agreed to call the meeting. The date of the meeting was set to coincide
with the annual meeting of the Sahitya Sammelan, which also took
place in Nagpur. This ensured that a large number of pro-Hindi people
attended the meeting, while it was secretly resolved that Hindi would
be declared the national language at the meeting. This was contrary to
the Congress decision of making Hindustani (the north Indian spoken
language which was written in either Urdu or Hindi script) the
national language.

It was after an upheaval had been caused over the affair that
Gandhiji realized his mistake in 1945, and he decided to create a
Hindustani Literature Board. Among the ten members of this Board
were, Dr Tarachand, Pandit Sunder Lal, Dr Zakir Husain, etc. My name
too was printed as secretary and member, but by now the doors of
conciliation had been closed. Gandhiji had under our very eyes,
destroyed a major bridge of Hindu-Muslim reconciliation. This is what
happens when literature and culture fall into the whirlpool of
politics.

The Sahitya Parishad meeting changed Maulvi Sahib's life and the
modus operandi of the Anjuman. When we reached Aurangabad, via
Hyderabad, the first thing Maulvi Sahib did was to throw away the
spindle, and put away his garments of homespun cotton. He also

removed from the shelf the jug that Lokmania Tilak had left behind when he was in hiding from his political foes. The normally gentle expression on his face had hardened, and a new resolve shone in his eyes instead of the usual cloud of worry. He would repeat, sometimes in anger and sometimes in sorrow, 'I used to believe Gandhi was sincere, and a proponent of national unity, but it transpires that he is bent on destroying the national language. Now we must be ready to make all kind of sacrifices to defend Urdu, and make the Anjuman a dynamic and organised institution.'

He put his changed perception into practice by stopping the work on the English–Hindi dictionary. The step did not make much difference as the work was only in its early stage and I had been busy working on the English–Urdu dictionary. When I sent for Indulal Yagnik's book, *Gandhi as I Knew Him* from Bombay, Maulvi Sahib read it and was aghast. He said, 'I did not know that Gandhi was so wily. This book ought to be translated.' And so Maulvi Sahib's reaction to Gandhi became stronger, which was only natural considering his boundless love for Urdu.

On the one hand my interests were altogether scholarly and literary, and language figured as no more than a vehicle of expression; on the other hand, despite my involvement with Urdu, I felt no hostility towards Hindi. I believed that every intellectual ought to fight the growing communalism, because it was retrogression in its worst form. It was different with Maulvi Sahib. He had seen the beginning of the confrontation between Urdu and Hindi in the days of Sir Syed, and could observe and understand the danger of Gandhi's challenge to Urdu with a more experienced eye.

Two things happened at this time that alarmed me, and forced me to think of my future. Maulvi Sahib had been mulling over a scheme of translating one hundred literary masterpieces of the world into Urdu. He had intended that a year later, when work on the dictionary would be completed, I would give all my time to this project. I became so enamoured of this scheme that I would spend my leisure hours preparing a list of titles to be translated. But one day Maulvi Sahib pronounced that the scheme would have to be shelved for the time being. While the disappointment was still fresh, I overheard him say, 'He is of such a restless nature that I have always been apprehensive that he may suddenly up and leave. But now that he is married he can't go anywhere.'

This one sentence made me quake. With Shameem Sahib's approval I decided to sell the Raipur property, and actually sold it off at a fraction of its value. Somebody has truly said, 'The price of a needy man's property goes down as his need increases.' Had I waited a while longer in Raipur before selling it, I would have sold it for twice the price that I did. The trouble is, my temperament is not suited to commercial activity. In short, after I returned to Hyderabad, having got rid of my inheritance, I had a few thousand rupees in my pocket, half of which I gave to my brother. Although lacking in worldliness, I was not short of courage and enterprise. It was now time to make some definite plans for the future. I decided to leave Hyderabad and go to Delhi, and to start an innovative new Urdu weekly there. There was such restiveness in my disposition that no sooner had I settled down peacefully than I felt the urge for change. So it was that, tired of the company at Hyderabad, one day I steeled myself and told Maulvi Sahib of my decision to leave.

I still remember that evening. He took a deep pull at his hookah, and said after a long silence, 'It is true that when you came here on my insistence you told me clearly that you would not stay for more than two years, but it is only the end of 1936, and the condensed version of the dictionary has yet to be completed. After that, the Anjuman will need your help in compiling and publishing it.' I assured him that I would provide this assistance regularly from Delhi. The advantage in my going there now was that making the preliminary arrangements for the magazine would become easier.

Naturally he was displeased at my obduracy. He had given Hameeda and me the warm affection that only a father can give, and in return we had treated him with an equal degree of deference. The fact of the matter, however, was that I was an employee of the Anjuman, and I knew that I would not be able to survive there for long. It was best for me to leave before there was confrontation or unpleasantness between us.

When I arrived in Delhi, I rented a flat in Sarbuland Jang's house in Darya Ganj, with the help of Shahid Ahmed. At the same time I applied for a declaration for the magazine. Minor officials however warned me then and there that permission for the paper depended on the report from Hyderabad, which would take time. I informed Maulvi Sahib of the position and became absorbed in work on the dictionary as well as matters concerning the proposed magazine.

The literary companionship that I formed with Shahid Ahmed during our days in Aligarh, continued through the musical gatherings in Karachi. Whenever I used to make my way to his upper storey office through the intricate streets of Khari Baoli in Delhi, his partridge, which performed the duties of a watchman for him, would attack me in a paroxysm of enthusiastic affection. The calligraphists would call out, 'Akhtar Sahib is here. Get him to give you his article.' Presently, all our friends—Ansar Nasri, Fazl Haq Quraishi, Sadiq ul Khairi— would gather. We would sing, and Shahid Sahib's classical singing would wane beside my light, popular songs. After a day full of article writing and pleasant chatter we would head towards the Jami Masjid in quest of kebabs. How can one forget the literary taste that Shahid Ahmed's magazine *Saqi*, and Salahuddin Ahmed's *Adbi Dunya* created among the readers of Urdu? The sincerity of the two men has left a deep impression on me.

After a two-month long period of waiting I was informed that my application for a declaration had been rejected by the authorities. I learned on inquiry that the report from Hyderabad was not favourable. The news stupefied me.

Some Aspects of Maulvi Abdul Haq's Personality

Much has been written about the visible aspects of Maulvi Sahib's personality, but his private life has remained obscure. His companions either remained ignorant of its state, or they chose to remain silent about it. His personality may come to light if his memoirs escape the exploitation of time.

He shunned practical politics, although having spent many years of his life in a princely state like Hyderabad he was decidedly well acquainted with the complexion of politics there. One of its aspects was the conflict between British authority and the independence of the Nizam. When the question of succession was raised after the death of Mir Mehboob Ali Khan, the British tried to intervene, and those who resisted their unjustifiable intervention became the target of their wrath. Maulana Zafar Ali Khan was exiled from Hyderabad and

Maulvi Abdul Haq was transferred to the isolated town of Aurangabad. Maulana Zafar Ali Khan has hinted at these occurrences in his poetry:

وہ کہنی مارنے والوں کا ساتھ اگر دیتے

نظام آج نہ ہوتا غلام ٹامی کا

Had he paid attention to those who signaled their advice to him
The Nizam would not have been in thrall to the British

Here and there in his verse, Mir Mehboob Ali has expressed his longing to be free of the British:

یہ کہہ رہی ہے پلٹ کر نگاہِ یار ابھی

زمانہ اور بھی بدلے گا ایک بار ابھی

My departing beloved looks back at me, and says,
'Time will take yet another turn'

Maulvi Sahib's real talent for politics was displayed, when after his arrival in Delhi, he secured the help of the Muslim League in the confrontation with Gandhi over Urdu, and allied it with concurring minds in Hyderabad.

I was curious to see the human being who was concealed behind the love of Anjuman and nature. Everybody knew that after a marriage lasting a few days and the divorce that followed, Maulvi Sahib had remained single for the rest of his life. One day when we came across a wedding band playing on the road, Maulvi Sahib clapped his hands and shouted, 'Yet another bird trapped, yet another bird!' When, taking him literally, I looked up at a withered pipal tree, he pointed to a grain seller who was preparing for his second marriage.

It cannot be said that Maulvi Sahib had something against womanhood. However he disliked the halter that Sheikh Saadi wore all his life, calling it the 'tradition of the Prophet.'

Once when I had just bought a gramophone, Maulvi Sahib brought out a decrepit old record from his safe and asked me to play it. The record had a lyric by a famous singer called Gauhar, who belonged to the town of Sholapur. There was such allurement in the voice, such feeling in the rendering! After he had heard it in silence two or three times, he said with a sigh, 'Keep this record'. I have kept that memento safely with me to this day.

عالم ہُو میں اک آواز سی آجاتی ہے
چپکے چپکے کوئی کہتا ہے فسانہ دل کا

In the wilderness a voice is heard
Somebody is confiding softly the sadness of his heart

It had never occurred to me that my fearless speech and writing in Hyderabad would have the consequences that they did. However many enlightened minds among the students of Osmania University were influenced by them. One of them was Makhdoom Mohyuddin, with whom my friendship was similar to my bond with Majaz in Aligarh. Later Makhdoom was revealed as a man of action as much as he was an expert at wielding his pen. Maulvi Sahib disapproved of him because of the university's politics, and tried to keep me away from him. We used to meet up either at Baba's flat or one of the tea rooms on Abid Road. Thus we founded a literary society that can be called the cornerstone of the Progressive movement in Hyderabad.

The mirage of a magazine that had brought me to Delhi had now vanished, and I needed to find a different path for myself. This was about the time when I met Sajjad Zaheer in Delhi. He has mentioned this meeting in his book, *Roshnai*, in the following words:

> I met Akhtar Husain, who had quarrelled with Maulvi Abdul Haq and come to Delhi. I was not satisfied with the state in which I found the Association of Progressive Writers in Delhi, so I asked him to take up the responsibility of looking after it, but he was not prepared to do so since he was set on becoming a great man.

It is surprising that a cultured man like Sajjad Zaheer could mention something that was so petty. It was not even true, because the excuse I had given him was that I was about to leave Delhi, for there was now no reason for me to stay on there.

In April Maulvi Sahib came on his annual trip to the north, and stayed at my house. When I declined to go back to Hyderabad, he expressed no annoyance, and instead, assured me that the Anjuman would always need my help in the publication and compilation of its works.

Maulvi Abdul Haq's Menagerie

There was much diversity in Maulvi Abdul Haq's personality. Despite his rejection of married and family life, he was full of a sparkling vitality and life. He and I shared a fondness for good food, love of reading, a sense of humour, a predilection for travel, affection for animals, and many other such characteristics and pursuits. Many years ago I wrote an article entitled 'Maulvi Abdul Haq's Menagerie' for the magazine, *Auraq*. I am including it in this book for the reason that nobody has thus far written about that aspect of Maulvi Sahib's personality.

In Hyderabad Deccan, Maulvi Abdul Haq would leave each morning for his walk, taking his accustomed route to Husain Sager. But I remember that at one time he began to head for Bagh-e-Aama, though this place was not far from his house. Once he was within the Bagh, he strode rapidly towards the cages in which tigers were kept, and would stand in front of one of them. A tigress would come and stand near the iron bars, look attentively at Maulvi Sahib, and put some question to him with a growl. Recently she had given birth to two cubs which the keeper would bring out of the cage and leave with us. Maulvi Sahib would be transported with joy, and would play with them for a long time. For me this was a new aspect of his personality with which I was unacquainted. At any rate I would join enthusiastically in the sport, and we would be playing with the cubs until one of them happened to collide with us and cry out in pain. Meanwhile, the tigress who would be watching our movements with high disapproval, and leaping up and down in her cage, would let out a furious roar. The keeper would laugh and gather up the cubs in his arms to take them to their mother. Maulvi Sahib would then pick up his walking stick and say to me, 'Let's go. We'll come again tomorrow.'

I had never seen or heard of Maulvi Sahib's interest in animals before this. When I told him as much he explained, 'A long time ago, before the First World War, when I was in charge of education in Aurangabad, I had acquired an Alsatian. I formed a great affection for that dog. You have seen how far away the bungalow next to the tomb is from habitation. I was living there in those days and that dog was my only companion in that whole desolate landscape. He would follow me like my shadow everywhere I went.

One day a hunter brought a tiny tigress that he had captured in the jungle, and left it with me. I had a large cage built for her and employed a man to look after her. The tigress grew fast and I became quite fond of her as well. But she couldn't stand the dog, and nor could the dog tolerate her presence. He would bark at her several times a day, and the tigress would tell him off with equal frequency. I tried my best to make peace between them, but to no avail. I was still trying to think of a way to settle this matter when death led the dog close to the cage. The tigress put out a paw through the bars of the cage and wrung the dog's neck. When I arrived on the scene I found the dog covered in blood, and lifeless. The incident grieved me, so after that I sent the tigress away to the public gardens and resolved never to keep a pet again.'

Whenever Maulvi Sahib recounted something like this, the whites of his eyes seemed to expand, and he would become quiet for a while, which was what happened on our way back from the public gardens in Hyderabad. Suddenly I had a compelling sense of his loneliness, and I decided that I would get him a dog of a good breed.

After a while, Maulvi Sahib said, 'I wouldn't be surprised if it is the same tigress.'

'That's not possible. A tiger doesn't live for more than fifteen or twenty years.' I replied.

'Well, maybe she is her daughter. There is a resemblance.'

Maulvi Sahib would now and then speak in this naïve way. He retained an element of innocence even in his old age.

There was a large empty area in front and at the back of Maulvi Sahib's house, and two tall pipal trees stood guard in front. I spread an iron netting around the tree trunks and introduced into this enclosure, birds of different colours, which I had sent for from various places. Maulvi Sahib was pleased with this arrangement, and would watch the antics of the birds for a while everyday, though at the same time he would say that birds should not be imprisoned in cages. In this connection, Iqbal's *Parinday ki Faryad* is a good poem. Of all the Urdu poets, the only ones Maulvi Sahib liked were Hali and Iqbal.

Soon we heard that Qazi Abdul Ghaffar's bitch had had a litter. In those days Qazi Abdul Ghaffar used to publish a daily paper called *Payam* in Hyderabad. Although he had named his bitch Moti, she had a western pedigree. Her magnificent get up was no less than that of an English memsahib. Qazi Sahib himself used to look after her and see to her adornment. I liked one puppy in her litter, and when it was a little older I asked Qazi Sahib to give him to me. I still remember his soft white and black curly hair, and loving, loyal eyes.

Maulvi Sahib jumped for joy when he saw him. Touching him carefully he said, 'He is certainly of a good breed. He should be given a good name.'

I suggested several names but he didn't like any of them. Instead, he called the dog Nazi. I protested that the Nazis were cruel people, what did this poor puppy have to do with them, but Maulvi Sahib had settled for Nazi and that is what we ended up calling the dog.

When his legs became strong enough to carry him around, Nazi decided to inspect the rooms in the house. In one room he found Maulvi Ehtishamuddin, Shanul Haq Haqqi's late father, absorbed in compiling the Urdu dictionary. When Nazi attempted to address him, he levelled his staff at him, and the poor puppy ran for his life. When he peered into the next room, he found Dr Abid Husain putting together the English–Urdu dictionary. Stammering with nervousness, he scolded the dog so harshly that the creature was stupefied. Nazi now realized that he had two guardians in that house. One was Maulvi Abdul Haq, and the other was I. However, I had given him to understand that Maulvi Abdul Haq was his master and his loyalty must lie with him.

When Maulvi Sahib would enter his study after breakfast, Nazi used to follow him, and sit down quietly behind his chair. Soon a servant would bring the hookah and Maulvi Sahib would take puff after puff from it. Nazi strongly disapproved of this activity. In the beginning the rumbling of the hookah used to startle Nazi, for he thought that it was an animal that was making the sound. The smoke played its part in alarming him, and he made such a racket that Maulvi Sahib lost patience and turned him out of his room. After that Nazi became more discreet. He would now crawl under Maulvi Sahib's bed and lie there only when Maulvi Sahib himself was resting on the bed. Maulvi Sahib would speak to him softly, and Nazi's ears would prick up with attention and pleasure.

From a distance one could take Nazi for a lamb. When Maulvi Sahib tossed the ball to him he would leap at it with the utmost agility, despite the considerable weight of his thick fur, and would seize it with his paws. At times he imagined that his tail was an object extraneous to his body, and he would run round and round trying to catch it. He would then head towards the garden where he buried his bones, and would sharpen his teeth on them. There were, in short, many interesting aspects to Nazi's shenanigans.

About this time I made a mistake. I used to drop by at Mrs Sarojni Naidu's, frequently in the evenings. She had a beautiful Siamese cat for a pet. Recently the cat had given birth. Mrs Naidu gave me one of the kittens to take home. It seemed to me that the kitten did not in the least resemble its mother. It looked like the progeny of a black monster. But Mrs Naidu assured me that every newborn kitten looks ugly, however, its looks improve as it grows up. So, in short, not disagreeing out of politeness, I brought the kitten home, tucked under my arm.

As soon as he saw it, Nazi raised a long wail of protest. Maulvi Sahib too, expressed his disapproval. 'A cat hardly qualifies to be a pet. Besides how can a cat and a dog, living in the same house, be expected to get along? I think you should return it immediately.'

The kitten meanwhile was sitting in its basket, listening to us with an utterly helpless expression on it frightened little face. Taking its side, I came up with a host of ideas: sang panegyrics to the beauty of the Siamese cat, counted the blessings of keeping a cat. I had not read Ubaid Zakani's poem, *Garbah-o-Mosh* (Cat and Mouse), at the time, but reminded Maulvi Sahib of Katherine Mansfield's essay in praise of the cat, which he too had read. When Maulvi Sahib was still not convinced, I got the servants to tell him that there were signs of the existence of mice in his library. On hearing this piece of information, Maulvi Sahib took back his objections and the kitten finally became a part of the household.

Without consulting Maulvi Sahib, I named the kitten Lama. I was certain that once he grew up, he would be as round and fat as lamas from Tibet. But meanwhile, he was thin and weak, and on his face there was such an expression of longing and yearning, that if somebody had seen him in 1947, they would have thought him a member of the refugees' caravan.

We spared no effort in looking after Lama. We protected him from Nazi's antagonism, and waited impatiently for the day when he would begin to show his Siamese good looks. But unfortunately, as he grew older, his ugliness only increased. Neither he nor his fur grew any longer. His complexion grew blacker by the day. His father must have been a black cat, and Lama had taken after him wholly. The reason for his confusion was that he could not hide this secret much longer.

Lama now had no standing in the house. Everybody would revile him, and Nazi would pursue and persecute him at will. He found protection only either in Maulvi Ehtishamuddin room, where he would hide behind a dictionary, or on my table, on which he sometimes jumped up and settled down with his eyes closed, to think of his Maker.

Lama always longed to have Maulvi Sahib pay attention to him. After all it was thanks to him that the mice had vanished from the library. Maulvi Sahib did indeed appreciate this service; as a matter of fact, when once Nazi tried to creep into a cupboard full of books, in imitation of Lama, Maulvi Sahib caned his erring canine. It was a scene worth watching: Maulvi Sahib had never struck Nazi before, so there were tears of complaint in the dog's eyes, while Lama's eyes sparkled with joy.

For his diligence in getting rid of the mice, Lama was awarded the right to share with Nazi the largesse which Maulvi Sahib dispensed from his table. The two would squat, one on either side of his chair, and Maulvi Sahib would throw pieces of bread, sometimes to one and sometimes to the other. He showed his partiality to Nazi by casting the food more often in his direction, and tossing him the choice morsels. But Lama would take care to remind him of his presence by tapping his feet with his paw, and in this way he would obtain his share.

Very soon Nazi began to feel that Maulvi Sahib was being quite liberal minded with Lama, even though his tolerance did not really amount to affection. It filled him with such an implacable vindictiveness and malice that he became Lama's mortal enemy. He persecuted him to the extent that the cat could no longer dare to enter the house, and spent his time in the garden, where lying on the grass he would watch the birds and the butterflies for hours. He crept in only when he could hear food being served, or at night when the blackness of his skin merged with the darkness of night and he became almost invisible.

By and by, Lama became quite shrewd, and realized that it was owing to Nazi that he had become a victim of injustice. He then decided to fight for his survival, and began to use the tricks and strategies he had inherited from his black African father. Sometimes he would hide under the sofa where Nazi could not follow him. If Nazi tried to peer in, he would scratch his nose, and while Nazi attended to his injured muzzle, he would strike his leg with his paw and make good his escape. Whenever Nazi chased him in the garden, he would play tricks on him, turn up suddenly from behind him, slap him, and leap into a tree to climb out of the dog's reach. Nazi's fury would then know no bounds. He would bark so loudly that everybody would be startled. Maulvi Sahib would then say indignantly that it was all Lama's fault. He would stroke Nazi lovingly and shake his fist at Lama who would be sitting in the tree, grimacing at him.

The effect of Lama's defiance was the opposite of what he had expected. He soon realized that nobody in the house was sympathetic to him anymore. When he was young, he was fed on milk and cream morning and evening, and everybody used to guard him from Nazi's onslaughts, but when he grew up people lost interest in his welfare. He therefore thought of a new way of protecting himself.

Many stray tomcats used to live in the neighbourhood. All day they used to be occupied in their search for livelihood, but at night they would gather in some open ground and exchange views loudly on the cruelty and heartlessness of the human race. I cannot say when Lama joined this band. We discovered Lama's involvement in it one night when suddenly we heard a piercing chorus of cats from among the trees in the garden. It was like a war song that was getting faster and faster. First there was a single cry, which then became an unbroken scream. In no time the whole house was reverberating with the thunderous sound. We stared at the trees with amazement, wondering what the matter was. Then, in the pale light of an electric bulb we caught sight of Lama, who was leading the chorus with rapt abandon.

Maulvi Sahib laughed when he beheld this spectacle. He yelled at the cats to drive them away, while we threw stones at them. The next morning when Lama presented himself at the breakfast table, he showed no signs of remorse, nor did Maulvi Sahib express indignation at his conduct. As a matter of fact he treated the cat with indulgence, saying, 'He is a rascal. If we do not fill that stomach of his, he will make a bigger nuisance of himself.'

When it became known that Maulvi Sahib was fond of animals, an acquaintance brought him a pair of young deer. They were kept at the back of the house, where they grazed freely and gambolled without fear. But as soon as someone looked at them, they were alerted, and would run away.

Maulvi Sahib took an interest in them for a few days, but was soon tired of them, saying, 'A deer's nature is too wild, too intractable. He can never be anybody's friend. The jungle suits him best and there is no point in keeping him for a pet.' However, whenever he was exhausted after a day's work, he would leave his study and come out in the verandah to watch the wild creatures. He would stand there for a long time and would recite the following couplet from Mir:

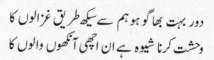

You have learnt the ways of the deer, and run far away from me,
Wildness is the manner of those with beautiful eyes

Maulvi Abdul Haq did not care for the genre of *ghazal* in poetry. Yet he admired Mir, and would unthinkingly recite from his ghazals. However, unlike the prevailing custom, he never quoted poetry in either his speeches or his writing.

Maulvi Sahib was usually home in the evenings, and that was the time when people came to visit him. Before his visitors arrived and after they left, he used to stroll in the garden. Sometimes he would stop by the aviary and listen for a while to the crooning of the birds, then go over to the backyard to take a look at the deer who would be chewing the cud, sitting comfortably close to each other. Finally he would sit in his armchair, smoking his hookah, absorbed in reading a book. He would then be quite unaware of his seclusion, because Nazi would be sitting at his feet and Lama would be wandering around nearby. This state of affairs was soon disrupted when I left Hyderabad and went to Europe, and Maulvi Sahib arrived in Delhi with the Anjuman Taraqqi Urdu office.

Many years later when this period was recalled, the whites of his eyes seemed to dilate. He took a deep puff on his hookah and was silent for a long time.

My other benefactor, Babu Molchand Agarwal, disapproved of my disassociation from Hindi. When he was informed of the desperate straits in which I found myself in Delhi, he wrote to me, inviting me to come to Calcutta, where, he suggested, I could either edit the Hindi monthly *Vishwamitr*, or work for the English daily, *Advance*.

Some days passed while I pondered over my options, then one day Hameeda suddenly came up with an idea. She said, 'Why do you worry? Let's go to Europe. If you earn a doctorate there, there will be no dearth of jobs.' I stared at her with astonishment, for the thought had never crossed my mind. We had been married for a year, and while she was as unworldly as I, she possessed a spirit as enterprising as mine.

I was not inclined to go to England because living with racial prejudice was unacceptable to my ego. Moreover, I felt such hatred for the tyranny perpetrated by British imperialism that the idea of spending so much time in what was its bastion was abhorrent to me. I therefore decided to go to France, which has been the cradle of art and literature for centuries, and now in the coalition government became the centre of the Anti Fascist and Progressive movement. Paris University had an acknowledged status among the oldest universities of the world. Not knowing the French language was no obstacle for me, since I was naturally endowed with a gift for languages and could therefore pick it up fast.

This was the time when few Indians travelled to the West, and the number of those who went there for higher education was even less. If one possessed a suitable university degree from home, admission in a European University was no problem. Also there were no restrictions on sending or receiving foreign exchange. One could send money orders from any part of the world or transfer money easily through a bank. A health certificate was unheard of, and every traveller was considered to be of sound health. The stamp of the British government on a passport ensured that visas could be obtained easily and quickly at the borders. The cost of living was so low that one could live comfortably on £20 (300 rupees) a month. Besides, in France all education was free. However money was at least ten times as expensive as it is today. Nobody provided scholarships for education abroad, unless in a rare case a raja or some other wealthy person decided to oblige someone who had made a special effort to obtain one.

On the insistence of Mrs Sarojini Naidu, the Diwan of Travancore State, Sir Ram Swami Ayer did decide to give me a scholarship, but at the last moment the arrangement fell through and I barely escaped a catastrophic let down. The Fazalbhoy Trust of Bombay too, ignored the recommendations of Allama Iqbal and Najib Ashraf Nadvi to sponsor me. In the end I had to depend solely on my own resources, which consisted of a few thousand rupees, barely sufficient to see us through a year, and beyond that, whatever I could earn by plying my pen.

However, the biggest problem of all was to obtain a passport. The government viewed me with such disapproval that even Zafar Omer Sahib was powerless to help. I had lost all hope when in mid 1937, the Congress cabinet of UP was formed, and Pandit Pant became the Chief Minister. He intervened, on receiving a spate of telegrams from Mrs Naidu and Dr Rajinder Prashad, and subsequently, a few days before our departure we received our passports.

Our ship was to leave Bombay harbour at the end of August. Mrs Naidu advised me to visit Gandhiji en route to Bombay, at Vardha, because he had been desirous of meeting me since he had encountered me at the Sahitya Parishad. I could not ignore her wishes.

My Meeting with Gandhiji

Gandhiji's ashram was in Sevagram, which is near the town of Vardha. The journey to the ashram could be made either by bullock cart or on foot. City guests like us were put up in a simple but clean house. However the 'nationalist' type of individuals slept on mats inside huts, and ate from banana leaves. Only Mrs Naidu and Maulana Azad were entitled to charpoys. Those of Gandhi's disciples who lived in the ashram used to occupy themselves with farming and spinning. During my stay I saw Khan Abdul Ghaffar cutting the grass in a flowerbed.

The day after I arrived, I presented myself before Gandhiji. He was sitting cross-legged in a small room, and was writing something. He responded pleasantly to my greeting and then took off his glasses and looked at me attentively. His eyes were the most interesting feature of his personality, in the sense that they had the power to keep their own secrets concealed, but to penetrate to the depths of their interlocutor's soul.

Gandhi said to me, 'I am pleased to know that you write both in Urdu and in Hindi, and that you are also familiar with Sanskrit. What do you plan to do when you return from Europe?'

'If I have the chance, I will try to dispel the mutual distrust between Hindus and Muslims.' I replied.

Gandhiji was pleased with my answer, and said, 'That is a good thought. The issue of national unity is very important, and it does not fall in the field of politics alone; rather, it deserves the attention of scholarship and literature as well.'

Gandhiji showed that he remembered this meeting when he nominated me Secretary of the Indian Literature Board in 1945. However, by then it was too late for me to accept the offer.

5

My First Trip to Europe

The sea cast such a spell on me that I spent most of my time sitting on the deck and watching the blue sky and azure expanse of water. In the middle of the ocean, the rising and setting of the sun, the twilight's reddening of the sky from horizon to horizon, the play of moonlight on the waves, were all ineffable sights.

One day I was sitting with a textbook of elementary French, and a map of Paris spread in front of me, when an elderly fellow traveller extended his hand and introduced himself in English as Dr Leclerc. He was accompanied by his wife, who like him was a medical doctor and lived in Paris. I introduced Hameeda to them and told him that we were on our way to Paris, where I intended to study for a higher degree.

Dr Leclerc asked me if I knew French and had acquaintances in Paris. When I answered his questions in the negative he was surprised, and said, 'Why don't you go to England, then? It would be much easier for you there.' I replied, 'I am so deeply conscious of being a member of their subject race that I don't like the idea of living in their land. I would much prefer the free ambiance of France; and as for the language, all it needs is some hard work, so it won't take me long to learn it.'

He liked my reply so well that he took on the role of our guardian for the rest of the trip, and was very kind to us during our stay in Paris as well. His cousin was the same General Leclerc who liberated Paris from the Germans, and whose name has been given to an important road there. Dr and Madame Leclerc were supporters of socialism, and had travelled across Soviet Russia from one end to the other to observe the system in operation. They had changed ships, and were now on their way home finally, after a voyage of several months. Describing the miserable and oppressed state of the Soviet people he said, 'Don't forget that it [communism] is the greatest social experiment in human history, and its result will be known much later because it is being tried not in an industrial country like Germany and France, but in a backward, agricultural country. Communism means the distribution of wealth, but how can wealth be produced immediately in a poverty stricken country like Russia? Moreover, the Russian people have not known democratic freedom, and therefore do not miss it. Prosperity and democratic freedom will come with industrial growth.'

It is true that every progressive revolution brings with it a similar reaction: The successor to the reign of the first four Caliphs was Muavia, that of the French revolution was Napoleon, and it was Stalin to whom the heritage of the Russian revolution fell. All such inheritors of progressive change are so absorbed in their efforts for the supremacy and prosperity of their nations that the main ideology becomes no more than a tool in the hands of the government. Furthermore, the Imam, the Church and the Party, all use ideology to justify their own character and actions. The one element that sustains hope in all this is the fact that no despot dares to say that the desire for equality and freedom is meaningless. The leader who deviates from this is singed, and finally destroyed by his own ego as was the case with Hitler.

The number of Indians who travelled to the west was small in those days. A few thousand farmers, labourers, and mercenaries had settled in Canada, America, and England. But in Europe there were no more than a few hundred of our people. There were barely a hundred and fifty Indians in France, the majority of whom were Gujrati traders, and the remaining twenty or thirty were students. There was neither air travel in those days, nor much tourism or trade. Nobody had money to spare. The people of Europe believed either that India was populated by ascetics and magicians, or by rajas and the fabulously rich. The truth about India became known only after the War; for in the olden days we were highly respectable. What I refer to as the 'olden days' is the period before the First World War as it was known in popular parlance among the people of Europe. The War drew a dividing line in the European memory as deep and indelible as the Partition of 1947 drew in ours. Eras of history are created in this way.

Maulvi Abdul Haq had informed Abdullah Chugtai of our arrival in Paris. The latter was engaged in research on the Taj Mahal, in the French capital. He met us at the railway station and put us up in a hotel in the Latin Quarter. This old neighbourhood is spread around the

university, on the left bank of the Seine, and shelters students and
wanderers. In those days the population of Paris was about four
million, at least one fourth of which consisted of foreigners, mainly
Eastern and Central European immigrants. Among them were men of
diverse temperament, manners and religion. There were exiled
Russians, Balkan intellectuals, German Jews, Hungarian Chinese,
Italian anti-Fascists and Arab labourers. In this hospitable and gracious
city, there was room for all, and the level of tolerance was such that
prejudice on the basis of race, colour and language was never hinted
at. However the British tourist was as much a target of ridicule as the
Sikhs are in our parts. If somebody was caught being rude, people
would comment that he was probably an Englishman. As for
Americans, they had the same status as a petty moneylender used to
have in our youth, in the company of the elite.

Imtiaz Ali Khan and Brijesh Singh used to live in the neighbourhood
of our hotel. Imtiaz was the nephew of the Nawab of Karnal, and a
cousin of Nawabzada Liaquat Ali Khan. Brijesh was the son of Raja
Kalakankar. My friendship with Brijesh began on the first day of our
acquaintance and lasted throughout our stay in Paris. As for Imtiaz,
our friendship with each other never diminished for as long as he lived.
Both of them had been living in Paris for many years, on the pretext
of acquiring higher education. Despite their taste for licentious living,
they had a strong faith in communism. It was Brijesh Singh who later
married Stalin's daughter Svetlana. When he died in Moscow, she had
him cremated and brought his ashes to India, from where she defected
to America.

Imtiaz married a Frenchwoman by the name of Vivienne who was
the owner of a strange underground cabaret in the Latin Quarter.
When she decided to divorce her first husband in order to marry
Imtiaz, there was quite an outcry, and I began to frequent the place in
order to provide moral support to my friend. Before the French
Revolution, this cabaret had existed in a basement by the river, and
there had been no change in its atmosphere since then. The names of
celebrities who had been frequenting the cabaret over the years had
been engraved in a marble plaque. Prominent among them were
Baudelaire, Oscar Wilde and Bernard Shaw. A special feature of this
place was that nothing in it betrayed signs of modernity. Old songs
and dances, aged structure, time-bitten chandeliers, furniture placed

any old way, waitresses in long rural skirts, large measures of wine, and such heaps of jars that one could hear Khaqani exclaim:

ساقی بدہ رطل گراں آں ہے کہ دہقاں پرورد

Wine bearer! Give me a measure of wine, large enough to satisfy a peasant

In a word, the Caveauboly had such a reputation that people would come from afar to experience it. The company was especially agreeable when friends from London—Himmat Singh, Firoz Gandhi, etc.— would arrive. It was the same Firoz who later married Pandit Nehru's daughter, Indira.

There were many places in Paris famous for their character and atmosphere. They are all gone now, or are going. There was one nightclub called Lumiere which I particularly liked. A couple of artists could always be found there, who would draw a sketch or cartoon of the customer.

One or two poets would also be there, ready to oblige you with a short poem in your honour. A violinist would play your favourite tune for you.

Khalida Adeeb Khanum

After we had checked into the hotel, I posted the letter Mrs Sarojini Naidu had given me for Khalida Adeeb Khanum. A few years ago Khanum had come to India at the invitation of the Jamia Millia, and a collection of the speeches she gave had been published under the title of *Turkey main Mashriq-o-Maghrib ki Kashmakash* (The Conflict of East and West in Turkey), drawing much acclaim from discerning readers. On her return from India she wrote a book about her visit, which she called *Inside India*. Its Urdu translation was published with the title, *Andaroon-e-Hind*. Khalida Khanum and her husband, Adnan Bey, were among the oldest companions of Ataturk, but they were living in Paris as exiles owing to political differences with the Turkish leader. Adnan Bey gave Turkish lessons, while Khalida Khanum busied herself with writing and compilation in English. She was a well-known writer, both in English and in Turkish, and many of her books had been translated into European languages.

Two days later, Adnan Bey called us on the phone to invite us for tea. There is a place in the south of Paris, known as Cité Universitaire, which consists of fifty hostels. Each of these hostels housed the students of one country or another. Altogether, about ten or twelve thousand students resided in the hostels. Hundreds of flats have been built in the vicinity for the teachers, one of which was occupied by Adnan Bey and Khalida Khanum.

Adnan Bey was a tall, frail and taciturn man of a somewhat melancholic temperament. As for Khalida Khanum, there was such dignity in her good humour, and such discernment shone in her eyes, that the very first glance conveyed to one the impression of a great personality. Her infinite kindness to Hameeda and myself sheltered us from feelings of loneliness at the worst of times.

Khalida Khanum advised us that the best way of familiarizing ourselves with the French language and culture was to be the guests of a respectable family who knew no English. This would put us in a situation where we would, perforce, learn the language fast, and also get to know the right kind of people. Subsequently, she arranged for us to stay with Madame Martin, the widow of a lawyer, and we stayed there very comfortably for a year.

I used to read the English newspaper early in the morning. I would then read the same news stories in a French daily, and look up the difficult words in a dictionary. On my way to my French lessons I would learn the names of items that were given in price lists issued by shops, and sought help from my hostess in putting me right wherever I made mistakes when I spoke or wrote in the language. In this way, it took me no more than a few months to speak and understand French effortlessly, and to become a competent reader in the language as well.

The easiest way to learn a language is to live among native speakers of the language. Not only does one's comprehension become more accurate and precise in this way, one also learns the subtleties of the language and becomes sensitive to its nuances. Gradually, when I had learned enough French to read its literature directly, without the medium of translation, I realized why French prose is peerless.

England has been called the successor to the Roman Empire because it has benefited from its constitution and laws, and imbibed its discipline. On the other hand France inherited the wisdom and artistic genius of Greece. Logic and reason permeate French thought, and therefore the splendour of French literature is manifest in its prose, rather than in its poetry. There is such harmony between word and thought that all ambiguity is banished, and the whole undivided character of the word creates beauty from the fusion of simplicity, brevity, and wholesomeness. It is a beauty that echoes reality.

The University of Paris, which is also known as Sorbonne University, is seven hundred years old. In the period that I was there, it had seventeen thousand students. The number has doubled now. It had become even higher, but diminished after several other universities came up in the vicinity. Education was absolutely free, and one even got considerable discounts on showing one's student's identity card at certain restaurants, stores, theatres, and the railway. There is one useful practice that could benefit our own educational institutions: In addition to the permanent teaching staff, the university invites and compensates experts in different fields of study to teach in the capacity of guest lecturers. A lay person can listen to a lecture without any constraint. Such practices enhance the scope of both teaching and learning, and the university does not remain insular and limited.

The topic I chose for my PhD thesis was 'Life in Ancient India' as it is depicted in Sanskrit Literature. I worked on this project under the supervision of the famous expert on Indian Studies, Professor Louis Renaud. In addition, I was guided in the sociological aspect of my thesis by Professor Marc Bloch, who was killed by the Nazis during the War. After he had approved the outline of my research thesis, and completed the list of reference books that he had recommended, it was decided that I would attend his lectures when I needed to, and meet him once a week to discuss issues arising from my work, which necessitated his guidance. About once a month I met him at his house as well, which provided the opportunity for a free exchange of views.

There existed a putative 'Indian Association' in Paris, the members of which belonged to two schools of politics. Most of the businessmen, and some students were pro-Gandhi Congressites, the rest were radical students. The person who was then the President of the association, later became the Minister for Information and remained in that post for many years in the government of Pandit Nehru, and was known as Dr Keskar. Soon after I arrived in Paris, a meeting of the association was called in order to either reelect Keskar, or elect another in his place. Keskar represented the views of the Congress.

قرعهٔ فال بنام ِ من دیوانه زدند

The lot fell to me—this imprudent person

With no inkling of what was in store for me, I found myself lifted from the corner where I stood, and placed on the Presidential chair. Brijesh and Imtiaz had, without my knowledge, lobbied for me and convinced the majority of those present to elect me the President of the association.

It was understood that the President's residence served as the address of the Association. Moreover the only possession of the Association was a writing pad printed with its letterhead. The meeting of the executive committee of the Association was held once a month in our favourite café, Sorce, whose proprietor, in order to please us, subscribed to the daily, *Bombay Chronicle*. A bundle of the issues of this paper used to arrive every month. The General Body meeting of the Association used to be called to coincide with the arrival of some famous Indian leader in Paris. The expenses of the meeting-cum-visit of the dignitary to the Association could then be defrayed easily through the donations received from the members.

As the President of the Association, I sometimes had to carry out some interesting duties. One day a newcomer from Madras said to me, 'I am a dancer. If you introduce me here, my work will get a boost.' In those days Indian music and dance were unknown in Europe. However, I asked the dancer to perform in the weekly dance night arranged by the University Union on Saturdays. On the day of the performance the man dressed himself as the Hindu god Krishna, with a small purple turban on his head, a flute in his hand, a garland round his neck, and a *dhoti* tied just under his waist. A couple of records of Indian music had luckily been found somewhere. When this individual stepped on to the stage, the large audience welcomed him enthusiastically. I gave a speech introducing and praising the dance and the dancer. Then as he began the first movement of the dance, one end of his *dhoti* got caught in his toe and came off, leaving the man naked on the stage and in front of the audience, dressed in nothing but the tiny loincloth which he was wearing under his *dhoti*. For a moment the silence in the hall was unbroken, then girls in the audience cried out 'Shame!' in French. When the wretched fellow began to wind his dhoti around him, I shouted at him, 'This is a city where women dance in the nude. Why are you so embarrassed?'

The man took the cue, and with hardly a stitch on his body put on such a lively performance that the audience was dazzled. When he exited from the stage I explained to the viewers that the dance depicted the feelings of the forsaken lover who, faced with his loss in the kind of hot climate we have at home, loses his marbles and tearing his clothes goes about dancing in the street where his beloved lives.

The Arrival of Pandit Nehru

When Pandit Nehru arrived in Paris in June 1938, his fame had spread beyond the frontiers of India. His articles in English had been published in London and won much acclaim. Moreover his criticism of fascism was quoted in newspapers. He stayed for a few weeks in Paris at the Hotel Napoleon, during which period I had the honour of meeting him several times. I was able to meet his daughter Indira as well, who had come down from Oxford.

The meeting organized in Pandit Nehru's honour by the Indian Association was chaired by me. The audience consisted of Indians, as well as a fairly large number of non-Indians. In my speech I said, in connection with complaints voiced by Muslims against Congress ministries, that if the circumstances that gave rise to them were not controlled the differences between the two peoples would grow, and chances of national unity would diminish. My statement infuriated Pandit Nehru, and he remarked that this was not the occasion to discuss the internal matters of the country. The real reason for his annoyance was that in 1937, it was he who had thwarted the establishment of a joint Congress and Muslim League ministry in UP, a move that intensified the tension between the two parties.

Raja Kalakankar had close links with Pandit Nehru, and through this connection Brijesh knew him well. He therefore took the Pandit, Imtiaz and me to a high-class restaurant after the meeting. After dinner, Pandit Nehru suggested that we have coffee elsewhere. Accordingly, we took a taxi to Montparnasse, a district which was famous for its coffeehouses which were patronized by intellectuals and artists. When we were sitting in the Café Rotunde, Brijesh said, 'Before the First World War, this was a small place. Lenin used to frequent it, and he was on such informal terms with the proprietor, Jacob, that whenever he was short of money he would send him a note asking him for a loan. After Lenin left France, he surfaced a few years later as the leader of the Russian Revolution. Jacob heard the news with astonishment and joy. He framed Lenin's notes and hung them up in the café, proclaiming that Lenin had patronized the place. The result was that the café became flooded with tourists and Jacob made his fortune. Subsequently he refurbished the café and gave it an altogether new look.

Panditji was most intrigued by the story and asked Brijesh where Jacob was and what he had done with Lenin's notes. Brijesh explained that Jacob had aged and it was his brothers who ran the business. However he frequently came to the café at night.

Fortuitously, we saw him sitting by the safe, drinking wine. When the Pandit expressed a desire to meet him, I went over to him and said, 'The Lenin of India has come here just to meet you. We'll be grateful if you meet him.' Jacob agreed to our request and came and sat by us. He then went to the safe and brought three or four framed notes of Lenin, written with an economy of words, and now blurred with age. We examined those rare documents for a long time, then Pandit Nehru said, 'Monsieur Jacob, these pieces of paper are of immeasurable value.' Jacob replied with a laugh, 'I've been offered millions for them. But once I sell them, what standing will I have left? Why would people like you then seek me out?'

Café Rotunde still exists, but it is many years since Jacob died. One does not know what became of those bits of paper.

A few days later, Pandit Nehru left for Madrid at the invitation of the Democratic Government of Spain. Soon, time would be up for democracy in Spain.

The Civil War in Spain

Everybody realized that the future of the world depended to a large extent on the outcome of the war between Progressive and Reactionary elements in Spain. In 1936, the man who instigated the revolt against the nascent democracy in the country was General Franco, the military ruler of occupied Western Sahara. He incited the Arab soldiers to rebellion by telling them, 'Seize the land of Andalusia from which centuries ago your ancestors were expelled at the point of the sword.' It was the kind of logic with which the British had inspired the Sikhs in 1875, when they told them, 'Go, capture Delhi and settle your scores with the Muslims.' Consequently Franco's army landed on the shores of Southern Spain and the civil war blazed forth.

The Arab memory of their expulsion from Spain is so intense that the descendants, in Morocco, of those who were expelled, have held on to the keys of their abandoned houses and the lists of their belongings, expecting to lay claim to them at the first opportunity. The news of Franco's operation reached India as well, and when Khwaja Hasan Nizami heard the name of his lieutenant, General Maula, he at once became convinced that he was a descendant of the Prophet, and issued a statement in his favour. Franco never forgot the loyalty of those Arab desert dwellers as long as he lived, and employed them as his bodyguards. Napoleon's personal servant was also an Egyptian Arab who was nicknamed Rustum.

Franco had the support of the church, the capitalists and landowners, and he had the backing of Hitler and Mussolini's military might. The democratic government was supported by left wing parties, whose mutual rivalries smoothed the way for Franco's success, in the same way as the mutual antagonism between the socialist and communist parties in Germany had assisted the Nazi government. In 1938 when the democratic government of Spain began to lose ground, Hitler occupied Austria, and France was so bounded by fascism on both sides that the Popular Front government collapsed. Meanwhile in Russia, Stalin had paralysed the Red Army, with consequences at the beginning of the War whose severity is common knowledge. In October 1938, by accepting Germany's domination of Czechoslovakia at Munich, Britain and France cleared the way for Germany's offensive in the east.

The Western governments refused to send arms to the democratic government on the pretext of neutrality, and Russia was so far away that it was impossible for adequate supplies to arrive from that quarter. At this juncture, the intellectuals, writers, and artists of the world organized the International Brigades, and confronted fascism with a courage that has no parallel in the history of the world. Among them were people like Andre Malraux, Hemingway, Orwell and Arthur Koestler. Their goal was in truth the altar where literature is created from the heart's blood.

My friend Alphonso de Fiagaredo was closely associated with the secret French organization that had links with democratic Spain, and procured supplies and equipment for it. He was the scion of an old Brazilian family and had been living in Paris for a long time. His father, Count Figuaredo had at one time been Brazil's ambassador to France. Alphonso had taken a prominent part in a military revolt against the Brazilian dictator, Vargas, and after the failure of the uprising, was spending his exile in Paris. He owned a flat of seven or eight rooms near the Gare du Nord (northern railway station). He had kept his involvement with revolutionary work a secret, even from his closest friends. He was cautious and taciturn, but his friendship with me has endured the tests of time and distance.

In Alphonso's company I had occasion to meet many famous people of Spain and South America. Once he introduced me to Picasso, who was arranging for the exhibition of his masterpiece, Guernica. Nazi bombing had devastated the Spanish town of Guernica, and in his painting, Picasso has depicted the wreckage of humanity and its values against the background of the ravaged town. Nobody had created a more poignant image of the destruction inflicted by war, since the terrible scene of Napoleon's attack on Spain painted by Goya. Picasso was about fifty years old then. He was of medium height and muscular body, had a sharp tongue, keen, insightful eyes, and sensitive features.

Pablo Neruda was working as an attaché in the Chilean embassy, and used to visit Alphonso's flat. He would recite the poetry of Garcia Lorca, who was killed by the fascists in Granada.

Alphonso and I shared a liking for chess. Our interest in the game would sometimes take us to Café Napoleon, which was close to the Opera. It was said that Napoleon used to go there to play chess. His gem-studded chair was placed on a platform in the centre of the hall, alongside a beautiful chessboard. It was a place where tradition drew chess lovers from all over the world.

One night I was waiting there for Alphonso, when my neighbour asked me, 'Do you want to play chess?' I agreed to play with the elderly, burly man, without being introduced to him. While arranging the chess pieces he said with a smile, 'How about a bet?' I guessed immediately that he was an experienced chess player, so I suggested coffee instead of money. In a little while, just before I was defeated, Alphonso arrived. He greeted the man and said to me, 'Who do you think you are playing with? He is Capa Blanca.' I apologized to the great chess player who had been, until the recent past, the World Chess Champion. I saw him play chess in the same place on many subsequent occasions. I have lost practice now, but there was a time when I could play the game with considerable skill.

I had occasion to visit the Spanish refugee camps many times, and witnessed many instances of rivalry among the Leftist parties. It is futile to recount those now. I was not able to go to Spain then, despite many attempts to do so. I did get an opportunity in 1962, but will give an account of it in a later chapter.

I pray to God that Colonel Wiedman is still alive. A few years ago, in Western Germany, he was still living. In 1939, when the ranks of the democratic forces had been routed, he somehow escaped to France. When I met him, he spent the whole evening abusing the insensitive people of the world in a mixture of German, French, and Spanish.

Wiedman was the hero of a failed revolution. During the First World War he was a Captain in the German army. After Germany was defeated, he became active in the Communist movement, and was a member of its Executive body. When the Nazis gained power he fled to Russia, and became associated with the high command of the Red Army in the capacity of an adviser. In 1938, when, tricked by Nazi spies, Stalin put to death countless officers of the Red Army, Wiedman fled to Spain, where he became a Colonel in the democratic army. It was during this period that his book on the Soviet army, *The Red Army*, became famous.

While issuing him a three-month residency permit, French officials warned him that if he did not leave France by the end of this period, he would be deported to Germany, where he would inevitably be put to death. He had made such a reputation as an international revolutionary that no country was prepared to grant him a visa. The poor man would haunt the embassies all day, and in the evening he would arrive at our house, exhausted. He would then denounce the tyranny of Hitler, Stalin and Franco. Once I hazarded a remark in defense of Stalin, hearing which he was ready to shed my blood.

His despair deepened with time, but one day fate befriended him in such a way that the adage of truth being stranger than fiction seemed appropriate. Wiedman was strolling on the footpath along the river, when suddenly a car drove up to him and stopped. A well-dressed man alighted from the car and asked him, 'Are you Mr Wiedman?' The addressee thought that the man was a messenger from doom. However when he replied in the affirmative, the stranger embraced him warmly and reminded him of a twenty-two year old incident, when after taking him prisoner in the battlefield, Wiedman took pity on him and let him go. The incident made such an impression on the man that despite the passing of many years he did not forget Wiedman's face. The man belonged to an influential family and through his efforts Wiedman was given permission to stay on in France for a long period. I still remember our celebration of this happy development.

Sir Shaikh Abdul Qadir

In 1938 I spent my summer holidays in London, where I needed to work at the India Office Library in connection with my research. Sir Abdul Qadir was residing in London during those days, in his capacity as a member of the Indian Council. One memorable achievement of Shaikh Sahib was that he gave new directions to Urdu prose and poetry through his magazine, *Makhzan*. His other feat was that he introduced the English speaking class to Urdu literature. Today many Western universities have arrangements for teaching Urdu, and radio programmes are broadcast and newspapers published in Urdu, but it was not so in those days. Dr Syed Husain had started a noteworthy journal by the name of *Yad-e Watan*, in America, and in London it was Shaikh Sahib who initiated the first gatherings of the Urdu Majlis. Its meetings were convened regularly under his chairmanship, and numerous lovers of Urdu were drawn to them.

Shaikh Sahib was such an admirer of Hafeez Jalandhari that he invited him to London and translated some of his poems into English in order to introduce them to the literary circles there. My association with Hafeez dates back a long time. I have known him since the Aligarh days, when he had been a guest of Rasheed Ahmed Siddiqui. Once when he was reciting a poem, the children in the house began to applaud him loudly. 'Why have you stopped?' Rasheed Sahib prompted him, 'That is your real audience.'

Actually, this is the true merit of Hafeez's poetry—that it appeals to all. It cannot be denied that the most successful attempts to absorb the delicate elements of Hindi poetry into Urdu were made by Azmatullah Khan and Hafeez.

Once when I casually dropped in at a meeting of the Urdu Majlis, Hafeez introduced me to Shaikh Sahib. Subsequently my relationship with him grew, and remained so until Partition. His magnanimity, discernment and eye for talent, continued to benefit all.

Once Shaikh Sahib took me to the Shafiq Restaurant, which was considered the best Indian restaurant in London. The plate in front of me was covered. Shaikh Sahib said to me with a smile, 'It contains something that you like.' I removed the napkin to find a large tomato lying on the plate. Shaikh Sahib said with a roar of laughter, 'Isn't this your favourite food?'

In some strange frame of mind I had once written, 'O God, I am convinced of Your benevolence, for You have created good things like woman and tomatoes.' The incident at the Shafiq Restaurant put me off tomatoes for ever.

Shaikh Sahib's mind was for ever looking for new expressions in scholarship and art. In a Soho café he said, 'Listen carefully. What is that gypsy singing on the guitar?' These were the words of the song:

Odray de ruk aar chirya kala and chirya kali
(There is a black male bird and a black female bird on the tree)

Undre de ruk aar pyaranoon and pyari ni
(Under the tree there is a lover and a beloved)

Shaikh Sahib spoke about Indian elements in the gypsy language in such a way that the subject attracted me, and later, after I had met gypsies in countries as far-flung as Hungary and Spain, it was further confirmed that they did indeed have their origins in our subcontinent and that numerous words from our tongue had found their way into theirs.

Shortly after our return to Paris, Sir Abdul Qadir came there with Hafeez. In his company we gained access to many notable places around the city. I became convinced of Shaikh Sahib's discernment.

One day he asked to go to a museum called Musée Guimet. Although I had spent a good deal of time in almost all the well-known museums of Paris, I was unacquainted with this place. It contained a large collection of Gandhara statues. When Shaikh Sahib sensed my ignorance, he spoke at length on the technical excellence of the Gandahara sculpture in the museum. Few people know how deep an understanding of the fine arts he possessed.

One evening I took Shaikh Sahib and Hafeez to visit Khalida Adeeb Khanum. We talked of this and that, and Shaikh Sahib translated Hafeez's poems into English. After they left, Khanum asked me what Hafeez did for a living. When I told her that poetry was his profession, she was incredulous. It was with difficulty that I could convince her that not just Hafeez, but many other poets depended on poetry for their livelihood, and that although the days of court ceremony and composing odes to the nobility were over, there were many other ways of earning a comfortable income. Khalida Khanum commented with astonishment, 'This is possible only in your country. In other places people are too busy to listen to poetry even if it is free of charge.'

Adnan Bey and Khalida Khanum were so conscious of their national dignity that they never mentioned their falling out with Ataturk to anybody. At the same time they had so much pride that they used to return the pension that the Turkish government sent them every month. Turks settled in Paris, some of whom were my close friends, had great respect for them in their hearts, but kept their distance, out of fear of their embassy.

One day Khalida Khanum casually brought up the story of the Indian Muslims who were overtly representatives of the Khilafat Movement, but were in fact British spies. One of them, a Mustafa Sagheer Muradabadi, conspired to assassinate Ataturk. He developed such good relations with influential circles that everybody trusted him. Then, somehow, his secret was divulged and he was shot dead. Among the Indian suspects who fled Turkey on that occasion was Iqbal Shedai.

Khalida Khanum suffered from being in a state of exile from her country, and her long separation from her two sons. When Ataturk died in 1938 he was succeeded by Ismat Inonu, who had no disagreements with her. I said to her, 'There can be no harm in your returning home now.'

She replied, 'It is possible only if Ismat Inonu invites us to return. And there has to be a reason for that.' Then she thought for a while and said, 'It can be done if you have my interview published in some English newspaper in India, and its translation is published in Turkey.' So she sat down and wrote a long interview (I still have the MS), which appeared in *Hindustan Times* under my name, and was then translated and published in Turkey. The result of this tactful appeasement was exactly what Khanum had reckoned it would be. A few months later the Turkish Ambassador in Paris came to Khanum's house for the first time in twelve years, bringing with him Ismat Inonu's letter.

After she had returned home, Khanum continued to write and compile. She died in or around 1964. Some of her pictures and letters, in which she has addressed Hameeda and me as her children, are our treasured possessions.

A description of how she familiarized me with the idea of Pakistan will come later in this book.

At the beginning of 1938 we heard the unpleasant news that I had become the victim of the tussle between the Education Minister and the Chief Minister of Tranvancore, and as a result my application for a scholarship was rejected at the last moment. That left me with just the remuneration from Anjuman Taraqqi-e-Urdu as a regular income. I used to send the Anjuman pre-agreed installments of work every month. Translations of *Shakuntula*, and Qazi Nazarul Islam's poems had reached Maulvi Sahib, and in addition, I had begun work on the short Hindi Urdu dictionary on his request. Suddenly, in March 1938 he informed me that the Anjuman would be shortly transferred to Delhi, and would thenceforth be organized on new lines. I was to stop work on my projects for the time being.

One setback followed another, but it was useless to complain, because it was a matter of an organization that came under a native state. If I had not been experienced in writing in English, the loss would have been great. After this episode I did not write a word of Urdu or Hindi as long as I remained in Europe. Journalism in English and my work at the university left me no time for it.

One misfortune upon another! When the English–Urdu dictionary was published, my name was absent from among the names of people who had contributed to the dictionary, mentioned in Maulvi Sahib's preface. For a long time I grieved over this incident, not because my hard work of two years was wasted, but because my greatest trust had been shattered. I adhere to certain fundamental principles and values in human relationships, and whenever these are ruffled, the relationship ends without my expressing any grievance in speech or in writing. I am thankful that although my relationship with Maulvi Sahib did cool down after this incident, it did not sour, and opportunities to serve him and the Anjuman continued to present themselves.

At the end of 1938, when Hameeda returned to India I moved to the old hotel in the Latin Quarter. A few months later, when my thesis was completed, the difficult stage arrived, of entering one hundred printed copies of it, according to the custom of that period. By the time I had completed this requirement it was June, and as per regulation the date for the oral examination had been fixed three months thence. It was on the result of this examination that the division for the degree used to be determined. In addition, two secondary dissertations had to be prepared under the supervision of tutors other than my main tutor. The topics for these two subsidiary dissertations were not to have direct connection with the central dissertation so that the breadth of the candidate's scholarship could be better judged. Based on these considerations it was decided that the oral examination would be held in October.

The City of Lights

Paris has been called the city of lights. To enjoy its lights one should view them from a height. If one observes them from the Eiffel Tower for example, they remind one of Shab-e-Barat or Diwali. This is one aspect of light, but it is different from the luminosity that centuries of art, science, and traditions of human liberty have radiated. The position that Rome had in ancient times, and Baghdad held in the Middle Ages, belonged to Paris in the Modern Age. Apart from being the centres of large empires, these cities were the hub of universal civilizations. Cultures cannot be captioned as feudal, bourgeois, or proletariat. Whatever of their genius survives the revolution of time, lightens the dark path of humanity and shows mankind the way ahead.

Everybody has sung the praises of Paris according to their own tastes. Women praised it for its fashions, men for its spectacles, artists for art and music, tourists for its architecture and gardens, gastronomes for its food and wine. All this was there before, and still exists. However, in the olden days, cars had not taken possession of the city. There was neither any turmoil, nor were the prices high. Tranquillity prevailed as it did in Delhi before the ravages of Nadir Shah, as a contemporary writer describes in his writing about Delhi. As the year 1938 began, democracy was breathing its last in Spain, Hitler had a tight hold on Czechoslovakia, and the clouds of the Second World War were gathering in such a way that everybody said they would rain blood in a matter of months. But despite the menace, the love of ease and luxury was such, and the pride in empire and wealth was so great, that nobody feared the imminent danger.

Science and art held a special position in French life, and their issues were given more importance than those of politics or commerce. The subject under debate in literature at the time was, to what extent it could participate in or stand aloof from political and social struggle. French literature should be called the laboratory of modern literary trends, but with the freedom to experiment, there was the condition that the material being tried should be authentic literature. I have described these matters briefly somewhere, under the topic, 'An Indian writer in Europe.'

Occasionally it happens that 'an empty house may capture a fairy', the shadow of a phoenix can confer prophethood or kingship. If the genie is benevolent, he can grant you the lamp of Alladin, but only a disturbed mind can be nurtured under the shadow of a fairy. From this there are two routes of escape. One of them is the one Maulana Abul Kalam Azad chose.

Writing in his book *Tazkira*, about an episode in his youth, he took refuge in penitence. The incident happened in Bombay, during the year or two that he spent in the company of Agha Hashar.

Amir Timur took the other route. He recounts that when once he marched to Mahmoodabad, which was a disrict of Gilan, in the north of Iran, he was told that the women there were so enchanting that nobody could escape their magic charm. Timur says that he had never feared an enemy as much as he dreaded this menace, and took flight in such frenzy that he did not allow his army to pause until they had left behind the city of love and beauty and arrived in a waterless desert.

14 July was the National Day of France. There was such a hullabaloo during the day, and such a hustle and bustle at night! But in one's heart, one had the apprehension that this might not be so next year, and that those who parted this year may never meet again. I was very eager to see Switzerland. Its attraction was so irresistible that at the end of the month I went there to spend my vacations.

Beginning of the Second World War

I have had occasion to see beauty in all its aspects. Of these, the beauty of women is the most transient, and as De Gaulle has said, it opens petal by petal, like the rose, and withers away in the same way. The beauty of art, character, and nature are immortal. Whenever human beings have hurt me I have looked for peace in the mountains or by the sea. I am especially attracted to snow-covered mountains. Although I had the opportunity to travel to Switzerland many times subsequently, nothing could match the first sight of it. The highest peak there is Jungfrau, which is covered in snow even in summer. The view cast such a spell on me that I stayed for a week in a small hotel outside a town called Interlaken, and spent my time strolling around the mountain from morning to night. Then, I travelled to Zurich, where my dear friend Nambiar was waiting for me.

Nambiar comes from a well known Brahmin family of Malabar. He went to England for his education after the First World War, and there he married Mrs Sarojini Naidu's youngest sister, Suhasini. As a punishment for marrying a non-Brahmin, his father cut him off, but the irony was that very soon the couple were divorced. After this, Nambiar did not return home. On finishing his education in England he went to Germany and lived there for a long time. After Hitler came into power he left for Czechoslovakia, and stayed there, but when the Nazis invaded that country as well, he fled to Paris. My friendship with him began in Paris, and has continued to this day. Nambiar had personal contacts with Pandit Nehru as well as Subhash Chandra Bose. During the World War, when Bose formed the Azad Hindustan Party, Nambiar became his ambassador to Germany. He occupied the same post under Pandit Nehru.

The names of two sisters were prominently linked with the anti-Nazi movement. The older sister, Louise, was the first wife of the famous

Indian revolutionary, M.N. Roy. The younger sister married a photographer by the name of Walter. This family settled in Zurich, and Nambiar was so close to them that I too was invited to stay there for many weeks. In their company I became familiar not only with the current German politics but also with many issues of Germany's intellectual and literary greatness.

Time sped past as we indulged ourselves with recreation and sightseeing. Then, in the last week of August, suddenly there was news on the radio of the German Foreign Minister landing in Moscow and entering into a pact with Russia. All of us held our breath and nobody said anything for a long time. This had happened at a time when Germany had completed its preparations for its attack on Poland, while England and France had guaranteed its security. War or peace now depended upon the attitude of the USSR. Had the Western countries come to a timely agreement with the Soviet Union, it is possible that Poland would not have been attacked, and the war diffused, but in their efforts to make Germany fight with the USSR, they forgot that there are no permanent friends or enemies in politics. There is a Persian proverb which says, 'Politics knows no accountability'. Much has been written on the causes and effects of the pact between Germany and Russia, both from a favourable and an unfavourable point of view. However, at the time even a temporary understanding between Nazism and Communism was considered impossible, and the anxiety and confusion it produced are unimaginable today.

Somebody commented that the German forces would enter Poland, and the Western Alliance would not be able to do anything about it, but our political judgment refused to accept such a possibility. Nambiar immediately suggested that we return to Paris in case war broke out and the borders were closed, in which case we would be stuck in Switzerland. And true enough, three days after our return to Paris, Germany attacked Poland on the first of September, and France and Britain declared war on Germany, in retaliation.

Martial law was promulgated in France as soon as war was declared. Blackouts which began then, went on for six years. Men between twenty-one and fifty years of age were conscripted and sent to the barracks. Owing to Germany's heavy bombardment of Poland, the same fate was expected for the towns of France, and fearing this Parisians fled the city in an unbelievable exodus. Immediately after the declaration of war, German bombers began to fly over Paris (though they did not drop bombs). The thunder of anti-aircraft guns frightened and discouraged rather than brought cheer to the populace. I have never witnessed such a mass flight in my life. Hundreds of thousands of people abandoned their homes and headed off, travelling in trains and motor cars. In a week Paris was a deserted city, with all its shops closed, its houses locked, and its roads bereft of vehicles, while a human figure walking down a street was a rare sight. However on every bend of the road, policemen could be seen, diligently checking the bonafides of people like us who comprised the leftover population of foreigners. All Germans, without exception, were arrested. The communist party was declared illegal, and its leaders went underground. Hundreds of thousands of soldiers in the French army shared their views, and were calling it an imperialist war. As a result, there was much confusion on the Western Front during the German attack in the month of May, and this fact has been regarded as one reason for the French defeat.

Along with everybody else, my professor too was conscripted and sent to the front. With the exception of Alphonso and Nambiar, all my friends were scattered. For the first few months exchange of correspondence with India came to a halt, and all sources of income dried up. My mind became numb as it did again in 1947 and in 1971. Alfonso said that it was not advisable to stay separately during such a crisis, therefore Nambiar and I moved to his house from my hotel room and Nambiar's flat. I have never met as pleasant a conversationalist as Nambiar. He has the quality of laughing off the worst troubles, and it is from him that I learned to laugh more than anybody else at my own mistakes.

One day, Alfonso lighted a fire in his fireplace, and placing two large trunks close to it, asked me to burn their contents, while he went off to look for food because restaurants and shops were closed. I opened one of the trunks and found it to be stuffed with passports, almost all of which were empty. The other trunk contained heaps of correspondence and reports. I realized that they had to do with the Spanish Republicans. These burned down to ashes in no time, but the hard passport covers were more troublesome. It took me hours to beat them down to fragments which would burn easily.

For some days we spent our time cooking, eating, and enjoying one another's company. Whenever we left the house for a stroll down the streets, we would find that an all-encompassing desolation had taken the place of the merrymaking, fun-loving crowds that had only recently filled them with their bustle. The nightclubs stood dark and gloomy, in the cabarets wineglasses lay overturned, cafes were deserted. Dusk to dawn blackouts created a daunting atmosphere, in which not a ray of light was allowed to escape. Policemen stood at every intersection, watching closely to see if one had one's gas mask under one's arm, and if one's identity card was genuine.

At the end of September, Alfonso quoted knowledgeable sources as saying that the following spring there would be war on the Western Front and that elderly soldiers would be sent back home from their barracks, and not only that, but a certain number of the city's inhabitants would gradually return home. We too therefore, would go back to our homes. When, in December, my professor came back from the battleground to the academic world, he fixed a date at the end of January for my viva, and so the matter of my obtaining my degree was settled.

During all of this period, Hameeda did not get my letters, and even if she did, she could not understand what I was doing in Paris. Sir Abdul Qadir had come to Paris from London as a member of the Viceroy's Council, but she made inquiries about my wellbeing from Sir Firoz Khan Noon who was India's High Commissioner in Britain. He got the British Consul in Paris to track me down. Having found me, the latter became bent on seeing me out of France. When finally he was convinced that I would get my degree at the end of January, he called me and said, 'A place has been reserved for you on a liner by the name of Count Biancamano, which will be leaving Genoa, and travelling to Asia at the end of February. Possibly, that will be the last available ship, for Italy's neutrality in the war is suspect.' It turned out that his guess was absolutely right.

Unwillingly, I acted on his advice, and dejected and unhappy, took the night train to Italy. The memory of those days has been captured in my two short stories, 'The cry of the body', and 'The darkness of the heart'. They are among my more successful short stories, and have been translated into other languages.

The next morning, when the train arrived in Genoa, I found the city much altered from about fifteen months ago, when I had last seen it. It remained the only escape route for people fleeing Europe, since the ships of neutral Italy could still cross the seas without danger. A multitude of anxious, dishevelled émigrés thronged the streets, and numerous were the gifts and inducements that they offered for hotel rooms and cabin space on the ships.

When I was leaving Calcutta I was like a deer who has spotted his hunter, but now one felt as though one were flying from a burning forest—a forest where a whole era, and the dreams of a generation, were turning to ashes. I did not experience the pleasure one feels on returning home, but rather, the agony one suffers when one sees one's homeland plundered. The ideas that had been nurtured in my soul ever since my youth were moribund, for my simple temperament could not accept the eternal conflict between the world of ideas and reality.

A new era of history had begun, and a chapter in the book of my life had ended. When I was leaving Bombay for Europe, my heart had been full of hopes and yearning. But now when the shores of Bombay came into view, my heart sank and I sensed that a new journey was beginning, the destination of which I did not know.

6

After the Return from Europe

When I returned to India in March 1940, life there had been affected by the World War. Its effect on politics was that Congress resigned from provincial ministries with the explanation that despite the fact that it opposed fascism, it could not support Britain without being given a decisive role in the central government. Within three years, these ministries had alienated Muslim public opinion to such an extent that it swung towards the Muslim League, and the League celebrated the occasion of the ministries' resignation, by offering prayers of gratitude. The matter had now gone beyond a question of minority and majority, and had entered the domain of separate nationalities. Consequently, on 23 March 1940, the Muslim League passed a historical resolution based on the two nation theory, which led to the creation of Pakistan in the next few years.

I still remember the day when I first heard the name, 'Pakistan'. It happened in 1929. I was working in the Hindi Calcutta daily, *Vishwamitr*. The editor of the paper, Pandit Mata Sevak Patekh pulled out a booklet from the bundle of foreign mail. As he began to leaf through it, his jugular vein distended, his whiskers stiffened, and giving me a stare, he asked me in a hard voice, 'Have you ever heard of a place called Pakistan?'

I spun the globe around mentally, but found no trace of 'Pakistan' on it. When I expressed my ignorance, Pandit Patekh passed Chaudhry Rehmat Ali's pamphlet to me. I took a look at it, without registering anything except the name 'Pakistan'. The social alienation of Hindus and Muslims from one another was an undeniable reality, and the biases of caste and class had hardened the barrier into a formidable wall. Yet, despite all this, the political division of the country on the basis of religion was then a totally new idea. Perhaps Lala Lajpat Rai was the first noteworthy political leader to have uttered it, a few years earlier. In those days he had left Congress and joined Hindu Mahasabha along with diehard Arya Samaj members like Bhai Parmanand, therefore nobody paid attention to his tall talk. But in 1930, when Allama Iqbal voiced his proposal from the Muslim League platform in Allahabad, for an independent country comprising Muslim majority regions, his demand soon grew into a movement. Muslim politics, which had been going helter skelter, sometimes towards Khilafat, and sometimes in the direction of Hijrat, were now finally concentrated on an established objective.

Meanwhile, Khalida Adeeb Khanum was the first to introduce the idea of Pakistan to the West. Her book, *Inside India*, which was translated into Urdu and published as *Andaroon-e-Hind*, by Jamia Millia, has been mentioned earlier. In 1938, when the new edition of the book was being printed in London, Khanum gave me its press copy to read. I was surprised to find that one of its chapters was devoted to an account of Chaudhry Rehmat Ali's idea, and Pakistan. The explanation that Khalida Adeeb Khanum gave me in answer to my question has left its impression on my memory:

> The chief political reality in India is not socialism, but nationalism, and this has not grown out of unity, but rather, from the conflict between Hindu and Muslim cultures. If Indian Muslims want to avoid the fate that the Arabs met in Spain, after ruling it for seven hundred years, or the Turks encountered in the Balkans after governing it for five hundred years, they have no option but to form an independent nation.

I had asked her, 'Can a nation be created on the basis of religion?' To which she replied flatly, 'It is not necessary for a nation to be created only on the grounds of colour, race, and universality of language. Are the hatred and conflict that these factors are capable of producing, superior to the human and moral values of religion?'

I remembered this dialogue, and was also aware of the experience of history of which it was an echo, yet the partition of my country was an unimaginable concept for me. In a tiny island of tolerance and open-mindedness amid the spreading waters of Hindu Muslim conflict, I covered my face and lay down.

درمیان قصر دریا تختہ بندم کردۂ
باز می گوئی کہ دامن تر مکن ہشیار باش

Having tied me to a wooden board in the middle of the river
You say to me, 'Take care! Do not get wet'

According to the Holy Bible, God was so displeased by Adam's liking for wheat that he was flung to earth and commanded that in future he and his descendants must eat bread made with the sweat of their brow. In addition to this was Karl Marx's statement that whoever does not work will not get bread. Artistic and literary work was not categorized as 'work' in those days, in the sense that it was not a means of livelihood. Institutions that published work in Urdu were better because they did not demand payment from authors for publishing their work. However Iqbal used to publish his works himself, and Premchand told me that his average monthly income never exceeded 200 rupees, and that too was thanks to his work in Hindi. As for Urdu, whatever work he published in it brought him nothing but 'dry fame', an expression that Ghalib used with some bitterness.

For three months I remained in a quandary as to what I should do. In those days nobody helped writers except the film industry and the radio, and both these institutions did not grant me their patronage. Bombay Talkies was held in esteem among film companies because it was controlled by a discerning director like Himansu Rai, and an actress like Devika Rani. The company needed a screenwriter and short story writer who was fluent in both Urdu and Hindi and had been educated in Europe. As soon as Devika Rani heard of my return to India she offered me a job, but the film environment did not appeal to me and so I did not accept her offer despite my indigence.

The Deputy Controller of All India Radio (later its Director General), Professor Ahmed Shah Bukhari advised me to consider joining the Radio since it had attracted many erudite people, did not impose restrictions such as were to be found in a bureaucratic environment, and was a place where one could criticize fascism to one's heart's content. Of course, if one did not want to applaud the British, that was all right, as long as one did not denounce them. The offices and studios of the Radio were located in two rented bungalows of Alipur Road in Civil Lines. One of them housed the Delhi radio station, where Noon Meem (N.M.) Rashid, Krishan Chandar, Saadat Hasan Manto etc. worked, the other accommodated the newly launched News Department, headed by a British journalist who already had three assistants, the fourth being myself. Translators of many different Indian and foreign languages, and announcers, used to be busy preparing and broadcasting war bulletins. In addition to compiling news bulletins in English and writing analyses of Indian news, my job was to supervise the work of the Dictionary Committee, which was responsible for creating easy equivalents for English idioms. The member of the committee who dealt with the Urdu translations was Chiragh Hasan Hasrat, while Watsain dealt with the Hindi translation. The latter had been implicated in the Delhi Conspiracy Case sometime in the past, and was now a companion of M.N. Roy.

I found a house close to my office. On one side of it was Qudsia Bagh, and behind it flowed the river Jumna. In this idyllic environment my tired spirit found some peace, and I spent two and a half years in the company of enlightened companions.

Free Verse and N.M. Rashid

My association with Rashid began in Delhi and lasted until our stay in Tehran. All of us were weary of working in the Radio after two years. Krishan Chandar, Manto, and others were drawn to Bombay by the allure of the film industry. Rashid and Hasrat became Captains in the army, and I found employment with the M.A.O. College in Amritsar. I renewed my contact with Rashid in 1959, when he was appointed Deputy Director (later, Director) of the Information department of the UN in Karachi. I had just been made the Director of the Regional office of the UNESCO, and sent to the same city. Later, when I was the UNESCO Representative in Iran in 1967, he was in charge of the UN Information Bureau there, and we were together again for four years. Different though we were in our views and temperament, our relationship of mutual respect never changed. I have known many aspects of his life when it was drawing to a close, but here I will dwell upon only the impression created by reading his poetry.

At the end of the last century, when free verse became popular in Western poetry, Bengali was the first language to accept its influence in the East. It did so through the virtuosity of Tagore, who had command over the music of language. This style had arrived as a reaction to classicism and romanticism, and was a precursor of impressionism and symbolism. Its aim was not merely to release words and meaning from the restrictions imposed by rhyme, but to find new connections between words and meanings. It became a common trend in Bengali poetry, and subsequently, experiments in free verse were made in Hindi after the First World War, and after many years of resistance, the style established itself.

Every style in literature and art reaches the summit of its potential, and then begins to decline. When Ghalib became aware of this fact he complained of the constriction that the *ghazal* imposes. At this point Dagh's *ghazals* did for poetry what the invention of *thumri* did for music. Great singers do not consider *thumri* worthy of attention because if it is not accompanied by illustrative or descriptive gestures it is not half as enjoyable. The same is true of Dagh's *ghazal*—it is the poetry of amour, coquetry, and enticement, and must not be recited in a harsh voice.

When Iqbal called Dagh 'the last poet of Jahanabad' he was taken to mean that Dagh was the last of the great *ghazal* poets. But about the same time the *ghazal* was going through a renaissance, and the style which emerged could be called Neo-classical. Hasrat Mohani was credited with being the leader of this movement, although it would be fairer to award this position to Shad Azeemabadi, since he was older than Hasrat by many years, and among his followers there were many great poets. However this movement too was exhausted by the time of the Second World War, and in the genre of *ghazal* the same decline that had appeared in the Persian *ghazal*, now appeared in its Urdu counterpart. The height to which a master like Iqbal took the rhymed poem (*nazam*) was so lofty that it left no room for improvement. The Urdu *ghazal* retained its vitality for 250 years, but the rhymed poem waned in half a century.

Around this time (1930–1935) experimentation in free verse began, and in the next forty years, most of the contribution, which it made in every direction of Urdu poetry, was owing to Rashid. In 1941, after he had given me a copy of his first collection of poetry, *Mavra*, he said to me with some hesitation, 'Have a look at it. It is the start of an experiment, not the end of it.'

Half of the anthology was influenced by the style of Akhtar Shirani, but beyond that a new voice could be heard, in which, despite ambiguity, there was allure, and an ability to echo in unexplored new directions. His art continued to perfect itself until he produced *La-Insan*, a copy of which he gave me in 1961, in Tehran. This collection of his poetry is his masterpiece. The preface he wrote for it can be called an excellent example of criticism in prose, and some of the long and short poems in the compilation will always be remembered in Urdu poetry.

This is not the poetry of mushairas and social gatherings, which is why it has been denied public acclaim. It is also lacking in subjects that deal with what befalls the body and soul on the battlefield of life, in the clear light of day. It holds those secrets and signs which the subconscious mind murmurs in the darkness or moonlight of life's night. This whispering creates new meanings for words, and the beauty of it grants a new harmony to language. This genre of poetry is difficult, and if Rashid succeeded in perfecting it, he owed this awesome achievement to his dedicated effort and practice. He had studied Islamic and Western poetry in depth, and to the end of his days he retained the capacity for curiosity and experimentation. He was by nature an extremist. When he fell under the power of religion, he became a Khaksar, and when he abandoned religion he became an atheist. But in reality he was a believer in humanism and individualism. If his poetry reveals a shade of misanthropy, it was because of the destruction of human values and the decline of the individual that were apparent to him. The bitterness in his tone should be understood as a dirge on devastated humanity.

Saadat Hasan Manto

Manto was a special friend of my brother, which was why despite our being about the same age, he treated me with a kind of affectionate restraint. He was first heard of in literary circles in 1935, when his name appeared as the editor of the Russian literature issue of the magazine, *Humayun*. When I wrote a rather strong and unfavourable review of it in *Urdu*, my brother Shameem Sahib was more unhappy about it than Manto. Two years later, on my way to Europe, when I heard in Bombay that Manto was working there for the newspaper *Mussavar*, I visited him.

During my stay in Paris I needed some published material from India for an article that I was writing for a newspaper. I wrote to Manto requesting him to send me the needful, and he responded immediately by posting the documents to me. When the newspaper gave me £100 for the article, I sent Manto £15 out of the sum I had received. He never forgot what I did, and thenceforth our relationship became closer.

When he came from Bombay to Delhi, and became associated with the Delhi Radio Station, we began visiting each other. He was exceedingly outspoken, and he wrote much as he spoke. His gift was such that he could write a complete short story or radio drama in one sitting. Like Premchand, he too believed in putting simple ideas in simple words, and did not waste time on stylistic refinements. Of all the masters of the short story he admired only Somerset Maugham. He was interested in the domestic life of the middle class, and he exposed its hypocrisy to the extent that he was undeservedly hauled up for obscenity.

In the development of modern Urdu literature there were other trends besides the Progressive movement, and those were headed by Rashid and Manto. They chose to ply their art, not on the subject of the evident conflict in society, but the inner struggle within an individual, and exposed hypocrisy by tearing up its disguises.

Late one night, Hasrat, Manto and I were strolling in the direction of the Jamia Masjid. On a field before us some travelling theatre company was showing *Laila Majnoon*. Hasrat said, 'I haven't seen such plays for a long time. Let's see what is going on.' The more I tried to stop him the more insistent he became. Finally Manto rendered the argument futile by saying, 'If we accept that we are not about to witness great art, but that we expect to find amusement for an hour or so, we will not be disappointed.'

And that is just what happened. In the play, Majnoon was walking through a desert holding the rein of a camel. Laila peered out of the litter and said to him, 'Dear Majnoon, I am hungry.' Majnoon replied, 'Food is not available here', but Laila insisted that she was hungry all the same. Finally Majnoon offered her his heart and liver. It now became evident that woman is a cannibal, for Laila accepted his offering. She then said to him, 'Dear Majnoon, I am thirsty,' whereupon poor Majnoon opened a vein and offered her his blood, of which she drank a cupful. Then Laila and Majnoon sang a duet of which the words were:

فراقِ جاناں میں ہم نے ساقی لہو پیا ہے شراب کر کے

Separated from the loved one, I drank blood, pretending it was wine

The audience was moved to tears, while we were laughing convulsively. People shouted at us angrily, and if we had not left voluntarily we would definitely have been thrown out.

Many years earlier, a similar incident had happened in Calcutta. The play *Prem Lata* was being enacted in the famous Maiden Theatre. Some friends dragged me there. The thwarted lover sang his valedictory song, plunged a dagger into his breast, and dropped down dead. The audience liked the song so much that they shouted, 'Once more!' An actor who got an encore from his audience was entitled to a bonus of 100 rupees. Since the 'dead' actor could hardly be expected to forego this windfall, he immediately came back to life, sang the same song again and committing suicide a second time, dropped dead once more.

One should not imagine that such incidents happened only in the past: Pakistani movies carry on the tradition even today, and there has been little change in the public's tastes.

The Rise of the Bourgeois Class in India

The spring of 1940 proved to be so inauspicious for Western Europe that within a few weeks, the swift as lightening German forces had attacked and defeated France and its allies, and were flying their flag in the heart of Paris. The British forces abandoned the battlefield and fled home via Dunkirk. It is a fact that if Hitler had not deluded himself that Britain would come to an agreement with him, and had made a decisive attack on them, the fleeing British forces would have been utterly destroyed. He had to pay heavily for this mistake, because despite their helplessness and lack of means, the British did not give in, and fought on alone for a year, until with Hitler's attack on Russia the fortunes of the war changed completely. The agents of history are very complex, and their interpretation is not as simple as it is made to seem. When Stalin was asked, 'What is the most decisive force of history?' He replied, 'The determination of man.'

Anyway, British imperialism was staggering from the reverses in war, and recruitment of troops and preparation for war were made in India on an unprecedented scale.

The problem of the educated unemployed was solved because hundreds of new offices were opened, where they were absorbed, or became officers in the army. Recruitment was made on an express footing. Numerous large and small factories had come up, and they manufactured goods of all kinds—some to be sent out as war equipment, and some for home consumption. Contractors, brokers, and shopkeepers were having a field day. Goods worth millions of rupees were being sold for the asking price, at the stroke of a government official's pen. The government resorted to deficit financing and inflation gave rise to high prices. The middle class, which had so far been known for their decency and contentment, set aside all niceties and flung themselves into the melee. Opportunism became the only code of conduct then. In the old system there was room for friendship and benevolence, but now Marx's words were proved right: Under capitalism human relationships turn into relationships of gold.

Things changed so drastically in a matter of a few years that spiritual, human, and moral values became things of the past, and when the war ended, this same middle class became widely involved in national trade and organizing and governing the country. Most of the newly liberated colonies are now paying the penalty for the greed and plunder learned and practised by this class. This preoccupation with money was gilded by the American view that progress is based on creating a consumer society.

This was the time when I became deeply conscious of the ineffectiveness of literature. On the whole, literary writers had proved to be courageous and enlightened. They wrote reams and reams against imperialism, fascism and hypocricy. But most of their readers were the middle class. In the same period the press, owned by the government and the capitalists, as well as the state-run radio, and the film industry, all typified by their clamorous and exaggerated style, were means of communication available to the public. The influence of literary writing remained limited by comparison.

For a time there was a stillness in Indian politics similar to the lull before a storm. The two main political parties in the country, the Congress and the Muslim League, were watching to see how far and when the British were going to accept their demands. Subhash Chandra Bose fled from Calcutta to Germany, and the movement he started under the name of the Azad Hind Hakoomat, changed the direction of politics in British India. In June 1941, the Germans attacked Russia and having captured a large portion of it, stood eyeing Leningrad and Moscow. At the end of the same year, after destroying the American fleet, Japan took over all the European colonies in South East Asia, and its victory appeared certain the following year. When Subhash Chandra Bose's Azad Hind army shouted slogans of 'March to Delhi', at Bahadur Shah Zafar's tomb in Rangoon, a wave of enthusiasm ran through India.

A few years earlier, Gandhi had expelled Subhash Chandra Bose from Congress. Now he was so awed by his valour that he too felt obliged to start the Quit India movement against the British. On the surface the British managed to crush it, but it had far-reaching consequences. Congress's greed for power increased. The spirit of revolt was engendered among the Indian troops. They no longer feared the government. The people heard news of bloodshed day and night, and therefore lost their respect for peace and humanity. As for the elite, they had already lost their fear of God.

Every school of thought has its own communalism. Therefore, as in the West, Communists in India began to express their opposition in religious language, calling their foes infidels and issuing fatwas against them. For the Communists the first enemy they needed to crush was not fascism but imperialism. But supporters of M.N. Roy were not of the same mind, and the priority of Congress socialists was the freedom of the country. The period of terrorism was over, and its devotees had either left practical politics or had joined other political groups.

One day, when I was passing through Chandni Chowk, I came across Phool Singh in a cloth shop. At one time he had been associated with terrorists, but during a short stay in Delhi in 1937, when Jamaluddin Bukhari introduced me to him, he had turned communist.

Phool Singh was a consumptive young man, who appeared to be burning in the fire of his own sincerity. Having sacrificed himself and all that he possessed for humanity, he died at a young age. I used to know him well enough to visit him at his shop now and then. One day he said to me, 'I am trying to reform some of my terrorist friends but my logic is helpless before their stubbornness.'

'I have nothing to do with any group or party. Please don't involve me in this tricky business.' I responded. But Phool Singh insisted on taking me to see his friends, saying, 'One of them is an old acquaintance of yours, who is very keen to see you.'

So, in the darkness of the night we drove through unfamiliar roads outside the city, and leaving our car in a small village, walked to a house. Phool Singh placed his lips on a closed door and said something. When the door opened we entered a darkened room where ten or twelve people were gathered. They could barely recognize each others' faces in the light whose source was a lantern. There are no introductions on such occasions, therefore Phool Singh did not introduce me to anybody and nor did he mention my name. But one of those present there got up and shook my hand warmly. I realized that it was the same Kundan Lal who while he was working with me in a newspaper office in Calcutta, had suddenly vanished.

For hours I kept giving arguments against terrorism to the people present, and they kept contradicting me. Later, in 1942, some of these people became active in the Congress movement and some raised the flag of Rashtriya Swayamsevak Sangh (RSS) at the time of the partition of India. The leader of this party, M.S. Golwalkar, had been trained in Germany and he patterned the RSS on the Nazi militant party, the SS. His party was in the vanguard of the massacre of Muslims.

One of the people I met in the All India Radio, an Iranian, is worth mentioning. I met him in Tehran again after a long time, and hope that he is alive and well. I will refrain from using his real name, and call him Aquai Takrimi here. At the beginning of the World War he returned to his homeland after taking a degree in engineering from the United States, and stayed in Zahidan to carry out compulsory military service. Once when he was sentenced to imprisonment as a result of his protest against the tyranny of Reza Khan, he fled to Quetta. There the British arrested him on suspicion of espionage and transported him to Delhi, but when he was proved innocent, he was forced to work for All India Radio's Persian programme. He was then interned in the Civil Lines. His confinement ended when I succeeded in my attempt to have him released. My relationship with him became warm and was renewed when, years later, we met again in Tehran. I will relate this later in the book.

Everybody who is familiar with the politics of the subcontinent, would remember the name of M.N. Roy. He was born in Bengal around 1890. After being associated with secret terrorist movements in Bengal before the First World War, he left for America. He took on the work for the organization that had been formed in Germany for the liberation of India from the imperialist power, during the war. After the Russian revolution he arrived in Russia, and there he won the confidence of Lenin, Stalin and others, to the extent that for years he became their special adviser on the affairs of India and other Asian countries. During Stalin's time, his luck ran out like that of many others, and when he returned to India in 1930, he spent many years in jail, imprisoned by the British. After his release he had no more links with the Communist Party, and spent most of his time in writing and compilation. I was able to meet him many times in Delhi. In my opinion, M.N. Roy was the foremost authority on Communism in the subcontinent.

My Stay in Amritsar

In June 1942 I fell seriously ill and was close to death. When I recovered I became conscious of a fundamental change in myself. My intellectual homeland, France, had been destroyed. Russia was struggling between life and death, and my birthplace, India, was standing baffled and bemused, at the crossroads of history.

امید و بیم نے مارا مجھے دو راہے پر

کہاں کے دیر و حرم گھر کا راستہ نہ ملا

Torn between hope and dread, I have been flung at the parting of the roads
Forget the temple and the mosque, I can't even find my way home

When I resigned from my job, everybody was surprised. Ever since my childhood I had scant interest in anything other than writing. Knowing full well that writing could not earn me a livelihood, and was only a preferred pursuit, I decided to start a literary journal, and obtained a declaration for '*Jahan Numa*' in Hameeda's name. I bought the paper and began to collect articles for the journal. All those who heard what I was doing declared that the project would not succeed, and advised me not to expect to make a livelihood from writing since it was an activity that was no more than an entertaining pastime. There were possibilities of better government jobs, but I did not feel inclined to take them up. Qazi Issa, who was related to me through my wife's family, offered me a job as an assistant editor of *Dawn*, which in those days was being published under the editorship of Pothan Joseph. In the meantime the M.A.O. College at Amritsar offered me the post of Vice Principal, which carried with it the position of Professor of History. I much preferred this job, firstly because it allowed me adequate leisure for reading and writing, and secondly because Pandit Sundar Lal had made me honorary editor of his magazine, *Vishwani*, when he was imprisoned by the British in August. I have mentioned this incident earlier. I was morally obliged to respect his confidence in his absence, and I could not have done so had I accepted a government job. And so I accepted the position at M.A.O. College and left for Amritsar at the end of the year. In the past, the Principal of this college had been Dr Taseer, and its Vice Principal Mahmooduzzafar.

At the college, I dedicated the time I had left over from teaching to literary activities. I had begun to translate the three volumes of Gorky's autobiography in Delhi, and I completed it in Amritsar. My work, *Adab aur Inqilab* was also put together and published in the same period. Many short stories which were included in a collection named *Zindagi ka Mela* were written in Amritsar. At the same time I carried on regularly with the editing of the Hindi magazine *Vishwani*. Amritsar is situated close to Lahore, at a distance of a mere 35 miles. Once a month or so I used to visit Lahore. Despite it being a business town, life in Amritsar had many interesting aspects. Just across from my house in Civil Lines was the bungalow of Deputy Commissioner Penderel Moon. I had got to know him quite well.

While I was still in Amritsar, he resigned in protest against mistreatment of political prisoners, and wrote a book called *Strangers in India.* He was one of those enlightened Englishmen who had genuine sympathy for the Indian public. A few furlongs away was the house of Dr Saifuddin Kitchlew. I met him many times and was impressed by his sincerity each time. I have mentioned this earlier in this book.

Between the cities of Lahore and Amritsar, was a boarding school called Preet Nagar. It had been established on the pattern of a commune by Sikh intellectuals who had returned from Canada. Their predecessors, Sikh revolutionaries, had brought out an Urdu magazine called *Keerti*, which however had been wrapped up, and now the journal *Preet Lari*, which was published in Urdu and Gurmukhi reflected modern educational principles. The institution was one of its kind in India, and I had a special bond with it.

In M.A.O. College itself, there was an assemblage of able teachers. Among them Khadim Mohyeddin (Zia Mohyeddin's father), Karamat Husain, Siddiq Kaleem, Hameed Naseem, and Rasheed are noteworthy. My friendship with Professor Rasheed has lasted to this day. Of my students, Saifuddin Saif, and Abdul Matin Arif made a name for themselves in the world of literature.

The quality of wrestlers that came from Amritsar had no equal in the whole country. The title of Rustum-e-Hind became the birthright of Gama and his family. My father-in-law once invited them to the Lucknow Exhibition, and lavished such hospitality on them that they became devoted to me too. This became evident in an interesting way which will be recounted further on in this book.

The city was not wanting in a taste for music, and masters of the art would cover long distances to participate in the celebrations at Holi. I still remember a musical gathering in which, despite their youth, Salamat Ali and Nazakat Ali made such a name for their school of music that a great musician like Pandit Onkar Nath Thakur took off his own shawl and put it around their shoulders. I was then already fond of Western music; I now acquired an ear for Indian music as well. It was the nectar that sweetened somewhat the bitter moments of life.

My Love for Mountaineering

In those days I developed a fondness for nature that, more than tourism, became a source of satisfaction for my aesthetic sense. The deep pleasure I derived from musical soirees, nature, and historical sites, is the treasure that I have gathered in life. Now I will describe my experience of a mountain that held me in its spell of enchantment. In July 1942, when I was unshackled from my employment with the Radio and my illness, I desired a change of air in the mountains. It so happened that at this very time I received an invitation from Nawab Nasser-ul-Mulk of Chitral. He wrote poetry in Persian and had a scholarly and literary bent of mind. On account of our common interests, he had heard of me. In those days few people ever visited the remote and perilous land of Chitral. But for me new places held such an attraction that not only did I immediately prepare for the journey, I also roped in my brother-in-law Shaukat Omer, an adventurous man like myself, to accompany me.

نہ سُدھ بُدھ کی لی، اور نہ منگل کی لی
اُٹھا اور اُٹھ راہ جنگل کی لی

I didn't care whether it was Wednesday or Tuesday
Simply got up and set out for the forest

I had read somewhere about Kafiristan, a part of which is in Chitral. I had heard that the view of the 24,000 feet, snow-clad peak of Tirch Mir that is visible from Chitral is unparalleled in its grandeur and beauty. A memento of this voyage is my short story, The Princess of Kafiristan. No writer had ever visited this area before me.

In Switzerland, the beauty of Jungfrau had awakened my sleeping soul. Tirch Mir endowed my weak frame with courage, and the innocent Kafir beauties taught me that true beauty never provokes lust.

My love of mountaineering and adventure took me to the valleys and hills of Kashmir in 1942 and 1943. In 1943 we climbed to the Zogi La pass beyond Srinagar and Soanmarg, where paths diverge in the direction of Ladakh and Tibet. At a height of 16,000 feet from there, we pitched our tents at the feet of the Kolahai Glacier. But that night there was such a blizzard that we were unable to continue climbing. Three weeks later, when we arrived at Nawab Jaffer Ali Khan Asar's house in Srinagar, our appearance was such that his servants recognized us with difficulty. Asar Lucknavi was a minister in the state of Kashmir.

He used to recite his poetry to all and sundry in such an unhurried fashion that being one of his listeners meant that one lost interest in Urdu poetry for a long time afterwards. In 1944, I went with the late Aziz Omer and Rashid to the Amar Nath mountain, which is beyond Srinagar and the valley of Pahel Gam, where Hindu pilgrims go to worship Shiva's lingum in ice. From there, despite the warnings of others, we crossed a broken mountain range, escaping death by the skin of our teeth. Twice my feet slipped on pebbles and I narrowly missed plummeting down to a ditch thousands of feet below.

The pleasure one finds in such expeditions is unknown to those who are used to the convenience of planes and motor cars. The real gratification of such journeys ends when one reaches one's destination. The sum and substance of their delights lies in navigating the pinnacles and gorges in the mountains.

Two Literary Battles

In March 1943, a literary meeting and mushaira was arranged in Muradabad, under the chairmanship of Sir Raza Ali. The numbers in which writers and poets flocked to the venue and the generosity with which their expenses were met, and hospitality dispensed, seemed to be a miracle wrought by the government's war effort. The late Ziaul Islam was organizing the convention in his capacity as the Chief of the Public Relations Department. The paper I read on 'War and Literature' is now a part of *Literature and Revolution*. It recommended that a war of the pen be waged against Imperialism as well as Fascism, and predicted, as perhaps nobody from our part of the world had done before, that in the future the danger would come from America's global imperialism. A pin drop silence prevailed in the meeting when I was reading my paper, and many government officials quietly slid off their chairs and left.

The students of our college had made a custom out of organizing a grand mushaira once a year, to which notable poets from outside the college were invited. In the middle of 1944, when the mushaira took place under my chairmanship, a crisis evolved for no real reason. Majeed Lahori read a poem on the recent famine in Bengal:

خدا سے پچھ نہ کہو ہاں، خدا سے پچھ نہ کہو

Say nothing to God, no, say nothing to God

Majeed's poem echoed the dirge, *God can Wait*, written by the famous English poet Anthony Lewis, on the same tragedy. Suddenly some people began to voice their criticism that the poem was disrespectful to God. I retorted that many poets, including Iqbal, had made complaints to God about the sufferings of man and His indifference to them; that such protests should not be construed as irreverence; and in any case, if people who were making these criticisms had no understanding of poetry and were more interested in moralizing, they should desist from spoiling the evening, and leave. When the condemnation became more vociferous, volunteers threw out the perpetrators, thereby opening a Pandora's box!

All the traditionalists in the town began to persecute me. The ulema printed *fatwas* of atheism and *kufr* against me in newspapers and posters. The college administration tabled a discreetly worded resolution, advising the faculty to abstain from hurting the feelings of others through their speech and writing. I called this a lack of confidence in me and resigned. And though Rasheed had nothing to do with the matter, he too handed in his resignation out of loyalty to me. The students organized a spirited demonstration in our favour, and when Gama, the wrestler, got to hear of the incident, he despatched his pupils to punish members of the administration. The latter were then left with no option but to ask Rasheed and me to withdraw our resignations.

On the surface the uproar had come to an end, but I had become disillusioned with Amritsar. At the end of the year, when Pandit Sundar Lal was released from prison, and he resumed the responsibility for his magazine, I breathed a sigh of relief. My personal circumstances were not such that I could afford to experiment with my life, nevertheless it had been brought home to me that involvement with Education was in keeping with my temperament, and that I should stick to this field, but that I should leave Amritsar at the first opportunity.

The following year, in 1945, when it occurred to Gandhiji to settle the Urdu Hindi controversy, he initiated the Hindustani Literature Board. I was offered the post of Secretary, but refused it.

At this junction the path that opened before me involved my working life permanently with the field of Education.

It was the view of the British government in India, that Agriculture, Health, and Education were the responsibility of the provincial governments, and it should not involve itself in these fields directly, except to give counsel and advice. Hence there was one common department at the Centre for all these three sectors. The adviser for Education was Sir John Sargent. He had neither authority nor staff, but he was richly endowed with perception and intelligence. He wrote the famous Sargent Report that prepared the blueprint for the post War development of Education in India. The Report had a decisive role in the history of Education in the subcontinent. Sargent did for Education what Cunningham and Marshall did for archaeology, and Greerson did for linguistics.

About this time the attitude of the British was changing. The War had ended, and along with Fascism, Imperialism had had its day. As a token of their good intentions, the British directed the attention of the Centre to Education, and in order to put into practice the recommendations of the Sargent Report, they created some more posts of Assistant Advisers in the Education Department. In those days the Department had its offices in Simla. When the Federal Public Service Commission advertised the posts, I sent in my application. After the interview, which took place in April, I was selected, and from July 1945, a new phase of my life began in Simla.

My new job was better paid and carried more benefits than my previous post, and I much preferred Simla to Amritsar. There did exist the danger that the involvements and the restrictions of the government job might interfere with my work of compilation and writing, but it was also possible that the reins of government would fall into the hands of the nationalist elements, in which case new paths would open before people like us for creative and constructive work.

7

Pakistan was Inevitable

The End of the War and the Death Throes of Imperialism

When I arrived in Simla, the War was almost over. Germany had already conceded defeat (in May 1945). In August of the same year, Japan, crushed by America's atom bomb, threw in the towel. And now commenced the era of history in which we live. Gone into the past was the age in which small countries in Europe had established large empires in the world, owing to their naval power and industrial dominance, and had amassed wealth by plundering them. Had giants like Russia and America not incapacitated Germany and Japan, the world would have found itself in the most fearsome clutches of exploitation and tyranny. The erstwhile imperialist countries, irrespective of whether they had been victorious or defeated in the war, had become so emasculated, that far from dominating their colonies, they had fears for their own survival in the future. Russia and America alone were left to fill the vacuum created by their rout. Those two countries had endless resources, their area and population were large, and their military might was immense. In addition to the inevitable rivalry between the two major powers, they embodied two opposing cultures and outlooks.

America's political and capitalist interest demanded that on the one hand, it help Western Europe and Japan to recoup their economic losses, averting a revolution in those countries, and making them dependent on itself for their survival; and on the other hand, handle the emerging political awareness of the colonies in such a way that while ostensibly their governments were no longer run by foreign powers, in fact the local governments that were installed there comprised of elements whose existence was linked to Western interests. Political freedom does nothing except hand over the administration of the country to native rulers, who are then held responsible for ending poverty. After that it becomes evident that the responsibility for all the ills in the universe cannot be laid at the door of foreign imperialism alone, but that the real evil is created by the tribal and feudal societies. Until a few generations commit themselves to working hard under a sincere and wise leadership, they cannot succeed in wiping out centuries–old economic and intellectual poverty, and in distancing themselves from the traditions of depending on prayer alone and claiming past glories. No matter what name they give it, newly liberated countries, eager to make progress, have no alternative but to opt for Communism, even if they give it a different name.

It is a miracle of the Russian Revolution that in one third of the world humanity has been set free from exploitation. It is the direct effect of this phenomenon that has forced Western capitalism to accept the concept of the welfare state, and taught colonized states to first leave the bondage of imperialism, and then to struggle for economic freedom.

Friends and foes alike have acknowledged the farsightedness and wisdom of Britain. For it did not take long for it to realize that after the War it would not be in a position to control its empire for very long. Consequently, it changed its stance so dramatically that in the history of imperialism there is no other instance of it. First in Asia, and then in Africa, it wrapped up its concerns so well that all the affected countries forgot its tyranny, and in fact the newly independent countries were proud to be members of the Commonwealth. Moreover they extolled its language and culture, bought its products, sought training from its experts, and treated London as their place of pilgrimage. The reason was that the rulers of these former colonies had received their education from the British. As an example of this, according to Lord Mountbatten, Nehru and Patel, when offering him the post of Governor General in free India, in 1947, asked him to teach them the business of governance.

India was the linchpin of the British policy, since it was the largest of its colonies, and whatever happened here was reflected in the reactions of the countries in the rest of the former British empire. The success or failure of the British policy was most clearly evident here. There is no doubt that British imperialism had thrived on the animosities it had created between the Hindu and Muslim communities, but it is equally irrefutable that when the British (ostensibly of their own accord, but in truth under compulsion), finally agreed to transfer power, they wanted to preserve the unity of the subcontinent at any price, and they continued to make every effort to do so until the very end. In this respect Britain and the Congress had the same goal.

The conference for which leaders of the Muslim League and the Congress gathered at the invitation of the Viceroy, Lord Wavell, in July, generated much activity in Simla. It was not possible to negotiate the steep roads of Simla by motor car. The most commonly used vehicle was the rickshaw, but apart from that, everybody walked. After I left my office in the evenings I used to stroll on the Mall Road, where sometimes I would see Mr Jinnah and his sister in a rickshaw, or Pandit Nehru riding a horse. Lord Wavell was trying to persuade Congress and Muslim League to form an interim, coalition government, but his attempt came to nought and the conference was a failure. The real reason for this was the issue of Muslim representation in the proposed cabinet. The Muslim League claimed that it was the party that represented the Muslims, while the Congress insisted that it represented the whole country, and since Maulana Azad was its President at the time, it was trying to induct Muslims for its seats in the cabinet.

No sooner had this episode ended than there were general elections in England in which Mr Churchill's Conservative Party was unexpectedly defeated, and the reins of the government were transferred to the Labour Party. At the end of the year when the Labour Party held general elections in India it came to light that a large majority of Muslims were for the Muslim League, and in fact, the Congress had the support of the Hindus only. Hodson wrote in his book, *The Great Divide*, that with 102 elected seats, the Congress won a clear majority, but the Muslim League swept the board in the Muslim seats.

After the election results came out, the new British Prime Minister, Attlee, decided to send a high-powered Cabinet Mission to India in March 1946, which had three members. It included the Secretary of State for India as well as the well-known Labour leader Stafford Cripps. The members of the commission had been instructed to persuade the Congress and the Muslim League to cooperate with one another in preparing a draft for the Constitution of independent India, and to form an interim, coalition government. It is unnecessary to give the details here as every knowledgeable person is familiar with the events that followed. The views of the three parties, i.e. the British, the Congress, and the Muslim League have been widely written about. I witnessed the political dialogues in Delhi and Simla, and I can say on the basis of both historical evidence and personal observation that in 1946 the creation of Pakistan had become inevitable. The points given below lend credence to this assertion.

1. The Labour Party which was openly opposed to the colonial system, favoured the independence of India, and was a supporter of the Congress. Much amity existed between leaders of the two parties. Nehru's close companion, Krishna Menon, had been residing in London for a long time. He had moreover been actively involved with the Labour Party. There were long time connections between Stafford Cripps and Gandhiji's confidant, Sudhir Ghosh. Consequently, when the Labour government came into power in Britain, Congress believed that it could impose its own conditions on both Britain and the Muslim League. It was Gokhale's observation that Indian politics was a triangle based on the British, Hindus, and Muslims. Its two sides combined would inevitably be greater than the third side. Britain and the Congress were in any case strong believers in the political unity of India, and this was only possible if the majority ruled the minority.

2. However, this common political principle did not apply to the subcontinent because the two political parties that operated here represented two nations, one of which was demanding its own independent state in the name of the principle of self-determination. This was not the occasion of an ordinary election, it was a war of succession, in which along with the departure of Britain it was to be decided whether the subcontinent would be one independent country or two.

Ireland had separated from England on the basis of religious differences, which exist to this day. Therefore the Labour government's objection to Pakistan's stand can be construed as two-facedness, especially because the very next year (in 1948), the same Labour government snatched half of Palestine from the Arabs, and through the agency of the United Nations, established on it a racial and religious state for the Jews. Not just this, it also handed over a province named Ogden, belonging to Somalia, to the Christian government of Ethiopia.

3. After its arrival in Delhi in March 1946, and holding dialogues tirelessly for months, the solution that the Cabinet Mission presented came to be known as the Cabinet Mission Plan. The aim of this famous plan was to create harmony between the idea of a united India and the demand for Pakistan. The Plan decreed that the powers of the Central government would be confined to Defence, Foreign Affairs, and Communications. The rest of the portfolios would be given to the provinces, which would be divided into three groups: undivided Bengal and Assam would be in one group, and undivided Punjab, Sindh, the Frontier Province, and Balochistan would be in the second group. In both these groups the majority would be of Muslims. The rest of the country would belong to the third group, where the Hindus would be in a clear majority. The Constituent Assembly was to prepare the Constitution for a free country under these principles. Meanwhile an interim government was to be formed at the Centre, in which the Muslim League and the Congress would be given an equal number of, i.e. six, seats each.

Muslim League gave its agreement to the Plan, and so did the Congress. But as soon as Nehru took over as President of the Congress (in June), he announced that his party would have the right to interpret the Plan, and Gandhi issued a statement in which he said that Assam should be kept separate from Bengal. Despite protests from the Muslim League, the Viceroy, in view of the Cabinet Mission's bias towards the Congress, not only ignored the unjustifiable attitude of the Congress, but even reduced the number of Muslim League seats in the proposed Cabinet of the interim government, from six to five, while maintaining the number of Congress seats at six. Consequently, the Muslim League had no alternative but to withdraw its agreement to the Cabinet Mission Plan, and give Muslims a call to wage a people's struggle. With this object, it announced its intention of observing 16 August 1946 as 'Black Day'.

Lord Wavell, in his Memoirs, has severely criticized the Labour government, the Congress party, and Gandhi in this connection. All impartial observers, including even Maulana Azad, have blamed the Congress leadership, and particularly Pandit Nehru for ruining the Cabinet Mission Plan, and held them responsible for the Partition of India.

4. The bloody communal riots that started in Calcutta on 16 August spread all over northern India. Countless innocent people lost their lives. The number of Muslims among the dead was very high because they were neither organized nor prepared to defend themselves. In November such a large number of Muslims were killed in the widespread riots that, as Gandhiji's Private Secretary, Pyare Lal put it, the concept of India's political unity had come to an end. Again according to Pyare Lal, after examining the accounts of all witnesses, Gandhiji had arrived at the conclusion that the Congress ministry in Bihar was responsible for the massacre of Hindus there because it had remained inactive and done nothing but watch the event.

In the Bihar riots the figure for Muslim deaths was anywhere between twenty and fifty thousand. Among them was my old aunt, Begum Asghar Husain, who after the death of her husband, had been living in a hamlet called Neemi, near Patna. She was the niece of Shauq Neemwi.

As a result of the mayhem caused by the riots, the capital city of Delhi remained under curfew for a year. Everyday there was carnage in one place or another. The worst affected area was Qarol Bagh, which was the den of the Rashtriya Swayamsevak Sangh and the centre of the Sikh refugees. I was residing in a government flat in this area. I had sent my wife and children to Aligarh and remained alone with a servant in these heartbreaking surroundings, listening all night long to Muslims shout battle cries of 'Allah o Akbar' and Hindus of 'Har Har Mahadev'.

5. When Congress had formed an interim government on its own, and had given the Muslim seats to opportunists like Shafaat Ahmed Khan, Ali Zaheer, etc., the Muslim League agreed to participate in the government as a measure of expediency. However it refused to be involved in the Constituent Assembly. There was so much mistrust, and the atmosphere had soured to such an extent, that it was impossible for ministers from the two parties to collaborate even on day-to-day administrative affairs. Now the Congress began to put pressure on Lord Wavell to either accept their resignation or expel the Muslim League from the government. The poor Viceroy was in a predicament, and he told the British government plainly that India's problem was unsolvable, and that it would be best to evacuate the fifty thousand British

nationals in India and hand over the government to the Indians allowing them to do what they pleased.

As soon as this danger alarm sounded in Prime Minister Attlee's ear, he invited Mr Jinnah, Pandit Nehru and the Viceroy to London in December. But when after racking his brains for a few days over the negotiations no solution seemed to be forthcoming, he changed his strategy. He dismissed Lord Wavell and appointed Lord Mountbatten Viceroy in his place. In February 1947 Attlee announced in the British Parliament that Britain would leave India by June 1948. During this period the Viceroy was to obtain the agreement of the two parties on either the Cabinet Mission Plan or some other acceptable arrangement.

Sudhir Ghosh has written in his book, *Gandhi's Emissary*:

Cripps told Nehru that if he felt that he and Mountbatten could work together, then he would do his best to get Mountbatten appointed Viceroy in Wavell's place. (Sudhir Ghosh, *Gandhi's Emissary,* London. The Cresset Press, 1967, p. 44)

Mountbatten arrived in Delhi in March. In May he secretly showed Jinnah and Nehru the first draft of the transfer of power document, and then sent it to London. After it was amended and approved, and returned to Mountbatten, he showed it to Nehru in Simla, despite protests from his advisers (and kept it from Jinnah). He had V.P. Menon incorporate changes in it in accordance with the objections that Nehru had made, and quietly took the document to London where the seal of approval of the British government was appended to it. This was the June 1947 edict under which the subcontinent was partitioned. Historians have written details of these events, but the text of the documents has never been published, which could show what the changes were that Nehru dictated and V.P. Menon inscribed. The important point is that Congress accepted the edict on the condition that the whole exercise of partition should be over in two months, that is, in August, in return for which India would accept dominion status and appoint Mountbatten Governor General of independent India for a year. The Muslim League also agreed to the time frame, but it refused to make Mountbatten Governor General of Pakistan. How strong the reaction to this was, has been expressed by Hodson in his book, *The Great Divide* on the authority of Mountbatten's diary:

[I (Mountbatten) told Jinnah], "It may well cost you the whole of your assets and the future of Pakistan". The great harm that Mountbatten did to Pakistan in revenge for this decision is well-known.

Some Months with Maulana Azad

The sphere of activity of the Government of India was so limited before the Second World War that a workforce of 500 officers and 5000 members of staff were sufficient for its needs. All of them used to spend their summers in Simla and their winters in Delhi—moving with the seasonal movements of the government's headquarters. However the extraordinary expansion during the War put an end to this needless traffic. The vital offices stayed permanently in Delhi and the peripheral ones in Simla. Their personnel maintained contact through the post, the telephone or the railway. Among the non-essential offices was the department of education whose employee I was. In July there was one department for agriculture, health and education, which was run by eight or ten officers and had a workforce of thirty to forty personnel. In October the three sectors were separated and three separate departments of agriculture, health and education were created, and a year later, under the interim government, each of them became a 'ministry'. Before this happened, a minister was known as a 'member of the Viceroy's Council'. Our 'member' was Jogindar Singh, a lover of Persian and Urdu, and a close friend of Iqbal. The latter addressed him in his poem, *Motor*:

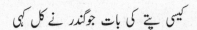

What a good point Joginder made yesterday

As soon as the government's attention turned to progress and planning, the department of education was speedily expanded. We were lucky to have a leader as enlightened as Sir John Sargent. Following his instructions I established the department of educational planning, and also laid the foundation of the Bureau of Education which was responsible for information and publications related to education. Every modern day department of education has its roots in the Bureau of Education. The provincial governments were responsible for education and the centre undertook to provide them with counsel and other help, and synchronize policy among them. To do this the centre formed a board of mutual consultation; ministers of education of all the provinces, vice chancellors of universities and recognized experts were members of this board. The annual meetings of the board were organized by turns in different provinces or princely states, while the meetings of its subcommittees were held in Delhi. I was responsible for supervising the office that coordinated all this work. The truth is that the experience I gained in those two years served me for the rest of my life.

Although many debates have left their impression on my mind, I will for the sake of brevity mention just one of them. The committee that was formed to discuss the need and the purpose for religious education included brilliant minds such as Dr Sarvepalli Radhakrishnan and the Nobel Laureate, Sir Chandrasekhara Venkata Raman. The former headed the committee (and was later the President of the Indian Union), and the latter was one of its members. I was the Secretary of the committee. There were many sessions of the committee, but no decisions were reached. When writing the report I had the problem of not knowing how to say that the committee had not agreed on anything. I suggested to the honourable President that he could say that schoolchildren should remember God silently in their minds for a few minutes everyday, in their own way. He accepted my suggestion, saying that conflict arises when views are expressed in speech; if they are confined to the mind and never expressed, what scope can there be for disagreements?

In January 1946 our department was moved from Simla to Delhi and was housed in the Northern Block of the Secretariat. However, for the next two years my office, along with those of the Minister and the Secretary, used to be shifted to Simla in the summer. After about six months, when the interim government was formed, the well known statesman Chakravarti Rajagopalachari (known as Rajaji) became the Minister for Education. I have had the opportunity to work with dozens of ministers in different countries but I have never known any that could compare with him in practical ability and astuteness. His was a frail body, dressed in a kurta and dhoti of homespun cotton. He had a *tilak* on his forehead, the sacred thread round his neck, a handloom kerchief across his shoulders, iron-framed spectacles, slippers on his feet, and a cane in his hand. He had the large chair and velvet sofa removed from his room, and substituted them with a wooden *takhat*, or divan. He would sit on this divan, leaning on bolsters, and study files and dispatch cases in no time. The custom that a minister dealt only with the Secretary had been discontinued, and now he could call the officer concerned, listen to him and give his own view of a matter. Rajaji therefore sent for me on several occasions.

In December, when I went to Bombay on a tour with Sir John Sargent, I heard two pieces of news. One day a newspaper carried the news that the Progressive Writers' Association in Delhi had chosen me as its President in its annual session. The very next day we heard on the phone the news that Rajaji was being transferred to a different ministry. His portfolio was being bestowed on Maulana Azad. Consequently, we immediately returned to Delhi.

I had been to see Maulana Abul Kalam Azad a few times in Calcutta, but the last such occasion had been twelve years ago. I was a student then, and there was no reason for a person as busy as he to remember me. I was therefore astounded by his memory, when, upon the secretary calling out my name, Akhtar Husain, after a formal introduction, the Maulana added 'Raipuri'! When I thanked him for his courtesy in remembering my full name, he said, 'I remember, when I met you in 1932, you had come to Calcutta from Aligarh, and despite attempts made by your Hindu friends, the landlord refused to rent out a room to you.' I wondered how he could remember such an insignificant detail. I observed the same perfection of memory in Sir Ross Masood. When Maulvi Abdul Haq introduced me to him he said, 'I saw him for the first time in 1932, when he had come from Calcutta to Aligarh for his admission to the college. When he entered my room to show me his certificates all the chairs were occupied, so, without hesitation he went and sat on the window sill.'

During his tenure as minister, Maulana Azad appreciated my work so much that without my realizing it, his good opinion changed the course of my life. Briefly, the detail of this is as follows:

During the War, when the government of India began to send people to America for professional training, an officer from the ministry of Education was posted in Washington to supervise the programme. Three years later, at the expiry of his tenure, he was to be transferred back to Delhi, and the question of nominating someone else to take his place in Washington came up. In the month of March, Sir John Sargent proposed my name for the post which was known as Educational Attaché, and passed the file to Maulana Azad. The Maulana was so kind to me that his acceptance was taken for granted, so the Secretary said to me, 'You had better leave in April because the state of affairs in the country is precarious, and there is no telling what might happen.' As soon as the news of my appointment spread my well-wishers started to congratulate me. Meanwhile Maulana sent for me, and pointing to my file said in his typical manner, 'My boy, I've only just stepped into this ministry and you are preparing to leave! You figure prominently in my mental blueprint for the ministry. Next month, that is in April, you are to accompany me to Simla. Until then I will not issue orders on this file. If after that you don't like my arrangement, you can go to America.' Well, since as they say in Persian, 'Orders from the Ruler are like sudden death,' I was silent, and in April I left for Simla to stay there for three months. The office there was in my charge and my daily routine went thus: I would take the relevant documents from the afternoon mail to the Secretary at the Cecil Hotel, and he would then select some of them for the Maulana, which I would carry to him. It had to be done this way because Maulana avoided speaking in English, and the two of them did not trust each other, while they regarded me as dependable; this daily attendance therefore fell to my lot. By five in the evening, after he had finished his work, the Maulana would arrive at the tea table. He did not eat lunch, and neither went out for dinner nor invited anybody for the meal. Visitors could join him at teatime, and be edified by his conversation, on subjects such as politics, history, and literature—a benefit they were unlikely to reap anywhere else. For three months I enjoyed this advantage; and I savour the pleasure of those sessions to this day.

The Maulana spoke and carried himself in exactly the same way whether it was in private or in public. He walked in measured steps and spoke in the same measured way. His deliberate style could conceivably provoke a suspicion of insincerity. Rhetorical speech was second nature with him, and he would express himself in this mode, both at home and outside. He was by nature a generous and elegant man. His *sherwani* was always made from homespun cotton, but it was tailored by a British tailor in Calcutta. I heard Saghar Nizami say that in 1935 he was once the Maulana's guest. When he was leaving,

the Maulana said to him, 'It's the tradition to give the fare for the
return journey to guests who are younger than oneself, so take from
me whatever is available,' and so saying he gave Saghar Nizami a
handful of eight anna and four anna coins. This was a period of
indigence for the Maulana. But when he became Education Minister,
my orderly Haji Mohammad was assigned to him. He told me that
Maulana would give the cook a hundred rupee note every day, and
never ask him for an account of the expenditure.

Politics and journalism of his era clearly bear his stamp. Yet Maulana
was always unhappy that he could not contribute much to literature
and scholarship. *Tarjuman-ul-Quran* will always be considered the
main work of his life, and will always bear witness to his perception
and wisdom. However the text of his *Tazkira* and *Ghubar-e-Khatir* had
less substance and too much style, while the style of his letters was
more businesslike than literary. It was in his speech that his talent
shone brightest. No matter what the topic, he could speak on it
eloquently and convincingly for hours. If someone in the audience
raised a point, he would listen attentively, and if applause was merited,
he would bestow it. Once when Western and Eastern poetry were
being compared, I commented that when I read Sanskrit poetry I felt
as though I were in a jungle which was full of many different kinds of
trees and countless species of gambolling animals and birds. European
poetry on the other hand ushered me into lush meadows and rain and
snow steeped landscapes. Persian and Urdu poetry evoked images of
city streets or else tracts of sandy desert. When he heard this, Maulana
was quiet for a while, and then said with some pleasure, 'This is a new
way of looking at it. You should expand on this theme in writing. Art
and literature are influenced not only by economics, but by geography
as well.'

When I was leaving for Simla, Maulvi Abdul Haq had told me that
land for the building in which Anjuman Taraqqi-e-Urdu was to be
housed, had been arranged, and Nawabzada Liaquat Ali Khan's
ministry of Finance would authorize a grant of five lacs on the
recommendation of the Education ministry. Maulvi Sahib then made
me responsible for getting Maulana's approval. When I subsequently
broached the subject with Maulana, he flew into a rage. 'Maulvi Abdul
Haq has dared to start such a serious linguistic controversy without
consulting the Anjuman's directors. Don't even mention him to me!'

'Sir this matter has to do with the institution, not with Maulvi Sahib.'
I ventured to point out.

When Maulana regained his good humour he told me to send for
Maulvi Sahib so that he could speak to him personally.

On my informing him of this, Maulvi Sahib arrived in Simla for a
day, at the end of April. When I took him to see Maulana, it became
apparent that the two of them were meeting after a long time, even
though Maulana had been a member of the Anjuman's advisory
committee. When Maulana complained to him that he had made an
issue out of the Sahitya Parishad conference, Maulvi Sahib pointed at
me and said, 'He was there throughout. You can ask him to tell you
what happened.' I then recounted the whole episode, after hearing
which Maulana said, 'I wish you had told me then (in 1937). I would
have got Gandhiji to see things in the right light.'

To cut a long story short, Maulana directed his ministry to
recommend the grant for the Anjuman, and to have the documents
signed by him and presented to the Ministry of Finance. The approval
arrived from Delhi in mid May, and after Maulana had signed it, it was
dispatched to Delhi. On 3 June, by the time Liaquat Ali Khan had
finished studying it, the Standstill Order was proclaimed, in accordance
with which, every new expenditure, appointment, promotion, and
transfer was stopped, pending the partition of India. Consequently, the
recommendation Maulana had made for my promotion stood
rescinded, and the file concerning my transfer to Washington became
ineffectual.

With the announcement of Partition, every government employee
was given the right to opt for India or Pakistan, and ordered to make
his decision known by the end of June. Quaid-i-Azam and Nawabzada
Liaquat Ali Khan sent out an appeal to Muslim employees asking them
to opt to work for Pakistan, without hesitation. When I mentioned this
to Maulana he replied, 'I have always said, and still maintain, that
Muslims have made a wrong decision, but since Pakistan is about to
become a reality, every experienced Muslim ought to go there and help
in its organization.' It is stated in Maulana's book, *India Wins Freedom*
that employees in his ministry were forced to go to Pakistan. This is
not true. None of us were 'pressured' by Pakistani authorities to go to
Pakistan. We either came here because we wanted to, or to save our
lives.

In post Partition India when Muslims became objects of displeasure for their support of the Pakistan Movement, Maulana lost his political clout. However, respect for his personality remained. Moreover owing to his good planning, education prospered. I had occasion to visit him twice on official business from Pakistan. It was then that I realized the extent of his powerlessness. At the time of Partition, Chaudhry Mohammad Ali had consented to (against my advice) not splitting the libraries belonging to the Central government between the two countries, and instead, agreed on behalf of Pakistan to receive one copy of only those books which had two copies. Later the Indian ministry of Education declared that they did not have a list of such books. Consequently an officer and staff were dispatched from Pakistan to compile a list of such books in Delhi, but despite the expenditure of lacs of rupees and many years' travail, nothing was achieved.

In 1952, I was sent to Delhi to persuade Maulana Azad to resolve the matter. The Maulana said, 'I have told them time and time again, but the Hindu officers refuse to comply. Take your team back to Pakistan because nothing will come of your efforts. However if both governments together ask Britain to transfer the India Office Library from London to the subcontinent, Pakistan's losses can be made up.'

On my return to Karachi, when I handed my report to the Pakistan government, it was decided to act on Maulana's advice. For years I remained busy, taking stock of the collection at the India Office, and finally in 1955, when Prime Minister Mohammad Ali Bogra went to Delhi to discuss various matters with Pandit Nehru, he took the Minister for Education, Abid Husain, and me with him.

During our formal meetings with Maulana Azad, his attitude greatly disappointed us. He said, 'The books that arrived here from the India Office will remain here. However we will give you copies of those that are of interest to Pakistan.'

I replied, 'Despite our lack of resources at the time of Partition we did not insist on the division of libraries. So it is only appropriate that the part of the India Office that is transferred should remain in Pakistan while you take copies of what you need.'

The matter was not settled and it was proved that Maulana had no control in any matter. He avoided supporting Pakistan even in a just claim, lest he was accused of showing partiality to it.

Nobody had any inkling that the partition would be carried out so soon after it had been announced. There was so much enthusiasm and passion that it was not considered necessary to assess its immediate and far-reaching effects; nor was there any time to make such an analysis. Mountbatten's Public Affairs Officer has quoted him as saying, 'From the administrative point of view the new government can be established in a brick house, a mud house, or a tent. We are putting up a tent for Pakistan.'

Congress had stipulated a period of two months for the Partition so that Pakistan would not receive a fair share of the country's assets, and in the ensuing confusion it would not have the time to secure a foothold.

When I returned to Delhi from Simla at the end of June, the last date for making known one's option had passed, and I did not know what to do. Until 1945 I had been under the delusion that Congress would not hesitate to acknowledge the legitimate demands of the Muslims, but the lack of principles it demonstrated put an end to all such illusions, and the events of 1946 made it clear to everybody that the establishment of Pakistan was the only way left open for Muslims to achieve political salvation.

What would be the fate of the Muslim minority left behind in India? They would most certainly have to face the vengeance and fury of the Hindu majority, since it was not possible for the limited resources and restricted area that Pakistan possessed to provide refuge to them.

Chaudhry Mohammad Ali was in those days Pakistan's representative in the 'Partition Council', Prime Minister Designate Liaquat Ali's Special Adviser, and the proposed Secretary General of the future Government of Pakistan. He called me and enquired, 'Why have you not opted for Pakistan yet?' I replied, 'To leave one's homeland for ever is not an easy decision to make. Moreover, Pakistan will be facing so many problems in the beginning that the spread of education will not be a priority, and so a person like me will not be of much use.'

To this Chaudhry Sahib's confident rejoinder was, 'Your apprehension is baseless. Pakistan has been created to alleviate the plight of the Muslim people, which would not be possible without education.'

At the same time many sincere non-Muslim friends warned me that a massacre of Muslims was being planned in East Punjab and Delhi, and advised me to leave for Pakistan without wasting time. When I had written out my agreement for employment in Pakistan, Qazi Abdul Ghaffar, Dr Zakir Husain and others tried to discourage me, and Maulana Azad expressed his disappointment. But after the September riots, when Muslims from Qarol Bagh and its surrounding areas were singled out and killed, or managed to flee only after they had been robbed, the same people told me when I met them on later occasions, 'You did well to leave when you did, for if you had not, nothing could have saved you from being murdered.' The staff of Jamia Millia in Qarol Bagh barely escaped with their lives during the riots, and many of them, for example Maulana Aslam J. Rajpuri, Hamid Ali Khan, etc. fled to Karachi for a few months.

On 22 July, Pakistan's administration was formally given shape, and it was settled who would be in charge of which ministry or department. At the session of the Pakistan Council, Chaudhry Mohammad Ali sent for me and announced that for the present the Education department would be put in my charge, since I deserved the position. The Government of India too had recommended my name for this post but the Stand Still order had intervened and the directive could not be implemented.

The congratulations that followed had not yet died down when the very next day Chaudhry Mohammad Ali chose somebody else for the post. The person he selected was not directly linked with the Education Ministry, but he did have the honour to be related to Chaudhry Sahib. My unhappiness over this incident was exceeded by the astonishment of others. When Maulana Azad commented wryly, 'This is just the first rap. You can still change your mind,' I recited the following couplet and departed for Pakistan:

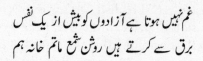

The free do not mourn for longer than the span of a breath
With lightening we kindle the light that brightens the house of mourning

The Perilous Journey to Pakistan

In the special train which carried Pakistani officers from Delhi on 10 August, a compartment was allotted to me. In addition to my family and me, it accommodated some of our essential belongings. Of the rest of our possessions some followed later and some were simply discarded.

At nine-thirty in the night, when we were passing the border of Patiala State, there was a great explosion and the engine was cut off from the train. There was the sound of some of the compartments crashing to the ground, while ours trembled but remained standing. The power lines were cut and there was pitch darkness all around. In the death-like silence the enemy stood hidden in the nearby jungle, ready to shed blood. Through the slats of our closed windows we could see the lights of their vehicles, and their guns pointed at us. Fortunately the few soldiers who were escorting our train turned their machine guns on the killers, who then did not dare to carry out their attack. After they had fled it was discovered that they had removed a portion of the track and placed a time bomb there. One woman died along with her small daughter. Some people were wounded, and the rest of us could do nothing but pray in that wilderness.

A detachment of the British army happened to be present somewhere in the vicinity. When they were informed of the incident, they provided a small train in which, somehow, all of us managed to fit, and proceeded, without food or drink, via Samasata, to Bahawalpur. There we boarded a regular train and arrived in Karachi on the night of 13 August. This incident was reported all over the world as it was the first armed attack on an official train bringing people into Pakistan. It then became a routine affair, and God alone knows how many innocent people fell victim to Akali Sikhs, Sevak Sangh murderers, Mountbatten's indifference, and Patel's apathy.

The older inhabitants of Delhi would remember the crazy old woman known as Allah Rakhi believed to be a 'majzoob', or one besotted with the divine. She used to frequent the house of our neighbour, the wife of the Principal, Mushtaq Ahmed Zahidi, and would sometimes visit my wife as well. I used to dismiss her chatter as a mad woman's drivel. When there was talk of my going to America in March, she said, 'First he will go to Madras, Hyderabad, Bahawalpur and Karachi, then he will go to America, and in fact he will travel so much that he will be tired of travelling.' It sounded meaningless at the time, but then suddenly, I had to leave on a tour of Madras and

Hyderabad. And later, I reached Karachi via Bahawalpur. The rest of her predictions too came true.

About the same time a vagrant palmist found his way into our compound, and reading my palm for free, he said, 'In about six months, you and your family will be in danger of losing your lives in the course of a journey.' That prediction too, came true. However the danger passed away and we survived.

The Early Days of Pakistan

Many simple people had imagined that as soon as the flag of independence was hoisted on 15 August, all the strife and violence would come to an end. Ram Raj or the rule of God would triumph in India while a golden age like the reign of the first four Caliphs would begin in Pakistan. They imagined the situation as though it was a lawsuit in the court of the British, and the judgement would be accepted without demur by both sides. But the bubble of this illusion soon burst. On 16 August Mountbatten announced from Delhi the partition of Punjab and Bengal, known as the Radcliffe Award. Radcliffe had been appointed Arbitrator in the division of these provinces. There is evidence that he completed the job between 9 and 13 August in Mountbatten's guesthouse, and having handed over the document of partition to the latter, escaped to England. He had assigned to India the Muslim majority district of Gurdaspur and several administrative divisions. India's border was thus drawn along Kashmir, and it also gained control of the source of three rivers. This of course opened the floodgates for the Kashmir conflict as well as the discord over the Indus water. Many analysts have held Mountbatten responsible for changes in the 'award.' During the war between India and Pakistan in September 1965, when a representative of the famous London newspaper, *Sunday Times*, asked Radcliffe why he had given the district of Gurdaspur to India, the latter replied that it had happened so long ago that he could not remember the details.

چہ دلاور است دُزدے کہ بکف چراغ دارد

How audacious the thief who holds a lamp in his hand

For the Muslims of East Punjab, the announcement of the award was no less than an apocalypse. Hundreds of thousands of them were butchered by Akali Sikhs, while forty or fifty hundred thousand were looted and driven into Pakistan. Meanwhile the frontier forces of the British and the Congress government witnessed all this in indifferent silence. About the same time a massacre began in Delhi and its environs, and a mighty wave of refugees flooded Karachi and the interior of Sindh.

While this devastation was under way, India attacked the princely state of Junagarh with the explanation that accession to Pakistan by the Muslim potentate of Junagarh was not acceptable to his Hindu subjects. India also invaded Kashmir on the grounds that the ruler there had decided to accede to India. Shaikh Abdullah enthusiastically supported the latter accession.

Meanwhile Khan Abdul Ghaffar Khan showed his hatred of Pakistan by intriguing with Afghan leaders when he visited Kabul in July, a step that turned the Afghans against Pakistan from day one. In short, the country faced nothing but problems and trouble, both inside and outside. As for its share of the assets, Pakistan was to receive 75 crore rupees, of which after the first instalment of 20 crores had been transferred, the government of India reneged, and refused to pay the rest. If Gandhi had not gone on hunger strike Pakistan would have been permanently deprived of its due share. Gandhi had to pay with his life for his sympathy with the Muslims, and was murdered by the RSS. With his martyrdom he regained his lost glory and greatness.

On 16 August 1947, the Government of Pakistan began to function on a regular basis in Karachi. Many people, like me, were newcomers to this city. When I left in the morning to look for my office, some local person informed me that it was located behind the Paradise Cinema. When I arrived there I found some barracks which were still under construction. Outside one tiny room was suspended a board that proclaimed it to be the 'Reception'. When I showed the reception clerk my identity card he handed me a bunch of keys, and pointing towards a two storied building informed me that it was known as the Sindh PWD Building, and certain rooms on its ground floor were reserved for the 'Education Department'. When I opened the rooms and looked in, I found them bereft of everything but a few tables and chairs. We had sent an advance guard from Delhi who had somehow taken possession of those few rooms. No sooner had we sat down to commence work than we heard the news that the goods train which had left Delhi for Pakistan, carrying piles of official files, had been torched just outside Delhi. This was the fate of the files; I have already recounted that of the books. We now had to depend solely on our commonsense, and improvise as we went along. Accordingly we bought paper from the market, and plucked thorns from the acacia tree to use as paper pins, and thus equipped we proceeded to take stock of our situation. If truth be told, this lack of means spurred us to action with extraordinary enthusiasm. It was as though our office was a battleground, where instead of a sword we were plying our pens to protect the trust of which we were the custodians. This spirit burned bright in the breasts of many in the early days of Pakistan.

Karachi was a very clean city in those days. Its population was no more than four or five hundred thousand. There was nothing but sand dunes beyond Kashmir Road and the Lyari River. As for the cemetery known as Gora Qabristan, there was such desolation around it that I declined to live in a house situated in its neighbourhood, saying that I refused to be the warden of this godforsaken graveyard.

I had just installed myself in a house in Napier Barracks, and fallen asleep when the barking of jackals woke me up and I discovered that the polo ground was their permanent habitat. In the beginning, the city was peaceful and serene, and the people of Sindh welcomed the immigrants from India warmly. Things took a nasty turn when people arrived, not to save their lives but to make money, and the interests of the newcomers clashed with those of the local inhabitants.

The initial structure of a government had barely been established, and about fifty thousand Hindus and Sikhs had crossed the border into India with their movable property while a corresponding number of Muslim refugees had arrived in Pakistan, when a year after Partition Quaid-i-Azam died—the foundation had just been laid when the architect passed away. Liaquat Ali Khan tried to follow in his footsteps and when the journey ended in his death, Pakistan was faced with the crisis which led to its division twenty years later.

The reasons for the ensuing crisis are obvious. First of all, the Muslim League had no blueprint for building the free state of Pakistan, once it had achieved independence. Secondly, the circumstances in which, and the suddenness with which Pakistan was created, made its survival a miracle. At the time of Partition, India was better off than Pakistan in many ways. If the political crisis there was brought under control with time, the reason was that for thirty years (1947–1997) the reins of government remained in the hands of the Congress, which maintained the continuity of policies and preserved links between the Centre and the provinces. The success of the Muslim League had depended on the personality of the Quaid and the political consciousness of the Muslims of India, which, from 1943 to 1947, clamoured to be liberated from the dominance of non-Muslims.

From the aspect of organization, the Muslim League's roots were weak in the region that was Pakistan, and this weakness became apparent immediately after the assassination of Liaquat Ali Khan. Bureaucrats and military dictatorship attempted to fill the political void that was subsequently created, and the poor state became like an orphan who after the death of his parents is left to the mercy of tyrannical employees.

If during the government of Liaquat Ali Khan the Constitution had been framed, the whole affair of evacuee property settled without delay, and the quota system for provinces ended, the country would have been safe from the flood of troubles with which it was confronted. India had settled all these three matters smoothly in its initial period as an independent state. In spite of the horrible destruction caused by the World War, Yugoslavia managed to draft a Constitution in a very short time, which has been working efficiently for the last thirty years despite linguistic and religious disagreements; and West Germany absorbed ten million German refugees from East Germany. If Pakistan was not successful in these matters, the real reason for it was that the exploiters' hold on the state had become tight, right from the beginning. Evacuee property entered Pakistani society like a deadly poison, and greed and avarice changed people's personalities. The nouveau riche, fraudulent characters and crooks had a field day. Many times, wandering gloomily on the streets of this alien city, I beheld stiff necks, beards whose aim was to deceive, and begums dressed foppishly and resembling female innkeepers. The late Agha Ashraf broke the spell of my perceptions when he said, 'If you become convinced that everybody was reborn in 1947, and are not what they were before, you will come to terms with what you see.'

What he said was true in many ways. No sooner had the genie of provincial prejudices risen from the bottle than national unity became an impossible dream, and the voice of people like us faded before the roar of the 'sons of the soil.' It then began to seem that the cultural heritage of Muslims was not what we had supposed during the Pakistan movement, nor were Islamic values as they had been interpreted by Allama Iqbal and Quaid-i-Azam—but that their meaning was understood only by tribal chiefs, landlords and capitalists; and moreover, anybody who opposed the interests of these people was the enemy of the nation and the state.

A few months after the establishment of Pakistan I met Sajjad Zaheer in Karachi. This was the period when the Communist Party had abandoned the policy of a united front, and had adopted the path that came to be known as the Zhadanov Line. According to this view, writers who did not align themselves with communist politics were no longer Progressive. I explained to him that this fledgling country needed stability. The axis of tribal and feudal systems was so powerful here that a progressive outlook could be assured only if all the enlightened groups were united.

To come back to the subject: here I was, sitting in an empty room of a derelict building, having left behind Simla's Girton Castle and the Northern Block in New Delhi. On 26 August, Mr Fazlur Rehman was inducted as the Interior and Education Minister. A few months later he was given the portfolio for Commerce in place of the Interior ministry. My association with him lasted for almost five and a half years. Mr Fazlur Rehman came from East Bengal, but he was a true patriot and had a deep interest in Education. He sent for me on his very first day as Education Minister, and discussed the issues of Pakistan's educational system for a very long time. Consequently, the historic Educational Conference, which could be called the first chapter of the educational history of the country, was organized in November. It was attended by the leading authorities on education, and I acted as the Conference Secretary. If one saw the detailed published report of that Conference, one would see in it the outline of the educational policy from every aspect. In order to achieve harmony between the provincial education ministries and the universities, two separate Boards were created at the recommendation of the Conference. It was I who framed the Boards and organized their annual meetings.

The History Commission and the Commission for Coordination with UNESCO were also given in my charge. In addition I was deeply involved with the Department of Education, Board of Secondary Education, and the early stages of the university in Karachi. The establishment of different cultural institutions, arranging grants for literary and academic associations and many other such matters were entrusted to me. In addition to Karachi, the educational responsibilities for Balochistan and the tribal areas of the Frontier province were assigned directly to our ministry.

How we, a handful of officials, along with our tiny staff and limited resources, were able to cope with all these duties is known to God alone. For years we worked from morning to evening, sometimes until nightfall, and frequently on the weekly holiday as well. However in those days Education had no importance in the eyes of the Finance Ministry. The authorities had no conception of the demands of freedom and progress. They were imbued with the British mentality. Our First Secretary was a member of the Civil Service. Whenever he was faced with an educational issue, he would tell the peon, 'Go call the Education people.' The peon would come to me and say, 'Sir, you have been summoned.' I would try to excuse myself by saying, 'There are other "Education people" too,' but he would insist, 'It's you he means'.

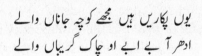

In the street of the beloved they call me thus,
Come here, O you with the torn shirt [the lover]

In 1953, when Ghulam Mohammad dismissed Khawaja Nazimuddin's cabinet, and dissolved the National Assembly, Pakistan's foundations were shaken. Then when he merged the provinces of West Pakistan into one, his associates said that the move had been made in view of the expected secession of East Pakistan. This change limited the scope of our ministry, and when the Constitution was framed (which was later annulled by Iskander Mirza), it no longer retained the status of a ministry.

Until 1955 it had never entered my head to seek employment with a foreign organization. Columbia University offered me a temporary position as a professor, Professor Bukhari found a position for me in the Information department of the United Nations, but I refused both. Instead I continued to discharge my responsibilities as Deputy Secretary in the Education ministry, as well as Head of the Secondary Education Board. However, at the end of 1955 it seemed as though my compatriots were racing towards the model of the early Caliphate of the Blessed Four, and in their enthusiasm had even outstripped their model, and reached an earlier period where Abu Jahal, or the Father of Ignorance was holding sway. Therefore when UNESCO offered me a job, I accepted and left for Paris. It was agreed at the time that I would return to the Ministry in two or three years, but instead, I spent almost seventeen years working for UNESCO, and am now a pensioner of the organization.

The Partition of the subcontinent is such an important event in the modern era that historians will continue to debate its causes for a long time. 'What if it had been thus?' is a permanent topic in the book of a nation's or an individual's life. When we look back at the past we say 'If it were not for that mistake, the First World War would not have happened.' And, 'If only such and such measure had been adopted, the Second World War could have been avoided.' However we learn from analysis that no serious crisis of collective life is created or terminated at one point or by a certain event. This same historical logic applies to the partition of the subcontinent. Individuals see its effects in the light of their personal gain or loss. But there were many people for whom Pakistan was not merely the Allotment Office, or a storehouse for the loot and plunder of Partition. They saw this country as a trust for those values which brighten the early period of Islam. Their desire was to build national life in the light of those values, but a conspiracy between colonial and reactionary powers extinguished that torch.

Sonamarg (Kashmir), 30 August 1944

New Year's eve in Karachi (1951) with Hameeda and friends

In Paris with Hameeda and
Shahid (1957)

With Hameeda, Irfan, Navaid and Shahid (Rome, 1958)

With Hameeda in Karachi (1963)

With Masai tribesmen in Kenya (1964)

Iran (1968)

At his son Irfan's wedding in Lahore (1972)

With Dr Jamil Jalabi, Shanul Haq Haqqi and Sehba Lucknavi (Karachi, 1974)

8

The World Changed

Ancient mythology tells of a bird that is destroyed by fire only to reappear, glowing with an even brighter life. An individual or a nation that passes through fire but is not capable of emerging more radiant than ever, rather than turned to ashes, is destined for nothing but annihilation. The Roman Empire was trampled and buried under the weight of the barbaric hordes of Northern Europe, and was not able to throw off the burden and rise, ever again. Consequently, for centuries the continent of Europe remained in the abyss of degradation which is known as the Dark Ages. Arab society met with the same fate after the Mongol onslaught. But after the destruction of the last World War, we saw the countries of the West and East recover, and regain their momentum through reconstruction and development. This was the miracle of modern man's courage and determination, and the marvel of science and technology. I came across the first example of it in the German city of Munich.

In 1948, I was on my way to attend an international education conference in Geneva as Pakistan's representative, when the Pan American aircraft was forced to make a sudden emergency landing in Munich because of some fault in its engine. The city was almost completely destroyed by Allied bombing, and in whichever direction one looked, one saw nothing but broken houses, bare-footed old women and half naked, ragged younger ones, wandering in and out of piles of rubble. Ten years later when I came again to Munich, the city's population had increased considerably, and there was such a flurry of activity in its buildings and on its roads that it was impossible to imagine that it had undergone disaster. I found it hard to believe that a defeated government and an unequipped people had reconstructed the city so rapidly. I happened to meet an American, who introduced himself thus:

It was in 1945, after Hitler had committed suicide and those of his troops that remained had laid down their arms, that I was an officer in the American army which invaded Munich. A good part of the town had survived destruction, and was still inhabited. Suddenly our General announced that the war was over, and commanded that since there was no point in taking the ammunition back with us, it should be used on the town. No sooner had the order been given than thousands of cannons disgorged their shells, and in a few hours Munich was leveled. This destruction was so gratuitous that my conscience could not endure it, and so after my discharge from the army I decided to spend the rest of my life rebuilding Munich. Many years ago I came and settled here so that I could atone for my sin by helping to revitalize the city we had laid waste.

The man told me that every German spends some of his leisure hours in volunteer work aimed at rebuilding a part of his shattered country.

Such was the fervour that gave a new lease of life not only to Germany but also to every other country wounded by the War.

On this occasion I remembered an episode from my own country which happened about 1950, at a time when groups of refugees were huddled together on roads, waiting for the arrival of angels who would lift them out of their destitution. Some British volunteers were trying to explain to them that they could build simple houses for themselves at very little cost if they put in the effort. But the refugees neither volunteered, nor cooperated with them in the work. One reason for our decline is that we leave all responsibilities to God and the government. The result is that the spectacle of inertness, apathy and insensitivity that one beholds here is rarely seen anywhere else.

There is no doubt that after the war the axis of power moved from Europe to America, and that if America had not helped out, the spreading flood of the Russian revolution would have inundated Western Europe. However time disproved the prediction that after the inner conflict of Capitalism, and the liberation of the overseas colonies the old culture of Western Europe would be demolished, and the flag of revolution would be fluttering confidently in its place. The creation of the welfare state retained democracy and at the same time combined and merged Socialism and Capitalism in such a way that people turned their backs on revolution. This was the state of affairs in Western Europe—which Karl Marx believed would be in the vanguard of revolution. By reducing the rate of population growth, increasing industrial and agricultural wealth, and strengthening political and social institutions, Western Europe chose a route which, ignoring all mutual rivalries, pressed on towards the goal of a united Europe. Besides challenging the political ascendancy of Russia and the economic superiority of the United States, the fundamental aim of this unity was to have a voice in directing the markets of the newly liberated third world countries.

The way in which this struggle influenced the United Nations was an experience I gained in the course of my long service in UNESCO. For nearly seventeen years my status was that of a diplomat, and as the head of the UNESCO mission in Somalia and Iran, my rank was that of an ambassador. This afforded me the opportunity to observe and understand, at close quarters, the forces that influence the relationships between rich and poor countries. Working with people from different countries also gave me the chance to analyse their distinctive traits. In this connection, the delicate stages I had to pass through can be fathomed from the fact that in Iran the thirty foreign experts who worked in the different parts of the country, under my supervision, included Americans, Russians, Englishmen, Frenchmen, Indians, and in short, people of many different nationalities and calibre. For fear of longwindedness, I will not dwell on their habits and character traits, but resume my account under other topics.

In the beginning of 1956 when I arrived in Paris, the UNESCO office was housed in a sizeable building located near the famous highway in Paris known as the Champs Elysees. Before the War, the Hotel Majestic used to be situated in that building, which became the headquarters of the German military government after the defeat of France. After the War, France confiscated the building and handed it over to UNESCO. In 1959, when our organization was shifted to its own magnificent building near Napoleon's tomb, the government reserved its previous location for international conferences.

Pakistan's Ambassador to France in those days was Mir Khan. This venerable gentleman came from Hyderabad Deccan and knew Ghulam Mohammad from the time when he was the Finance Minister of that state. He came to Pakistan after Hyderabad state had been crushed, and was made Ambassador at Ghulam Mohammad's recommendation. He seemed to have absorbed some of the tightfistedness of the Nizam of Deccan, Mir Usman Ali Khan. He lived alone in a large house where he was served by two Hyderabadi servants. In Paris there is no dearth of uninvited guests from our part of the world. Mir Khan had devised an unusual strategy for avoiding them, which was that as soon as a guest was expected, he would leave on a tour, and the servants would tell the guest that there was neither food nor drink in the house. If the guest asked the servant to get the supplies from the market and offered to pay for them, the servant would refuse, saying, that his master would be enraged to know that he had taken money from a guest. In a day or two the poor guest would be so distressed that he would pick up his bag and baggage and leave for some other destination.

The person who first introduced the sitar to Europe was Inayat Khan. This gentleman had arrived in Europe shortly before the First World War and demonstrated his skill there. The sitar was foreign to Western ears and they failed to appreciate it, but a rich American woman was so stirred by it that she fell in love with Inayat Khan and married him. Once this event took place he gave up all thoughts of returning to India and settled down in Holland. Abandoning the sitar he turned to Sufism. One does not know how well he understood Sufism, but there was such charisma in his personality that many people became his disciples. After he died, his two sons, Hidayat and Wilayat exploited his esoteric vocation well, and founded Sufi centres in many cities of Europe. I met Wilayat in Paris. At that time he was altogether ignorant of Eastern learning, and his knowledge of Sufism was limited to a few Western books that he had read. On my suggestion he went to Turkey, Iran and Pakistan in quest of Sufis, but failed to discover an ideal mentor. With time however, he acquired maturity in his learning and experience. His sister Nora was executed by the Germans during the last World War, for spying for the British.

It is important to clarify here that the Inayat Khan we have mentioned above was not the same person as his namesake, who became famous in northern India as a sitar player, before the Second World War. It is not possible to find in the present age sitar players like his two sons, Wilayat Khan and Amrit Khan, in the subcontinent.

France's pride in her importance as an imperialistic and military power was crushed by the humiliating defeat it suffered in the World War. The northern part of the country which had been the battleground was still occupied in repair and recovery. For its Indo–China debacle the army was avenging itself on the Algerian Arabs, who had staked their lives for liberty. It was no longer the same France I had known in the days when I was a student there. It dawned on me then that no individual or nation has a permanent temperament, and that they change their form with the circumstances. It was impossible to convince anyone that Algiers had as much right to freedom as did France, and that racial prejudice is contemptible, whether it afflicts the Nazis against the Jews, or the French against the Algerian Arabs. Not only were the lives of Arabs living in France in danger, but even people like us who because of our complexion were taken for Arabs, were not safe. The police were trying to track down the secret Algerian organization and would go looking for its members in coffeehouses. My identity papers were searched a few times on the suspicion that I was an Arab. The famous Indian journalist, Khushwant Singh (the former Editor of *Hindustan Times*, Delhi) used to work with me in UNESCO. French pedestrians chided his sons on the suspicion that they were Algerians—despite the fact that they were wearing their Sikh turbans. Defeat in the war, the end of the empire, and economic decline created such an atmosphere of uncertainty that every third or fourth month the government would change. Nevertheless the foundation of the administrative structure was so strong, and there was such a deep sense of duty in the workers that bribery, black-marketing, and social crimes were rare. This state of confusion ended when General De Gaulle broke his vow of staying away from politics, and once more took up the reins of government. I still remember the month of May in that year, when he emerged from his village and stayed in a hotel that was situated opposite my office. I used to see him in the midst of his supporters every evening, in the hotel lobby. A few days later, with the help of the army, he became the President of France. The new life which he vouchsafed the country is an important event in the modern age.

Everyone has acknowledged De Gaulle's farsightedness, courage, and sincerity. His mastery over the spoken and written word was perfect, and his autobiography ranks as a masterpiece. It was under him that, despite the opposition of the army and the people of France, Algeria was granted independence, and the NATO headquarters were moved out of the country, thereby disengaging France from the yoke of American domination.

By and by De Gaulle began to inspire such awe that swarms of prostitutes disappeared from the streets either of their own accord or because police censors forced them to earn an honest living. De Gaulle was also a master of the fine irony that is a special feature of French culture. On a pilgrimage to the magnificent Parisian cathedral, Notre Dame, Jacqueline Kennedy who took pride in being an expert on art, observed to De Gaulle, 'What a lot of money must have been spent on the construction of this building.' De Gaulle replied with a smile, 'Thousands of years of culture have been spent on its construction.'

An inhabitant of modern Europe is different from his predecessors in many ways. Life before the Second World War was not as tough and costly as it is now. Moreover, people of pre-war Europe were more tolerant and considerate. Values and ideals have now been replaced by consumerism, and harshness has taken the place of refinement. When I was introduced to the great French intellectual, Sartre, as someone who had been a student of Paris University before the War, he at once asked me, 'What difference do you find in the Paris of those days and Paris as it is today?' I replied unhesitatingly, 'There is no sign of values in today's life.' Sartre remarked with a laugh, 'In the eyes of the new man, a washing machine is more useful than values.'

If economic issues are analysed from a purely materialistic point of view, it would be said that means of production should be controlled not by individuals but by the whole human race, so that they can be used in the best possible way to ensure the greatest advantage to all mankind. There is no room for divergence with this modern day point of view, whether or not it is implemented. However, it does not answer questions such as, what is the place of the individual in society, and whether it is his destiny to become an eternal prisoner of a government, an institution or a belief. While it is ridiculous for an individual to believe that he is the centre of the world, or that this insignificant earth is the centre of the universe, yet does he not have the right to live in an environment where he can use his constructive and creative abilities, and establish a healthy relationship between the society and himself? In other words, is there a fundamental difference between the demands of communism and democracy? Personally I believe that the contradiction is impermanent, and future generations will find their salvation in a merger of these two movements.

On the face of it, after the Second World War, the spell of imperialism had broken and the colonies had gained political freedom. These newly independent states, which number more than one hundred, have caused the continents of Latin America, Africa, and Asia to be labelled the 'third world'. However this perception is really an illusion created by the apellation, because in reality the world is divided into just two parts, that is: the rich countries which have experienced the industrial revolution, whether they adopted the path of communism, or of capitalism, and the poor countries, or the 'third world', who are trying to move towards the industrial system from the agricultural system, regardless of whether they have adopted the path of communism, like China, or of capitalism, like the South Asian countries. The helplessness of the third world is such that they look to their old masters for technical and financial help. But those wily old hands know better than to let backward countries become their rivals by helping them make progress in industry. So, the purpose of the Western countries' union is not only to block the onslaught of communism, but also to prevent the third world from becoming united. No matter how hard we try, we cannot find a permanent solution to the serious problems facing poor countries until we understand that by artificially dividing this tiny planet into hundreds of large or small states, man has violated that principle of nature according to which all human beings have an equal right to the earth and its resources. A just distribution of wealth among nations is as important as it is among individuals within them.

But regretfully, it is not possible to ignore the bitter reality that the focus of modern politics is nationalism. The population of Maldives may be only one hundred thousand, but the country is as proud of its national indentity as is China, with a population of one billion. If any part of the earth calls itself a nation by waving the flag of independence and putting into place a government, its people will sacrifice everything for the sake of their separate identity. Every government claims to have an ideology, a religion, or a principle, but its primary aim is to defend national interests.

However, the fear of the terrible devastation that a future war may cause has forced governments to cooperate with each other in different fields through the agency of international bodies, and maintain some balance in their relationships as far as possible. The loud call of internationalism is rarely heard now, and has been replaced by the concept of regional cooperation. Two influential examples of this are the Western organization NATO, and the Warsaw Pact which unites Socialist countries. In the Third World too the idea of regional cooperation is being recognized. For example, there is the Pan American Union in the continent of America, the regional institution of the African countries, and the Islamic Conference. The reason for the failure of all three of them, notwithstanding their good intentions, is that their members are fundamentally weak and lack the mutual trust that cannot be created without the wisdom of history and political acumen.

When we speak of unity among the Muslim nations of the world, we forget that such a concept is present also among other fraternities of the world. Take South America for example, which comprises dozens of nations, and until the beginning of the nineteenth century, was ruled by Spain and Portugal. On gaining independence, this region was divided into many nations, although its inhabitants apart from Brazil share a common religion, language, and culture. Yet there is less accord and more discord among them. The same is true of black African countries. While it is correct to say that Western imperial power encourages such discord, the real fault lies with the shortsightedness and corruption of the local rulers.

Against this background, the circumstances of Muslim countries should be analysed. Their political and economic aspects relate directly to other Third World countries. They too must form the organizational, industrial, and political institutions without which no nation can prosper. The kind of thinking which draws its strength only from past traditions or the power of individuals, cannot provide a strong foundation for nationhood. It is hard to stay free, but harder to make progress. A people learn lessons from the past, but their hopes are linked to the future and this route can be negotiated only with constant struggle. The Caliphate of the first four Companions is considered the brightest period of Islamic history for the reason that it established the great traditions of equality and egalitarianism. Democratic and welfare institutions of our day interpret those traditions and keep them alive. If we abandon these concepts, our past would not possess any feature that could distinguish it from the histories of other nations. On the one hand we proudly preach adherence to the great traditions of equality, justice and egalitarianism, and on the other, we want to retain dictatorships, feudalism, and allegiance to pirs or professional 'spiritual guides'. Every day we repeat Quranic injunctions that knowledge is the goal of life, yet when someone dares to criticize obsolete and superstitious beliefs, we cut him short with the clamp of fiqh. It is these attitudes that have lead us to our present straits, despite the geographical extent over which we are spread, our individual strengths and material resources. Indeed they have landed us in a situation that caused Iqbal to cry out:

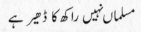

Not Muslims, we are merely a heap of ashes

Nevertheless we should not see our future as bleak. The tide of history is like the current of a river. No boat can sail against it. After many centuries of decline, Muslims too are beginning to awaken in this century as others are, and the time may not be far off when history will toss reactionary forces into its dustbin.

9

The Globetrotter

There is a marked difference between travel, tourism, and expedition. One travels to accomplish some job in hand. One engages in tourism for sightseeing and for the sake of entertainment, and one undertakes an expedition in order to discover some unknown and hazardous part of the world. In the olden days it was not possible to distinguish between the three, owing to the diffculty in obtaining supplies and provisions, and the perils to life and property. Poets encouraged others to undertake journeys, but few of them took the trouble to stray far from their own homes. Khwaja Atash counselled:

سفر ہے شرط مسافر نواز بہتیرے

It is travelling that counts; there are plenty of those who are hospitable to travellers

And Ghalib opined:

کہ چشم تنگ شاید کثرت نظارہ سے وا ہو

Profusion of view could broaden a narrow mind

However Atash never strayed far from Lucknow, and Ghalib did not venture anywhere except Calcutta.

As for Mir Anees, he stayed home after declaring:

ہوتے ہیں بہت رنج مسافر کو سفر میں

A traveller has to face much anguish in the course of his journeys

Only Nasir Khusro and Saadi travelled for many years and put up with the hardships of travel. So they can justly be called 'adventurous'.

The world of today is different. Just everybody seems to pick up a suitcase and speed away for the Haj pilgrimage, or the even greater pilgrimage to Europe or America. Tourists rummage around in the world like swarms of locusts, seeking bargain goods and cheap hotel accommodation. There is no shortage of travelogues which describe the activities of a few weeks or a few months, things that you could read about in guide books without leaving your house. When Ibne Insha used to return from a few days' trip to some place, and write an article in the paper under the title of 'On the trail of Ibne Batuta'—detailing his argument with some custom official, commenting on the indifference of hotel employees, or setting out prices of goods in the market—I would laugh at him. He would respond by saying, 'If I were to follow you in your love for the difficult, and your parsimonious use of the pen, I would not be able to produce any writing all my life.'

What places in the world did I not go to in the course of earning my livelihood; what dangers did I not face in fulfilling my passion for mountaineering, and my wanderlust; and how numerous were the abodes I visited in order to satisfy my love of knowledge and art! It is impossible to go into the details of all this, especially since there is neither the need nor the time to do so. However since these were my pursuits over a long period of time, I cannot ignore the subject. Therefore I will briefly mention those experiences and observations here, though they have been touched upon in other chapters of the book as well.

Two Years in Africa

In the beginning of 1965 when I was appointed the Representative for UNESCO in Somalia, I left on a prolonged tour of the country on the advice of the government, so as to acquaint myself with the conditions there, and also in order to assess the work of the experts in my organization. Besides the driver, the one person who accompanied me in the jeep, on those nameless roads and through the endless desolation, was Mahmood Ali, a Somali intellectual who had been educated in England. When we arrived near the Ethiopian border in the north, Mahmood Ali had the car stopped and looked out at the plain where thousands of camels were either grazing amidst the acacias, or chewing the cud under them. Mahmood Ali then said to me, 'Those pastures belong to my tribe, the Hazar Maut, and many of the camels are mine.'

'How can you recognize them?' I asked him in surprise.

In reply he descended from the jeep, and made some strange noises with his mouth. Some of the camels then pricked up their ears. They first looked attentively at Mahmood Ali, and then rushed at him. They embraced him with such fervour that he fell to the ground, and then he whispered to them for a long time while I looked on in amazement. Mahmood Ali told me, 'Africa has not yet cut its links with nature. Animals, plants and humans are used to living together harmoniously here, but the interference of the white people is breaking up this relationship and it is likely that with time we too will become involved in the curse or blessing of the machine and urban culture that you Asians have begun to follow.'

At our next camp we found a crowd of tribesmen and women jeering at a few whites who were cutting a channel from a hill stream to bring the water to the nearby fields. These were young men who had arrived from America, full of enthusiasm to serve poor nations. But Africans were not ready to accept the fact that anybody would want to work for their good, disinterestedly. Therefore in the vernacular, the young whites were known as white slaves, and the tribesmen praised their government for its cunning in avenging the enslavement of their own people by doing the same to the white men.

As evening falls, the African land and sky take on an appearance that is different from anything one has seen elsewhere. The European and American sky is either covered in clouds or wrapped in a blanket of thick mist at this time, and rarely can one witness the dazzle of stars on it. But in the place where I was, countless stars were throwing their radiant loops on the earth. All one could hear in this desolate stillness, besides the cries of wild animals, was the silent lament of Mother Earth.

The real Africa begins south of the Sahara, which is the home of the black tribes. Western Africa was first dominated by the Arabs, and after their decline the Europeans took their place. However in eastern and central Africa their control did not last beyond a hundred years or so, and after the Second World War the process of gaining political independence started for these colonized countries, and is now near completion. The exploitation wreaked by Western imperialism on the African continent in this short period has no match in Asia. The plunder was not confined to the export and import of goods, it was shot through with the racial violence that knew no distinction between the slaughter of wild animals and the massacre of innocent and helpless blacks. This same vile impulse nurtured the culture that destroyed innumerable Native Americans on the American continent and countless aborigines in Australia. Even now the itch reappears, and despite noble protestations, we see it wiping out innocent men, sometimes in Vietnam, and sometimes in Algeria or Palestine. At all times in Africa I felt, like other sensitive foreigners, that we were living among a people who had been wounded by history.

The problems of birth, marriage and death in which our life is entangled, had no special significance for them. My servant Abukar was very fond of his brother Wahid, and when the latter fell ill he served him to the best of his ability, but the day after he died Abukar returned to me and resumed his duties as though nothing had happened. When I expressed my condolences he replied that there was no remedy for death, and it was futile to mourn for the dead. On another day he suddenly said to me, 'I got married yesterday.' When I asked him why he had not informed me and not asked for leave, he said, 'Actually it was to be an engagement, but the village elders said why not have the nuptials as well.'

In short, like birth and death they see marriage as an accident of life. Life does not make them happy nor does death grieve them.

Living in Africa I became an admirer of the qualities of wild animals. In forests unfrequented by human beings, and where hunting is prohibited, animals act according to the laws of their nature and are rarely afflicted by the selfishness, duplicity, prejudice and hostility that characterize civilized man. If a lion's stomach is full, it will suffer a deer or an antelope to pass by at close quarters without giving it a glance. Most wild animals are not carnivorous. Once I saw two lion couples hunt a zebra. After they had killed it, the couple that had given it the deathblow first had its fill of the corpse, while the other couple stood by, waiting for its turn. After half the zebra had been devoured, the first lion couple turned away and it was the turn of the second couple to eat. Such elegant restraint is not seen at buffets, where people practically snatch food from one another. I remember the time when Nawabzada Liaquat Ali Khan had thrown a party at his Karachi residence. A variety of food was served on tables which had been laid out in the garden. While the guests attacked the food voraciously, Maulvi Abdul Haq stood aside, plate in hand and bewildered. The Prime Minister came up to him and enquired, 'Maulvi Sahib, why are you not eating?' Maulvi Sahib replied peevishly, 'Sir, I am waiting, with my begging bowl in my hand.' The honourable host was embarrassed and had food laid out for him on a separate table. I went and sat with Maulvi Sahib at his table, and was treated during the course of the meal to his detailed views on the absurdity of buffets.

Thinkers and scientists have racked their brains over the nature of time, but they never discovered a clue to it. Yet every grain of the universe is imbued with the miracle of time. What it decrees, people call their destiny, and astrologers and palmists claim to be its confidants. I will mention my own experience of prophecy here since it was directly linked to my stay in Africa, of which I did not have the slightest foreknowledge.

The episode happened in August 1962, when I was coming from Europe to Karachi, where I had been put in charge of organizing and managing the regional office of UNESCO. En route to Karachi I stopped at Istanbul where I ran into Fatima Khanum, who had been my classmate in Paris University twenty-two years earlier. During this whole period we had never communicated, nor had she known anything about my activities. In her house that evening, where I had been invited for dinner, I was introduced to a Greek lady, and was told that the lady could read a person's future in his coffee cup. After dinner when I had finished my coffee, I turned over my cup on the saucer. She regarded the few drops that still adhered to the cup and told me three strange things. Two of them concerned my private life and proved to be true to the letter. As a result, the third prediction kept bothering me. What it foretold was as follows: I was involved in work that took me away from my homeland repeatedly. After that day [when the prediction was made] I would travel abroad six times, and after my sixth journey my head office would transfer me to a country where at first I would refuse to go, but would have to go there willy-nilly. Gradually, I would begin to like the place so much that when I was transferred to a better country I would be extremely reluctant to leave.

But once again I would have to go where I was sent, albeit with great reluctance.

The Greek lady's prophecy turned out to be exactly correct. When I returned to Karachi after my sixth trip abroad, the UNESCO chief ordered my transfer to Somalia after informing me, 'All the efforts of our institution have proved futile there, and we have no better man than you to put the situation right.' So, in short, I had no option but to go there. But then, very gradually and without my realizing it, Africa cast a spell over me, which was something only those who have spent a long time there can comprehend. Life in the West can be dazzling, but time dulls its radiance. On the other hand, the magnetism of Africa takes long to be felt, and lasts longer.

About a hundred years ago, colonial Britain had found it expedient to occupy northern Somalia because it was situated on the mouth of the Gulf of Aden and the Red Sea, and it was considered necessary to control the Indian Ocean from Aden to Singapore in order to guard their South Asian empire. In the beginning of the century Italy occupied Southern Somalia, but at the end of the Second World War and with the establishment of the United Nations it was decided that the two parts of the country would be united, and made independent. On this occasion Britain displayed its habitual duplicity by handing over the Somali province of Ogaden to Ethiopia as it bowed out of the region. Thus was the conflict between Ethiopia and Somalia born, which has continued to the present day. Though the Western countries demonstrated no religious prejudice in Africa, history is witness to the fact that in practice they worked as far as possible for the suppression of the Muslims and in support of the Christians.

The Somalis have no equal in Africa as far as their physique and looks are concerned. They are nomadic and talkative to the nth degree. It is a small matter for them to go off on a hike of hundreds of miles, or spend the night reciting poetry or telling tales. In gatherings where poetry is recited, the chairperson suggests a theme: for example, thunder, a storm at sea, or, a lion hunt, and the poets present recite extempore couplets on the given topic. When the inspiration of one poet runs out, another continues from where he left off, and so the improvisation continues ceaselessly all night. The same is true of their predilection for covering miles on foot without giving it a thought. My watchman, Abdul Qadir, once told me that his marriage was being arranged with somebody who lived about four hundred miles away, and he was expected to go there so that the girl's family could look him over. He then picked up his walking stick and started on his journey which was to take him through thick inhospitable forests. A month later he returned, hale and hearty, with his mission accomplished.

Somali men and women have good, regular facial features, of which their teeth are the most attractive. Perhaps nobody else in the world has such clean, gleaming teeth. Sometimes during the night when the power broke down and the lights went off, I would say to Abdul Qadir, 'Open your mouth so that I can look for the matches in the light from your teeth!'

Somalia's capital, Mogadishu, is situated on the shores of the Indian Ocean, and has been mentioned by Ibne Batuta in his travelogue. It used to be visited by wild animals at one time, though that is no longer the case. Instead, now it is pythons that sometimes show up there. One of these reptiles caught the lower part of a car belonging to the Indian Ambassador, Dr Sinha in such a tight grip, that despite continual efforts by the driver, the vehicle would not budge, and all the poor Ambassador could do was to stay in the car, stunned and imprisoned.

Now and then, during a drought, there would be radio announcements that hungry monkeys were raiding a shop in some place, or that hordes of elephants had invaded another place and hunters were solicited to help drive them away.

Although I beheld many interesting and strange spectacles in the jungles of Eastern Africa, my most difficult and memorable expedition was one that took place on the sea near the border between Somalia and Kenya. I had gone in quest of wild animals in the company of an English friend, to a jungle called Ofmogo, where they were to be found in great numbers, and where they led an untroubled life, away from the reach of human beings. When we flew into a small port named Kasmayo, we were informed that it was impossible to approach the forest, for it had been raining there for the past few days. Since there was no other way to pass the time, we took a sailboat to the desert islands which are scattered in the ocean across a long area. We entrusted our precious lives into the boatman's keeping, and for five days drifted on the open sea as the waves rose and fell, our hearts in our mouths every second of the time. We lacked the courage to open our eyes and see our boat tremble on the peak of a mountain of water, and each moment we were afraid of being drowned. In the evening, when an island of rock or sand emerged from the depths of the water, the boat would be anchored and we would lie on the sand, exhausted. Only in two places did we find signs of a fisherman population. We even found an aged Chinese, who for some unknown reason had decided to settle there. When the night would become saturated with dew, and the cold would wake us up, we would open our eyes in an ambiance made inexpressibly and ravishingly beautiful by the starlight. No sound could be heard except the lapping of the waves and altercation among the fishes. In that environment it became easy to believe in the superstition of negro tribes, according to which when human beings fall asleep their spirits leave their bodies and wander over seas and mountains to breathe the air of freedom. Expeditions of this kind may tax the body, but they also impart pleasure to the soul.

When I think of Africa, the image of Mount Kilimanjaro's 20,000 feet high peak, looking like a sky-high black monster with a cap of snow on his head, rises in my mind. I am reminded of the illusive desert mirage when I think of the salt lakes near the mountain. I remember also the giraffe who stood alone and helpless in a north Kenyan plain, silently beseeching someone to remove the arrow embedded in his neck. I remembered a saying of Gautam Buddha, 'The immediate need is to pull out the arrow that pierces the soul of wounded humanity. Who shot that arrow and why, are questions that can be answered later.' My heart cried out at the giraffe's pain, and stopping the car I went towards it intending to pull out the arrow. But the animal ran from me in fear, since I was a member of that same human race that considers it a cultural distinction to murder animals.

I also remember the people of the warlike Masai tribe, who drank the blood of cows mixed with the same animal's milk, because this was their favourite fare. Their women plastered their naked bodies with so much fat that bees built their hives on them. How can one forget the lions, who had got into the habit of sleeping on trees, or the elephant which blocked the path of our car near the Nile in Uganda, and was signalling with his leg, the threat that it would push it into the water. Or the army of crocodiles who awaited their prey with bated breath, on the banks of the Nile. Or the formations of colourful song birds that can be seen nowhere but in this region. Many such memories are stored in my mind.

The proximity of animals and birds have created such a combination of ferocity and innocence in the African temperament that foreigners find it hard to understand. The reason is that the latter are distanced from nature. Modern civilization does not teach man to cooperate with nature, but rather, to challenge it. This is one of the reasons for the decline of human values.

I met Prime Minister Abdur Razzaq immediately after my arrival in Somalia. During the course of the conversation he elucidated why there was no follow up on the schemes initiated by UN Advisers and Experts. The real reason was that the government was short of financial resources as well as manpower. The Prime Minister told me, 'Our educational system is weak in every way. You can call for whatever support you need for its improvement. However don't expect any increase in the budget.'

As a matter of fact, like other African countries of those days, Somalia suffered from a mind-boggling backwardness. Most teachers were untrained, the Somali language had no script, the textbooks were published in Europe, there were no buildings to house schools, and there was not a single university in the whole country. The United Nations had had a hand in the supervision of the country for ten years, and Somalia had been independent for four years; I was now given the responsibility to produce results immediately. I am justifiably proud of the way the work was accomplished.

Every educational system has four important components: the teachers, the syllabus, the textbooks and the school environment. Under the plan I made for training Somali teachers, UNESCO and UNICEF could render this service without burdening the government. I persuaded the Russian government to arrange for the publication of course books written by Somali authors, and had UNESCO experts review the syllabus from beginning to end.

The problem of accommodation for the schools was solved when I dispatched the young Americans who had arrived in Somalia to serve humanity, but had so far spent their time wandering in the jungles or diving in the sea, to far-flung villages, where they set up small structures to house the schools, with the help of the local people. It was an uphill task to bring the plan to fruition, but I redeemed my promise to Prime Minister Abdur Razzaq, by demonstrating that determination and not money is the seminal factor in achieving one's goal. The Somali university, which I had planned, also materialized, though it did so a few years after I had left Somalia.

The Somali language had no script at the time, a disadvantage that was deeply felt. New thinking was all for having the Roman script, and was supported in its preference by the Western embassies. The traditionalists on the other hand favoured the Arabic script, and were backed by the Arab governments. There were also some Somalis who would have liked to invent a new script for their language. To settle this controversy, the government turned to UNESCO, expecting sound advice on the issue from foreign experts of the Somali language. But when I realized that the problem was political rather than linguistic, I tried to keep my organization out of the matter, leaving the responsibility of the decision to the Somali government. However, UNESCO did send a mission of European experts, who quite predictably, declared the Roman script suitable for the Somali language. Demonstrations against this decision erupted in the city, and violence was feared. The experts whose advice was responsible for the situation had left the country, and I, being the UNESCO representative on hand, had to bear the brunt of it. The Secretary of the Cultural Association wrote a letter to the United Nations General Secretary, General U Thant, which contained a threat to kill me. A copy of this letter was sent to my headquarters in Paris. Without my becoming aware of it, a crisis was created. Our organization summoned the Somali Ambassador in Paris and showed him the letter, making the Somali government responsible for my safety. As soon as the Ambassador informed the Somali government of the matter, two guards, dressed all in white, were posted at my residence, quite unknown to me. The Somali who was after my life was taken into custody. A few days later, when I became acquainted with these details, I visited my enemy in jail, and removed his misunderstanding. I even had him released from prison on my own responsibility. Many years later the government solved this difficult problem by introducing the Roman script on the one hand, and making Somalia a member of the Arab League on the other.

I will end this account by relating an unforgettable experience. My office was situated in two rooms inside the building of the Education

Ministry. One room was reserved for the experts who assisted me, while my secretary and I occupied the other room. My secretary was a Somali by the name of Abshir. In those days experienced stenographers, fluent in English, were hard to come by. Abshir had spent some time in London and had worked for the British Embassy, and so was useful in every way. However, he suffered from a bizarre malady. Every other year, with the coming of spring, a strange madness would come over him, and he had to be sent away to Somalia's only mental hospital which was situated in a faraway place. But even the insane can be quite clever where their own interest is involved. A few months after he arrived at the hospital he would get one of the doctors to certify his sanity and get himself reinstated in his job. When I read this in his secret dossier I was very surprised, but expediency required that I did not rock the boat. For a year he worked with such commitment, and dealt with such forbearance with unruly Somalis that my doubts were allayed. Then came spring. The trees around us were sprouting new leaves and birdsong was echoing in the air. Now a change came over Abshir that brought him close to a condition much referred to in Urdu poetry. His eyes shone with a strange light. He would hum something under his breath. He started making incorrect entries in the file register, and would uncharacteristically forget instructions. This state of affairs continued for many days so that I began to suspect that his madness was coming on. One morning when I entered my room, Abshir jumped up and bolted the door, and sitting down across from me, began to stare angrily at me. It occurred to me that if this giant decided to hit me or throw me out of the window, there was nothing I could do. However, I remain imperturbable in the face of the most dangerous situations, therefore, I smiled at him, lighted a cigarette, and asked him what he wanted. Abshir answered angrily, 'I know very well that you want to sack me.'

I said, 'You are wrong. On the contrary I have just extended the period of your employment. In fact you typed out the letter yourself.' Saying this I brought out the file and laid it before him.

Abshir was still not satisfied. He said, 'Why didn't you recommend an increase in my allowance?'

I replied, 'There too you are wrong, because a copy of my recommendation is lying in this very file.'

Abshir was still trying to think of a new accusation to level at me when there was a knock at the door. When he unbolted the door my Indian assistant, Dr Lakhani entered the room. Abshir shook hands so warmly with the frail gentleman that he screamed with pain, and I immediately went out of the room to inform the Education Minister Yusuf Kanadid of the episode. His assistants overpowered Abshir with great skill and put him on a plane which took him to the mental hospital. I thanked God for my deliverance, but those who knew the man cautioned me that I had not seen the last of him yet, and he was bound to surface again. It turned out that they were right.

Foreigners who visited the city used to find that the hotel Joba offered them the most suitable accommodation. I too was staying there. Late one night, when I entered the hotel lobby, Abshir suddenly sprang at me from out of the dark, 'I have been waiting for you,' he said.

Perceiving the peril, I greeted him with a smile and asked after his health. He replied bitterly, 'I was never ill, and you will realize as much in your office tomorrow.'

I now discovered that he was staying in the same hotel. Back in my room, when I called the Italian manager of the hotel and told him about Abshir, he instructed his staff to guard me at night. Much later, after it was all quiet in the hotel, Abshir silently advanced towards my room, knife in hand. I had bolted my room from inside, and had been kept awake by the sense of impending danger. As soon as Abshir reached my door the hotel staff caught him. The police was informed immediately and Abshir was sent to the lock up. At first he was to be tried for attempted murder, but in the end he was sent back to the mental hospital. I am not aware of what became of him after that.

By the end of the year 1966, it was two years since I had been living alone in Somalia. My work had pleased both the Somali government and the UNESCO chief. The two expressed their appreciation in different ways. The government tried to stop my transfer—a step in line with my own wishes—but my headquarters had decided that Iran needed me, and so I was transferred to Tehran in January 1967, as the Head of the UNESCO mission.

10

Four Years in Iran

The Muslims of India inherited their religion from the Arabs, their government from the Turks, and their culture from the Iranians. In our childhood Iran was mentioned in old Muslim families as though it was our real homeland. The body grew up in India, the mind was nourished in Iran, and the soul wandered in Arabia. The story of Rustum and Sohrab was on our fingertips, and Shaikh Sadi's *Gulistan* and *Bustan* formed a part of our earliest lessons.

In 1959, when I had to go to Tehran for the first time in connection with my work at the UNESCO, I had no inkling that I would be going there every year, and would even stay there continuously from 1967 to 1970. I have still not forgotten my first visit there. The bid for the era of prosperity and progress that Dr Mussadeq had made by nationalizing oil production, a few years earlier, had only just begun. At present the area between the Shamran hills in the north and Shah Abdul Azeem's Mausoleum in the south is thickly populated, but in those days the city had three distinctly different parts, which were separated by large unpopulated spaces. In the south were the remains of the ancient city of Ray, destroyed by Chengiz Khan, and now inhabited by the poorer section of the population. In the centre was Tehran, to which the Qajjar kings had moved their capital from Isfahan, two hundred years ago. The rich had their villas in the Shamran hills, where, especially in the summer, there was much bustle and activity. Between these three inhabited areas there were large unoccupied spaces, which however were speedily populated.

This was Iran in 1959. Isfahan and Shiraz were desolation itself. Ever since my childhood I had heard that 'Isfahan is half the world'. When my enthusiasm drove me there, I was disappointed to see a small, old-fashioned town, covered in dust. This was what Agra was like forty years earlier. However, like Agra, Isfahan's historical buildings are peerless. As for Shiraz, there was not even an airport there. The aircraft dropped us in a field near the town, and suitcase in hand, we had to wait for a taxi by the roadside. Yet it has to be admitted that in the short space of a few years, not only these cities but the whole country made dramatic progress.

At this time I was transferred from Paris as Director of the regional office of the UNESCO, based in Karachi, which controlled the organization's activities in the South Asian countries. When there was a proposal for the extension of its operations into other countries, the first country to be included was Iran, followed by Afghanistan, Nepal, Thailand, Malaya, etc. I had occasion to visit these countries many times, but it was Iran with which I felt a deep-rooted intellectual closeness. There I made many friends, with whom my friendship has survived the ravages of time. This was the attraction that drew me to Iran from Somalia, in 1967. Not for a day did I feel that I was a stranger there. My knowledge of Persian poetry and Iran's history, combined with my extensive travel to every part of the country brought me an exquisite pleasure.

Who could have envisaged at that time that the Pehlavi era would soon be over? Although every dictatorship survives on the shoulders of the army and the police, if the country has resources that can be converted into wealth, the cosmetic effect of apparent prosperity can temporarily conceal social ills. Therefore nobody could guess then, that the volcano of revolution was soon to disgorge the lava of discontent that was even then raging underground. However, there was a prophecy in the earliest edition of Shah Nematullah's collection of poetry, which was compiled immediately after his death, according to which Iran's last dynasty of rulers, consisting of only two kings, would be terminated at the end of the fourteenth century of the Hijra calendar. This prophecy can be found in the famous poem which has prophesied events that took place in the past five hundred years, and although it has been altered with the passing of time, its most authentic version, mentioned above, was extant twelve years ago in the ancient library of Imam Raza's mausoleum in Mashhad.

It cannot be denied that during the reign of the Pehlavis, measures taken to preserve the name of old poets give the impression that those poets were the real standard bearers of the Iranian cultural heritage. Every city, large or small, had roads named after Firdausi, Sadi, Hafiz, etc. Not just that, mausoleums unsurpassed in their splendour, were built over every dilapidated grave of a famous poet. The trend was started fifty years ago, by Raza Shah I, when Firdausi's one thousandth anniversary was celebrated. Six hundred years earlier, Tamerlaine, who was an admirer of Firdausi, had had the poet's grave repaired under his personal supervision. But that was the last time anybody tended to it, until Raza Shah had a magnificent mausoleum built over it in Tus. The wall of Firdausi's original house has been preserved in the same enclosure.

Like Tamerlaine, Raza Shah was not interested in any poet except Firdausi. Once when he was in Shiraz, and was passing by the grave of Hafiz, he happened to see a copy of the poet's collected works, which was suspended from a chain at the door to the tomb. Accompanying the king on that occasion was the Education Minister Aqai Ali Asghar Hikmat, who later recounted the incident to me. Raza Shah did not believe that the *Diwan* (Collected works of poetry) could predict the future for those who opened it with a query about what was in store for them. However, just to test the traditional belief, he shut his eyes and opened the book at a randomly chosen page. He opened his eyes to find his finger resting on a couplet which contained the name of his dynasty—Pehlavi.

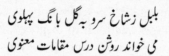

On a branch of the Cypress tree. The nightingale is reciting from the Pehlavi (Persian) Gulbang
Lessons of luminous depths

Stunned by the coincidence, Raza Shah ordered the renovation of Hafiz's tomb. Consequently, the tomb is now surrounded by a beautiful garden. Shaikh Sadi's tomb, which is situated at a short distance from it, has also been restored and its beauty enhanced. The river Ruknabad, mentioned in Hafiz's *Diwan*, now flows through its enclosure. Subsequently, the fortunes of Omar Khayyam and various other poets also took a favourable turn, and their tombs too were rebuilt. In this connection I too was able to render a good deed. In 1959, when I was setting out on my first journey to Iran, my late brother Shameem said to me, 'When you go to Isfahan, visit the tomb of Saib and say a prayer there on my behalf. My brother was a great admirer of the poet Saib. And so, after I had visited some noteworthy buildings, I asked my guide, Aqai Karbalai to take me to Saib's tomb. The latter answered with some surprise that Saib was not buried there. However on my insistence, he set out to look for the little known tomb, and brought news the next day that Saib's grave was still extant in an orchard which was situated on the outskirts of the town. With much difficulty Karbalai and I were able to find the place and I completed my mission by paying my respects to the great poet.

On my return to Tehran, when I related this incident to the Minister for Education, Dr Mehran, he was surprised, and also sorry to hear about the neglect of the tomb of such an eminent poet. He suggested that I write a letter on behalf of UNESCO, so that a suitable tomb could be constructed on the poet's grave. I at once wrote an appropriate letter and sent it to him. A few years later when I happened to go to Isfahan, I was delighted to see that the government had bought half of the orchard and built a beautiful mausoleum over Saib's grave. In addition, a library had been set up next to it. During the same period I heard that signs of the famous poetess Quratul Ain Tahira's grave had been found in the courtyard of an old house in central Tehran. Accused of propagating the Bahai religion, she had been brought to the court of Nasiruddin Shah Qajar. However the king set her free, saying, 'We forgive you for you have a beautiful face.' But the king's mother had her murdered and buried in some unknown spot.

The remains of Quratul Ain Tahira were now brought to Yusufabad, a neighbourhood in the north of the city, and interred there. I was disappointed to read in the biography published by Bahai poets that the Persian poems that had brought fame to Quratul Ain Tahira, were not really her work.

The Pehlavi family were not only indifferent to Islam, they lacked any feeling for the cultural heritage of the country. This was the root cause for their blind imitation of the West which alienated the common people as well as the intellectuals in the country. The Shah's younger sister Fatima married an American. His older sister Shams married an Armenian doctor, Pehelbud. The latter retained the post of Minister for Culture, for many years.

It was said about the Shah's twin sister Ashraf, and about the Prime Minister Abbas Huveida, that they belonged to the Bahai religion.

In biographies of kings we read about *murshidzadas*. These were people who were in some indistinct way, connected to the kings. Once in Isfahan, I was strolling with friends on the bridge known as Khajo, over the river Zindarode, when somebody pointed to a kebab vendor, whose face wore an expression of dignity and nobility. My friend then told me the following interesting story: When the founder of the Pehlavi dynasty, Raza Khan, was a general, posted in Qazwain, he contracted a 'temporary marriage', and by this marriage he had a son. When the period specified in the contract came to an end, he paid the *meher* to his erstwhile wife and as is usual in such cases, disassociated himself from her. He then moved to Tehran where he later seized the throne and established a new dynasty. Meanwhile the woman, who had been his wife for a brief period, died, leaving her son a defenceless orphan. With neither education nor proper training, there was little that the young man could do, and so he became a kebab vendor. After the elder Raza Shah died, his successor tried to help the man, but he refused to accept assistance.

The Shah indulged non-Muslim minorities and foreigners to such a degree that native Iranians began to feel dispossessed. Oppression wreaked by the secret police negated the good work of the Pehlavi era. The arrogance of members of the royal family spared neither the elite nor the common man. I was personally witness to several such incidents, though here I will relate just one archetypal example. A certain minister, Dr Hidayati and his wife, gave a dinner in honour of the Shah's eldest daughter, Shehnaz. My wife and I were invited to the function along with many ambassadors and other highly placed officials. As specified in the invitation we arrived at the Wang Hotel punctually at 8:30. The lower floor of the hotel had been reserved for the occasion, and since protocol demanded that nobody should be sitting when the princess arrived, all chairs had been removed from the lobby. The hosts were standing at the front door, ready to welcome their guest, and the back door had been locked by the secret police. All the guests were standing in the lobby, waiting for the princess. Our feet were numb from standing so long, and we were perspiring from the exertion, but that good lady did not turn up until midnight, and when she did arrive, she neither apologized to Hidayati, nor bothered to respond to the greetings of the tired guests, but walked off haughtily to the dining room. That insensitive lady never stopped to think how unpleasant the occasion had become for both the hosts and the rest of the guests. In truth, it is useless to expect courtesy and polish from the nouveau riche. As Saib puts it:

امید مہر ز نو دولتاں مکن صائب
کہ نونہال کجا طاقتِ ثمر دارد

Oh Saib, do not expect graciousness from the noveau riche
For how can an immature sapling possess the power to bear fruit?

Despite the passing of the era, justice demands that I do not hesitate to communicate what I observed. Owing to the Shah's interest, UNESCO was paying a lot of attention to adult education, 'Sipah-e-Danish', and the preservation of archeological relics. In this connection the king gave me audience several times, and I was also able to meet Queen Farah and Princess Ashraf many times.

I should mention here my meeting with the Shah when he came to Pakistan for the first time, in 1949. Deen Mohammad, who was Governor of Sindh, was hosting a dinner for the Shah one night, and he decided that the event should have a cultural character rather than be merely a formal affair. Therefore he asked me to compose an address of welcome in Persianized Urdu, and have it inscribed by a calligrapher. He also asked me to arrange a cultural programme to be presented after the dinner. I accomplished this assignment competently, and when after he had read it out, the governor presented the address to the Shah, the latter looked at it for a long time in surprise. When I was introduced to him he said to me, 'I didn't know Urdu and Persian were so similar'. He then asked me, 'Have you ever been to Iran?' When I replied in the negative, the Shah said, 'You will definitely be given an opportunity to do so.'

Many years later, during an audience with the Shah, when I reminded him of that evening, he recalled it immediately. For a long time he talked about the cultural programme after the dinner, during which Omar Khayam's quatrains were rendered with dance and music.

Iran and Japan are the only two countries where culture has suffused the common people in the true sense. The same standards of conduct and manners prevail among all Iranis, whether rich or poor, educated or ignorant.

Iran's other great characteristic is that there is hardly a place in all of the country that is not interesting for some reason or the other. Travelling through barren mountains, devoid of any sign of vegetation, one's tired eyes may suddenly come to rest on a lake or a meadow. Or, the remains of an ancient fortress or palace, telling a forgotten tale, may be discovered in the middle of a lonely desert. On one side of the country, the vast Caspian coast with mountains and forests in its lap, offers a spectacular prospect, and on the other, Isfahan and Mashad present the best examples of Islamic architecture.

I have seen every inch of Iran. The area that lies along the Caspian, and spreads for hundreds of miles behind the Elburz Mountains, is the most beautiful part of the country. Shiraz and Mashhad are historical cities, with whose attraction all tourists and pilgrims are familiar. However there are also some far-flung places that still preserve their traditional charm. Among them Hamdan, Khurramabad, and Kirman especially come to mind. Here in the subcontinent we are familiar with the name of Kirman through the people of that city who migrated here. What caused them to relocate here is an instructive story.

About two hundred years ago, when Agha Mohammad, the founder of the Qajar dynasty, drove out Lutfullah, the ruler of Isfahan, seized his throne, and pursued him with his army, Kirman was the only place where Lutfullah could find sanctuary. Agha Mohammad, who was notorious for his cruelty, warned the people of Kirman that if they did not hand over Lutfullah to him he would not spare them. When the people of the city refused to entertain his demands, Qajar's army forced its way in. Agha Mohammad then ordered that the adult male population of the city be blinded. This command was carried out with such ruthlessness that long after the incident Kirman was still known as the 'city of the blind'. A few hundreds of the inhabitants managed to escape the mutilation, and they fled to India. One of their descendants is still avenging his ancestors.

The mention of Kirman reminds me that there I met one Ismaili family who claim relationship with the late Aga Khan Mohammad Shah. Their grandfather was the brother-in-law of Fateh Ali Qajar, and the governor of Kirman province. He quarreled with the king and fled to Karachi, arriving there at a time when the British had conquered

Sindh. When a reconciliation was effected between the late Aga Khan and the Pehlavis, his ancestral property in Kirman was restored to him, but he renounced it in favour of those of his relatives who had continued to live in Kirman. The latter then had legal battles among themselves for their share in the property, which were still waging while I was in Kirman.

The late Aga Khan was a very mature statesman. It occured to him to realign his sect with mainstream Islam, and remove misunderstandings about it by publishing the earliest Ismaili manuscripts which had so far been undisclosed. To carry out this undertaking he chose an Islamic scholar of Russian descent who lived in England. At the Aga Khan's invitation, the scholar, Ivanov, established an institution in Bombay, and there, after 1930 he produced some major work on the history of Ismaili philosophy, which earned fame in Western countries. However the work stopped after the death of the Aga Khan, and Ivanov moved to Tehran with his library. It was apparent that neither Iran nor any other Muslim country was interested in his research, and when I came to know of him he was living a life of obscurity in a corner of Tehran University. After I had heard of him, I would sometimes visit him and listen to his interesting accounts of Ismaili history. I also became aware of his concern for the fate of the precious collection of books in his keeping. Ivanov had neither relative nor friend in the world, so when he died the library was closed. God alone knows in what condition it is now. The Ismaili movement is an important chapter in Islamic history, and it is the duty of unbiased researchers not to let this treasure be lost once again.

The taste for poetry prevails not just in the urban centres of Iran, but also in its rural areas. The fact is that the character of Persian poetry has changed radically in this century. Leaving behind its classical tradition, it first metamorphosed into revolutionary poetry, and is now inclined towards free verse. At present there is no shortage of poets, but none of them can claim greatness.

In spite of an untroubled and comfortable life in Iran, I was at times deeply conscious of a spiritual and intellectual vacuum. Although I was on intimate terms with many Iranians, they took care never to mention politics in their conversation. At the slightest hint of it they would say meaningfully, 'Walls have ears'.

I tried several times to go to the southern part of the city which was inhabited by labourers and poor people, but was always warned that it was inadvisable for a foreigner to do so. The agents of SAVAK or the secret police were active everywhere, and I knew that one of them was a member of the Iranian staff in my office. Up to that time I had found no trace of a secret revolutionary movement. I held Dr Mussadeq in great esteem and wished I could get in touch with his friends and admirers. It is common knowledge that during his tenure as minister, foreign monopoly on Iranian oil was brought to an end. In retaliation for this the American CIA, in league with the Shah, overthrew him and after much bloodshed, sentenced him to a lifetime of house arrest.

At the beginning of 1967 he became terminally ill and was sent to his son Ghulam Mussadeq's house for treatment and care. While he was there, the house was surrounded by a heavy police guard, and every day, while I travelled back and forth to work, I would observe the place he inhabited with longing. When he died he was buried quietly in the village. People in Iran held him in great respect in their hearts, but feared even to mention his name aloud. As my circle of acquaintances grew wider I was able to meet people who had been his associates and helpers. Saeed Fatmi who was the younger brother of the Foreign Affairs Minister, Hasan Fatmi, and Mussadeq's right hand man, became a close friend of mine. Considering the present circumstances I will mention the real name of neither the secret revolutionary organization nor the friend who put me in touch with him. I will refer to my friend by the pseudonym of Aqai Takrimi.

Many years ago, when I was working for All India Radio in Delhi, we became friends, and were highly compatible in our ideas, even though he was my subordinate. Then, for a long period we were out of touch with one another, until one day I came face to face with him while walking down a road in Tehran. Only a sensitive person can fully appreciate what pleasure there is in unexpectedly coming upon an old friend in this manner. Aqai Takrimi was an experienced engineer, who had worked in many different countries, married a European and settled in Tehran. He was the only Iranian with who one could discuss the internal politics of his country.

After we had resumed our connection, a strange incident occurred. One night he came to see me at a time when my servant had retired and I was alone, reading. He seemed a bit troubled, and said to me guardedly, 'Your help is needed.' When I asked for details, he said, 'A fugitive revolutionary needs shelter for two or three days, and your house would be the safest place he could find.' I thought apprehensively of the risk I would be running if I agreed to shelter the man, but was fortified by the memory of similar situations in the past. In the days of the British government I had had to conceal people in my house on three or four occasions, even though I had no direct links with them. In such matters the only principle I followed was that the people who risk their lives for a great cause, deserve our sympathy and help.

Confronted with a secret organization, the rule is not to probe, but to ask only those questions that elicit answers necessary for meeting the immediate need. Therefore I asked Aqai Takrimi, 'Where is the man?' and he answered, 'He is sitting in the car downstairs.'

With my permission the man was brought upstairs, and lay down in a spare room. Luckily he had an entirely European appearance and could speak the French language fluently. I instructed him on no account to speak to me or my servants in Persian, and to keep to his bed as though he were ill. A few bottles of medicine and some books in French were placed by his bedside. Takrimi then left, promising to take the man away in two or three days, as soon as his passage abroad could be arranged, and I kept looking out of the window nervously for informers who might be lurking on the street below. Three days of anxiety and tension came to an end when Aqai Takrimi returned and took the man away. With this incident I began to have some idea of the secret organization that was actively and with great risk to the lives of its members, engaged in overthrowing the Shah.

At the end of 1970, I was transferred to Paris. My stay in Iran had been extremely comfortable, but just as I was leaving, I was beset by two misfortunes. My brother died in Karachi after a long illness. To this day I have not got over the pain of my separation from him. Shortly before he died he had compiled an anthology of the Persian poetry of subcontinental poets, under the title of *Farsi Poetry in India and Pakistan*. The book was published by the Iqbal Publishing House in Tehran, and drew much appreciation from discerning readers.

The second misfortune that befell me was the depletion of vision in my right eye at about the same time as my brother's death. Nothing that the local doctors could do made any difference.

Having said good bye to the beloved land of Iran, I left with mixed feelings of hope and despair, and headed once more for the city with which many of my memories are linked.

11

A Few Weeks in Palestine

In July 1971 I had the opportunity to go to occupied Palestine with the UNESCO organization that works in collaboration with UNRAWA (United Nations Refugees And Works Agency) to monitor the working of Arab refugee schools, supervises the annual examination of the twelfth or graduating high school class, and ensures the availability of their textbooks, which are produced in Egypt. The process is accomplished with the help of Israel, whose objective is to ensure that educated young Arabs go abroad in search of livelihood or higher education, and do not stay home to join the freedom fighters engaged in combating Israel.

With the exception of one other person who was associated with the World Health Organization in Beirut, I was the first Pakistani to enter this area after the June 1967 War. I was given a special permit to do so, and the Israeli visa was stamped on it. My stay was of two weeks, of which I spent ten days in Gaza and its surrounding areas, three days in Jerusalem and the region west of the river Jordan, and the last day in Tel Aviv waiting for the plane to fly me back.

It is only now that I have the chance to document my impressions of this memorable trip. While it lasted there was neither the time nor the desire for rest or entertainment. For me it was a pilgrimage to a place of sacrifice, where, indifferent to victory or defeat, man has been sacrificing himself, from the times of the prophets Abraham and Jesus, to the present day.

About a hundred miles to the east of Tel Aviv lies Jerusalem, and the Lod airport is between the two cities. I had deliberately taken the El-Al flight from Paris to Jerusalem, but the experience was not a pleasant one. As soon as we reached Geneva, a threat to bomb the plane was received, so we were taken by a long underground route to another plane, which transported us stealthily to Zurich. The El-Al plane which we had abandoned in Geneva was also brought to Zurich and it then flew all its original passengers to their destination. The UN representative met me at the airport and conveyed me to the National Palace Hotel in Jerusalem, without any trouble. On the way he counselled me not to comment on current affairs and to remember that many of the local Arabs were spies [working for the Israelis]. The hotel management was Arab, but there were throngs of Western tourists, and in the evenings Jewish celebrities such as Moshe Dayan were present in the hotel lobby.

The entire population of Jerusalem numbered about three hundred thousand, and this may be considered the sum of the residents in three towns. The most recent community of settlers was the Jews, who were making clumsy, unattractive houses at the western end, with great speed. Against the beautiful and historic background of Jerusalem, these houses stand out like patches of sackcloth on satin. Western countries have criticized this unsightliness, but when have wayward offspring paid heed to degenerate parents?

The old Arab town nestles in the hills, and there is a haunting attraction in its houses and gardens. It was built in the reign of the Turks, and its architecture is reminiscent of Istanbul and old Cairo. There is a certain quality in its gentle, pleasing, air, and though Europe was warm at the time, the weather here was cool. Next to the Arab quarter is the historic walled city which is known to Muslims and Christians as the Holy City, and to Jews as the House of God. It is flooded with enthusiastic pilgrims and tourists in every month and season of the year.

It is a place where time seems to have stopped. Old houses have been standing unchanged and undisturbed since the crusades, and the discerning eye can spot the footsteps of history on every stone. In the streets can be seen Jewish rabbis, Christian priests, and Arab dervishes—all busy with their own rites and practices.

I spent hours in Haram Sharif where the mosques of Sukhra and Aqsa face each other, symbols and reminders for Muslims of determination and tragedy. How can one praise the refinement of Caliph Abdul Walid's taste enough for building the peerless and magnificent structure that is Sukhra? In order to attract tourists, the government of Israel projects Sukhra in the same way as the Indian government projects the Taj Mahal.

Inside the Aqsa it is forbidden to visit the spot where the pulpit had been set on fire some time ago. The guards inform one that repairs are in progress on that side of the building. Near the back of the enclosure is the Wailing Wall of the Jews. According to Jewish belief it is a part of the ruins of Solomon's temple which was destroyed by the Romans two thousand years ago. In remembrance of this brutal act, the Jews express their sorrow by wailing by the wall. They consider it a fundamental duty to rebuild Solomon's Temple, and are digging here in search of its foundations.

The Aqsa Mosque is popularly known as the Mosque of Omar, because after his conquest of Jerusalem Hazrat Omar said his prayers at the site of this mosque, believing that it was the place from where the Prophet had begun his *miraj*. In the Sukhra, enclosed by a grille, is the rock on which Hazrat Ibrahim had stood when he promised God that he would carry out the sacrifice.

Within the city wall but at the other end, there is the enclosure which contains the empty grave of Jesus within the famous church that is the holiest of all Christian places of pilgrimage. Work on the construction of this church was begun in the fifth century, at the command of the mother of Constantine, the founder of the Eastern Roman empire. Sultan Salahuddin Ayubi gave the key to the main gate of the church to an Arab aristocrat, whose descendants hold it in their possession to this day. The present heir of the family is an old gentleman who opens the gate every morning and bolts it every evening. Holding his cane, and in the company of his attendants, he diligently checks all visitors to the church. I have myself seen him stop two Western women from entering the church because of their exposed midriffs. It is fortunate that they knew no Arabic, for the gentleman had called them 'unchaste' and 'whores' in that language. When I embraced him with the Arab greeting and told him in Arabic that I came from Pakistan, he was very pleased, and whispered into my ear that the guide who accompanied me was a spy and I should be careful.

According to research carried out in modern times, the apparently lifeless body of Jesus was exhumed by his disciples, who then carried it outside the city in the darkness of the night and tried hard to revive him. When their efforts failed, and Jesus actually died, they buried him in a little known garden.

God alone knows the truth.

Along with the pilgrims, I too followed the footsteps of Jesus in the Street of Sorrows, and I too felt the weight of the cross that I have been carrying for years in my grief for oppressed humanity. The burden of my cross disturbs even my two recording angels. However I have not sought the assistance of disciples to mitigate the load I carry.

تا کجا اماں یا بد از ہجوم جاں بازاں
گوشہ گیر فانوسی بہر سوختن تنہا

How long can the candle find refuge from the reckless throng
It has retreated into the glass shade to burn there all alone

East of Jerusalem, the chain of dry, waterless hills, picturesque settlements, and desolate plains runs as far as the river Jordan. Beyond this, the territory belonging to the state of Jordan begins. In 1948, when Palestine was partitioned, Jordan gained control of this area, and retained it until the 1967 war, when the Israelis occupied it. The latter then drove out hundreds of thousands of the inhabitants and appropriated their possessions. Arabs who could manage to do so, stayed on, but we could sense that they had become slow and apathetic. One can see the Israeli army's trenches and homes of the new settlers everywhere. There are several small towns like Nablus and Ramla whose planning and layout are reminiscent of southern Europe, giving the lie to Israel's claim that Palestine was a stranger to culture and progress before its creation. The truth is that the Palestinian Arabs are not inferior to the Jews in their ability and drive, and if they were to gain control of an independent state, they could prove to be the leaders of the Arab world.

Our main work lay in Gaza, which is situated 65 miles to the south of Jerusalem. The occupied territories are under martial law and they are administered by the military. Only cars belonging to the government and the military ply the roads in Gaza. We were driven in a car belonging to the United Nations, under a special permit from the Israelis. Our car was escorted by armed Israeli soldiers who rode in front in a jeep. We could see no traces of habitation on either side of the road. However there were clusters of trees and some vestiges of orchards. Foreigners resident in Jerusalem who were accompanying us told us that this fertile region was once inhabited, but its Arab inhabitants had been banished, and they were now living a helpless existence in camps around Gaza. Looking through binoculars I could see signs of bulldozed houses.

Towards evening we entered Gaza. This ancient city nestles in a fertile valley by the sea and its population numbers about 150,000. The total population of the valley is about 500,000, out of which a large portion is of refugees who arrived here after the 1948 war. Ever since the 1967 war, the valley has been under a dusk to dawn curfew. In occupied Palestine, Gaza was the most important centre for the struggle for freedom. Every refugee camp was a kind of autonomous fortress, in the secretive atmosphere of which freedom fighters were trained, and at the same time a whole dispossessed generation was growing up in an environment of unemployment, despair, and vengeance.

Gaza was named after one of the goddesses worshipped by the Arabs before the advent of Islam. It used to be the hub for caravans arriving from Hijaz, Egypt, and Syria, and as such it commanded considerable importance at the time. And then it was overtaken by a period of such decline that for a long time it had shrunk into a small settlement. However, after the creation of Israel, when it came under Egyptian control, its fortunes looked up again. A new town was built, and a series of roads, schools, and markets extended its limits. But after it fell to the Israelis, an atmosphere of gloom settled on the town.

Gaza had just one comfortable hotel, which was situated on the seafront, and which had been reserved for officers of the Israeli military. A mile from this place was a guest house belonging to a Turkish widow by the name of Nahid Hadem, where employees of the UN were accommodated. Despite her seventy years Nahid Hadem was a very alert and spirited lady, and never hesitated to give the Jews as good as she received. She had spent half her life in Gaza, and at every opportunity, she would give me eyewitness accounts of British and Jewish highhandedness.

I stayed in her hotel for ten days, along with my colleagues. Our daily routine was to attend the meeting at the UN office early in the morning, and then leave on an inspection tour of the educational institutions where the school-leaving examinations of the twelfth class were being conducted. When we finished with this duty, and returned to the hotel at two o'clock, we had lunch and were free to go where we liked. While the others mostly made for the beach, I used to head for the town for it was the only time of the day when one could get aquainted with its life, since curfew was imposed early in the evening, every day, putting an end to all public activity.

Gaza has existed for thousands of years. During this period it was destroyed and rebuilt many times. Its few existing historical sites are worth mentioning: On Hashim Road, enclosed within a protective wall is the tomb of the ancient hero, Samson. At a short distance from this, in the courtyard of a mosque, is the tomb of the Prophet Muhammad's (PBUH) grandfather, Hazrat Hashim. A dilapidated house in an old neighbourhood is said to be the home of Imam Shafaee. Close by is the Jamia Masjid, which has been adapted from a club. It must have been a temple to the goddess Gaza at some point of time, for images of the deity are still discernible here and there on the walls of the mosque. The roads of the town were heavily guarded, and armed soldiers could be seen patrolling the streets in jeeps or trucks. Some of these men had Arab features. On inquiry I was informed that they belonged to the Druze sect, who worship the Fatmid Caliph, Hakim, and since they are not close in their beliefs even to the Ismaeli sect, it is not clear whether they are Muslims or belong to some other faith. During the Crusades they had supported the Christians, and now (at least in this area) they are on the side of the Jews. Since these people are Arabs, racially and linguistically, the Jews exploit them.

In many places in the town, there were signs of destroyed houses. Whenever the Jews wish to punish an Arab, they flatten his home with a bulldozer. This practice leaves the town looking pockmarked. On a few buildings I could see the name of a cinema or a bar, but all such buildings were locked. I surmised that Israeli officials were responsible for this, but was informed by Arabs that after the 1967 war, they themselves had closed down all places of entertainment. When a nation is engaged in a conflict of life and death, it can hardly have time for entertainment. I noticed that no Arab addressed a Jew. Despite the unremitting oppression that they encountered, the Arabs retained their spirit and were staunch in their faith. I saw many examples of this.

There was a girls' school named Az-Zehra on Hashim Road, where several hundred girls were taking the examination. There was a boundary wall surrounding the school building, and at its gate were soldiers armed with machine guns. Within the enclosure there was also a small bungalow dating from the Turkish period, which housed the office of the school principal. At the end of the eighteenth century, when Napoleon Bonaparte defeated Egypt, he arrived in Gaza in pursuit of Murad Bey, and while he was there he stayed in this bungalow for a few days. I sat in one of the rooms in the bungalow, checking the syllabus and going through the textbooks, and then took a tour of the school, where the students were diligently answering their examination questions. Suddenly there was a hue and cry because the soldiers guarding the gate had entered the school grounds. The girls came out on the verandah and started abusing them, refusing to go back to their exam until the soldiers left the premises. I had got to know the Arab principal of the school quite well, and he told me that under similar circumstances the previous year, the soldiers had resorted to beating the students, which led to turmoil in the town. When I heard this I rang up the Israeli Inspector of Schools. He came at once and spoke to the soldiers in Hebrew. The result was that they left the school grounds and went up to the roof of the building.

Every day during our stay in Gaza, hand grenades were thrown and a few people were injured or arrested. This had become a routine there.

Occasionally of an evening I would go and sit in the United Nations' club by the sea. Before the Israeli takeover there was much activity in the small harbour there. Hundreds of Egyptian tourists would arrive, and boats would throng the harbour. But now boating was strictly forbidden and silence and desolation reigned in the area. Every evening, when it grew dark, a military jeep with a trailer would smoothen the sand, the idea being that if somebody disembarked on the beach under cover of darkness, his footsteps would leave marks on the sand, which would help trace and capture him.

There used to be crowds of Jewish soldiers in the hotel near the club. One evening they began to shoot tracer bullets from their guns, lighting up the dark night. Simultaneously they started firing their machine guns, although it was no time for target practice. My German companion thought that a skirmish was imminent that night, and suggested that we leave. For several years he had been running a technical school in Gaza under a United Nations programme, and so was well acquainted with the conditions there. The bullets were being fired in the direction of the Habalya Camp in the north. The German surmised that the Jews were warning the residents there of some impending danger. His conjecture turned out to be correct, because after midnight we were woken up by the sound of continuous firing. The battle lasted until morning. We learnt more about it when we saw a crowd of people gathered in front of a hospital. We were told that some freedom fighters had hidden two of their comrades in a deserted building. The previous day, when the Israeli army got wind of it, they surrounded the house and issuing dire threats, demanded that the freedom fighters give themselves up. When the latter refused to obey, the Israelis attacked the building during the night, and a heavy battle ensued, in which some of the freedom fighters were killed and some injured. The rest fled in the dark. We could not ascertain the number of the Israeli dead.

I saw one of the fugitives while inspecting a school. A room was locked from outside, but I caught a glimpse of someone within. I had grown quite popular with the Arabs in Gaza in the week that I was there, because they had become convinced of my sympathy for them. So an Arab employee of the school told me confidentially that the brother of the freedom fighter had been killed in the skirmish the previous night, and the man had taken refuge in the school. The bandaged hand of the young freedom fighter I had glimpsed, had been resting on a table, and he was gazing into the void, as though searching for someone. I had not been able to think of a way to comfort him.

An examination centre for about 150 students, girls and boys, was set up in the Gaza jail. Since schools in the occupied areas generally lacked textbooks, and laboratories for scientific experiments, such resources could hardly be found in a jail. Among the students there were convicted political prisoners and detenus. The moral courage of all of them was admirable, but I can never forget the girl who had been sentenced to a long term of imprisonment for bringing supplies to freedom fighters, and was confined to a narrow cell where she was taking the exam all alone. My purpose here is to recount what I witnessed in the occupied territories, and not to list the brutalities of the Israeli government. To learn about the latter one should refer to the United Nations' special report, which is published in New York from time to time. The committee that is responsible for it has been compiling gruesome accounts of Israel's brutal treatment of the Palestinian Arabs for years, albeit their revelations have received little publicity.

After we had completed our assignment in Gaza and were preparing to return, the Israeli army suddenly embarked on a forcible operation of building roads through the refugee camps. Thus a strategy for destroying the camps and disbanding and dispersing the refugees was adopted, in contravention of UN resolutions. The latest reports from the area convey that Jewish settlers are gaining control of the fertile lands in the Gaza valley.

I had the opportunity to make a hundred-mile journey to the south of Gaza, beyond which is the Sinai desert, and past which point no civilian is allowed to go. I saw no lightening flash over the summit of Mount Tur. All I heard was the echo of the Voice that turned down Moses's request to see Him.

Before my departure a local Arab gave me a farewell lunch, to which he had invited some of his friends. Without being told I realized that they were members of a secret organization of freedom fighters. Not wasting any time they brought up the subject of the rebellion in East Pakistan. Their information however was one-sided, and despite their sympathy for Pakistan, it was obvious that they were under the influence of Indian propaganda. Another problem was that Palestinians at the time hated Jordan's King Husain, who had a warm relationship with General Yahya Khan's government in those days. I could proffer only the views of the Pakistani public in answer to their questions; on the expediency and deviousness of those in command I had nothing to say. When the issue of Palestine came up, the discussion started with the First World War. On the subject of the partnership between Christian imperialism and Jewish capital I remembered some lines from Iqbal's poetry, which I translated for them, much to their delight.

تاریک ہے افرنگ مشینوں کے دھوئیں سے

یہ وادی ایمن نہیں شایانِ تجلی

ہے نزع کی حالت میں تہذیب جواں مرگ

شاید ہوں کلیسا کے یہودی متولی

The West is dark with the smoke of machines
It is no Valley of Sinai to be worthy of the brilliance of God
Its young civilization is already dying
Perhaps the Jews will become the trustees of the Church

تاک میں بیٹھے ہیں مدت سے یہودی سود خوار

جن کی روباہی کے آگے ہیچ ہے زور پلنگ

خود بخود گرنے کو ہے پکے ہوئے پھل کی طرح

دیکھئے پڑتا ہے آخر کس کی جھولی میں فرنگ

Long have the Jewish moneylenders lain in wait
The strength of the bear pales before their cunning
About to drop like a ripened fruit
Let's see in whose lap the West will fall

Addressing the Palestinian Arabs, Iqbal had said:

زمانہ اب بھی نہیں جس کے سوز سے فارغ

میں جانتا ہوں وہ آتش ترے وجود میں ہے

تری دوا نہ جنیوا میں ہے نہ لندن میں

فرنگ کی رگ جاں پنجۂ یہود میں ہے

سنا ہے میں نے غلامی سے امتوں کی نجات

خودی کی پرورش و لذت نمود میں ہے

I know that in your being is the fire
That has singed the times
Seek not your remedy either in Geneva, or in London
The jugular of the West
Is in the grip of the Jews

I have heard that freedom from slavery for nations
Lies in their nurturing their pride, and their taste for life

Our host commented that these lines were written forty years ago, and both of Iqbal's prophecies had come true. Industrial grossness had caused such turmoil in the West that they were not able to find a solution to it. Moreover, the Pope had declared that mysterious demons and not the Jews were responsible for the crucifixion of Jesus—which approximates 'Jews will become the trustees of the Church.' In other words, the crime for which Christians had been punishing the Jews for two thousand years was in effect never committed. And now, as atonement for this historic blunder, the Christians were assisting the Jews in exploiting the Arabs. At this assessment, one of those present remarked that the shrewdness of Western politicians deserved to be praised, for in an instant they had turned the direction of the two thousand year old blaze of vengeance in the heart of the Jews towards the Arabs—people who had always shown them tolerance.

When I was taking my leave my heart was overflowing with respect for the Gaza Arabs. On the one hand they were fighting imperialism, on the other they were in the vanguard of the forces clashing in a modern version of the crusades.

In the afternoon we were taken to Tel Aviv by car, so that it would be easier for us to reach Lod airport at night for our return journey. Tel Aviv was founded 65 years ago on a desolate plain by the sea. It now resembles an American city. No Arab is allowed to live here, and non-European Jews appear only in the lowly roles of sweepers, cobblers, and peons. The place is so expensive that a room in a hotel costs $30. Along with the furnishing, there was a concealed microphone in my room. Guests were warned in writing not to open the window that looked out on the road, for that would endanger their lives.

There was hustle and bustle on the streets, and the shops were well stocked. Jews are astute businessmen anyway, and with the fat donations from Western countries coming in, there was prosperity and abundance. In modern times this is the only example of a nation crossing the seas to occupy the lands of another, expelling the old inhabitants, seizing their possessions, and as a reward for their behaviour, being showered with gifts—to the extent that West Germany pays them compensation. The dispossessed Arabs then become targets of wrath for not accepting their fate with gratitude and equanimity.

Having seen the city from various aspects, I found nothing exceptional about it, apart from the fact that it was new. I felt an urge to see Bahaullah's tomb in Haifa, but was refused permission to go there since the Israeli navy has its headquarters in Haifa.

That night there was no time to sleep as we had to leave the hotel at 2 a.m., in order to reach the airport early in the morning. The magnificent lobby of the hotel was crowded with Jewish tycoons, and its ballroom echoed with sounds of mirth and exultation. Untouched by these spectacles my heart bled for my distant home, which was in those days a country torn by civil war, and was heavy with the grief that my visit to Gaza had filled me with.

Even today Palestine is burdened with the cross, the weight of which made Jesus a martyr.

12

Glimpses of Spain

If you look towards the south of Granada, you will see at a distance of a few miles a mountain peak, which is known in the Spanish language, as 'The Moors' Last Sigh' (Lade Nier Supiro De Moro). Tradition has it that this was the spot where in 1492, the Muslims lost their Spanish dominions for ever. In return for sparing his life, Amir Abu Abdullah handed over the Alhambra Fort to the Christian conquerors, took one last look at Granada through his tears, sighed, and departed for Morocco. His infuriated mother said to him, 'O coward, when you could not defend your country with your blood, what good will your tears do?'

Abu Abdullah wrote his memoirs, which have been published in Morocco, but I have not had the opportunity to see the book. To this day some descendants of the refugees who fled from Granada and sought shelter in Morocco, possess title deeds and keys of their ancestral properties in Granada. The Christian conquerors, King Ferdinand and Queen Isabel dispatched Columbus on the expedition that resulted in the discovery of the New World, thus putting an end to one historical era and ushering in another. The way Muslims in Spain were massacred, and Indian tribes in occupied America exterminated, on the instructions of the Roman Church, is a horrifying chapter in history.

In 1964 I had occasion to spend a month in Spain, most of which was spent in Andalusia. Even after five hundred years, the society there bears the mark of Arab culture. In their appearance, dance, music and every other aspect of life, the influence of the Arabs is apparent. The present inhabitants of Andalusia mention the Arab era with pride and deem it a golden age in their history.

In many places in Spain, and especially in Andalusia, ruins of bridges, forts, and fortifications that were built by the Arabs can be found. Among famous examples of architecture still left standing are the Alhambra of Granada, the mosque at Cordova, and the Alcazar at Seville. In the older part of Granada, within the citadel, the old neighbourhood of Zako is worth seeing. Its houses are in the old Arab style, with fountains playing in their courtyards, the men's quarters in front, and the women's quarters next to the back garden. Though the streets are paved with stones, they are too narrow for a motor car to drive through them. But they are dotted with stalls where *jalebis* are deep fried or kebabs roasted. The church has conceded to the extent that Muslims are allowed to say their prayers in a part of the mosque at Cordova. This is the place which inspired Iqbal to write his stirring poem, *The Mosque of Cordova*.

In the five hundred years since the departure of Muslims from Spain, there have been many changes in the Spanish language. Yet even now a great number of Arabic words exist in it. Many names of places have an Arabic sound, and people use the word *Illah* frequently, which is their version of Allah. The word *Ustad* is used for Mr. In the south there is a town called Juarez. Its name is a variation of 'Shiraz'. A popular rice dish is known as *paella*, a corruption of pillao. Arabic influence is dominant in the style of music and musical instruments. Not only the folk songs of Andalusia but also its literature mourns the age that has passed. *Don Quixote*, the novel that ushered in modern Spanish literature, is much influenced by the *dastan* style of narrative that prevailed in the East. Azad, the hero of Ratan Nath Sarshar's novel, *Fasana-e-Azad*, and Khoji, his servant, have been inspired by the character Don Quioxte and his servant Sancho Panza.

The oldest Spanish poem is *El Cid*, its title probably a distorted version of Saeed or Saiyid. This poem is dominated by Arabic conventions. Even the Eastern variety of poem known as the *ghazal* had made its appearance in some Western languages. For a long time poems written in a similar style, and known as *zajal*, were produced in Provencal, the language of southern France.

Granada is situated in the lap of mountains. The city itself is positioned on one prominence, while the crumbling buildings of the Alhambra are scattered on another. Between the two is a steep valley, through which flows a river. Notable among the few remaining buildings from earlier times, is the 'Madrassa', which I have seen being used as a police station, though now I believe it has been handed over to the university. In the mountain caves outside the town, live gypsies, said to be the descendants of Arabs who became nomads in order to escape the oppression of the Christian church in the fifteenth century. After the heat of the Inquisition cooled down, they stayed on in the caves and made them their home. These caves now have electricity and are visited by crowds of tourists attracted by the gypsy songs and dances. When I spoke a few words in the gypsy language and told them that I belonged to the subcontinent, the gypsies were delighted, and lavished hospitality on me. Many researchers feel that these gypsies come from the region that is now Pakistan. Their assumption is strengthened by the language that these people speak. In the beginning of the Christian era, when warlike tribes from central Asia began their invasions, the early inhabitants were forced to flee to the south. It is very likely that many of these people mingled with the invaders and travelled west, adopting a nomadic life. In Spain I heard gypsies speak words like *pani*, and *kala chiri*, which have the same meaning in their language that they do in Urdu, i.e. water and blackbird.

The Alhambra evokes a romantic sense of the grandeur of bygone cultures. In keeping with the architectural style prevalent in the Middle Ages, the Arab elite of Granada kept erecting buildings inside the citadel until this 'royal space' became entirely self sufficient. The court of the rulers there became the hub for craftsmen and artists. However, the depredations of time have so changed this lively neighbourhood that now its fame is confined to the palace known as the Alhambra. In the eyes of the experts this building is unrivalled in its location and artistic qualities. The opposite side of the town is reserved for the public audience hall and the king's administrative centre. There are numerous windows in its tall marble wall, through each of which the city of Granada can be seen in its entirety as though set in the horizon. Embraced by fountains, a colourful path takes one to the women's apartment at the back, from every casement of which a panorama of snow-covered mountain peaks is visible. The old Alhambra garden has retained its original appearance, with seven hundred year old cedars imported from Lebanon still standing there, engaged in a lamentation for the past.

One of the buildings within this crumbling enclosure has been turned into a hotel. I stayed there for two days, and during this time I wandered in the ruined courtyard, heard old tunes on traditional instruments, and listened to the local people tell the old tale, the last page of which was written here.

The Civil War in Spain had ended more than twenty years ago, yet its wounds were still fresh. Nobody dared to say anything of significance to strangers, and General Franco's fascist dictatorship had put a stop to freedom of speech and writing. However, there were few apparent signs of the depredation of war. Like Madrid, many cities were transformed. In the reconstruction of Spain, the Germans who had fled Germany with their capital after the defeat of the Nazis had had a hand.

I am reminded here of an interesting episode. It was the year 1957. I had been working in the UNESCO office in Paris, when the phone rang and Mir Ghulam Ali Talpur was on the line. He had been Pakistan's Education Minister for some time, and was truly a personage in the old style. The doors of his residence, which faced the Karachi Gymkhana, remained open from morning to afternoon so that anybody who wanted to could walk into his dining room and ask the bearer to bring him breakfast or lunch. Meanwhile Mir Sahib would be busy chatting with his companions upstairs. Whenever I entered his room with an important file, he would say, 'All these people are my confidants. You can say what you like without hesitation.' When I excused myself from complying on the grounds that the matter I wished to discuss was a delicate one, he would get up and accompany me to the verandah, where he would sign the documents without reading them, saying, 'I trust you completely.'

I was sincerely happy to hear his voice on the telephone, and went to see him immediately. He told me that he was accompanying President Iskander Mirza to Spain, and had stopped en route for a few days in Paris. Iskander Mirza and his wife were the guests of Prince Aly Khan. My apartment was close to Aly Khan's house, so after tea Mir Sahib suggested that I accompany him there and be introduced to Iskander Mirza. Later I learnt that Iskander Mirza had gone to Spain on General Franco's invitation, in order to study the form of government there—this is a clue to the plan which materialized as the martial law of 1958 in Pakistan.

Here it would not be out of place to mention the Spanish diversion, of which the Urdu expression 'Come bull, stab me' serves as a good description. It is surprising that this memento of a barbaric age is flourishing not only in Spain but also in South America which is populated by the Hispanic race. Readers must have learnt from books and movies how irate bulls are brought to the arena, where they are jabbed with spears until they have no alternative but to attack their tormentors, who then put an end to them quite effortlessly. There is neither an aspect of courage nor of entertainment in the pursuit. It is a different matter that the spectators enjoy it in the same way as hunters enjoy killing innocent animals.

Madrid and Barcelona are the two large cities of Spain. The difference between them is the same as that between Ankara and Istanbul. After the devastation caused by the Civil War, the government paid special attention to rebuilding Madrid since it is the capital of the country. Like Ankara, Madrid is situated in the dry region, in the interior of Spain, and its ostentatious splendour smacks of the nouveu riche. On the other hand, Barcelona is situated by the sea, where it stands proud of its antiquity like some aged aristocrat.

It would not be incorrect to say that the most beautiful city in Spain is Toledo. It is located on a hill, fifty or sixty miles west of Madrid. The embellishments in the interior of the ancient church here are as striking as the grandeur of its exterior. They are actually an excellent example of Arab architecture, and the same delicate proportions are visible here as those in the pillars of the mosque at Granada.

Facing Toledo is a high mountain, known as Almanzar. It is said that Al Mansoor, the vizier of Caliph Abdur-Rehman lll, is buried here. A second reason for Toledo's fame is that it was the home of the great sixteenth century artist, El Greco. His house has been converted into a museum, and contains most of his masterpieces. Western art has four main schools of painting: Italian, Dutch, French, and Spanish. Pablo Picasso, the greatest painter of the twentieth century, was a native of Spain.

It did not take the Roman Church more than a hundred years to erase all vestiges of the 700-year Muslim rule in Spain. In 1605 the government of Spain made it illegitimate for a follower of any religion but Christianity to live in Spain. This rule was amended after the Second World War. It can be considered a miracle wrought by affluence that the same Arabs who had been banished from the soil of Spain are now welcomed there with open arms, and have settled on the eastern coast of the country, and especially Andalusia, in their thousands.

The road behind my hotel in Barcelona was called Casa Omar (Omar Street). When I became acquainted with the proprietor of a café there, I asked him how the road got its name. He told me that at the end of the Muslim rule this neighbourhood was the property of a wealthy Muslim called Omar. Although the owners had been constrained to change their faith from Islam to Christianity, they remained affiliated to the Muslim culture for a long time. The proprietor of the café was himself a descendant of Omar.

An old man who was listening attentively to our conversation, then spoke up. He said, 'There is no doubt that the church was very oppressive in those days, but is the government of General Franco today less tyrannical?' He then turned to me and said, 'I used to be a university professor, but as a punishment for opposing dictatorship, not only did I have to give up my job, I had to put up with the harsh conditions of imprisonment also, and now I have no shelter except this café.' The man continued with a bitter laugh, 'How ironic for a caretaker to appropriate a house he is supposed to guard with the excuse that the inmates are not capable of running it!' I have written earlier in these pages how in 1957, the Spanish dictator taught Pakistan's President Iskander Mirza his mode of government.

13

Impressions of Italian History and Art

If somebody asked me to choose just one country that could speak for the past and present of the West, I would advise him to go to Italy. This country was the hub of the Roman Empire and the cradle of the Christian religion. It was here that the Renaissance began and turned the direction of history towards the modern age. Moreover, in sculpture, painting, and music, Italy can be regarded as the teacher of the Western countries. My love of nature drew me deep into Europe, but nowhere did I find as much variety as in Italy. Indisputably, the mountains of Switzerland are taller and its valleys and lakes more enchanting, but the country has neither a shoreline nor the marks of historical and cultural grandeur which are found abundantly in Italy.

My first opportunity to visit Italy came in 1938, while I was a student in Paris. I stayed for a day in Genoa, which is renowned only for its harbour and its beautiful cemetery. The graveyard is like a large and handsome garden in which the graves have been carefully arranged. By contrast, the graveyards in our country are so unkempt and badly organized that they make one reluctant to die. Turkey is the only Muslim country where I found the dead treated with enough respect to warrant straight rows of graves in a necropolis. The sign of a cap is made on graves for men, and women's graves display the sign of a flower.

My first visit to Italy was made at a time when the country was dominated by Fascism and Mussolini headed the government. However signs of oppression were not apparent to foreign tourists.

The two most beautiful Italian cities are Florence and Venice. The latter has canals instead of roads, and boats or gondolas are the means of transport. Although every Italian city and town of any size possesses rare specimens of art, the most precious collections are housed in the museums of Rome and Florence, while the museum and library of the Pope at the Vatican are peerless.

Wandering alone in the streets of Rome I was overcome with exhaustion. It was then that I spotted Iqbal Shedai. Readers may be acquainted with his name. He was one of those people who migrated from India after World War I, arrived in Soviet Russia via Kabul, and after spending some time there left for Europe where they settled down. I had met Iqbal Shedai accidentally in Paris immediately after my arrival there in 1937, and had been impressed by his attractive personality. Soon after, I called on Khalida Adeeb Khanum, of whose kindness to us I have written earlier in these pages. To my amazement, during the course of conversation when I happened to mention Iqbal Shedai, Khalida Khanum flared up. She told me sternly, 'You must never meet that man again. Don't you know that he is a friend of the same Mustafa Sagheer who the British government dispatched to Ankara to assassinate Ataturk? The conspiracy was discovered in time and Mustafa Sagheer was hanged, while people like Iqbal Shedai were expelled.'

I had not known of this incident. The details of this synopsis are that the British government sent Mustafa Sagheer of Muradabad to Ankara in the guise of a member of the Khilafat Committee. There Sagheer gave away hundreds of thousand of rupees in charity in order to bolster his image. He was waiting for an opportunity to attack Ataturk, but was apprehended in time and paid his deserts. I do not know whether or not Iqbal Shedai was directly involved in this conspiracy, but when the British king was expected in Paris, he was among the suspect foreigners banished by the police. I was aware of these facts when I met him accidentally in Rome, and we sat together for a while in a coffee house. Iqbal Shedai spent much of his life in Italy. He married an Italian woman and died many years ago.

During the Second World War he enthusiastically propagated 'Azad Hind Hakoomat' over the Italian radio. After the partition of India, he stayed in Karachi for a few years, where I occasionally ran into him in the artist Nagi's studio.

The largest industrial centre in Italy is a city called Milan. Its Cathedral is as magnificent as its Opera House is stately. Opera itself was invented in Italy. We could call it *Sangeet Natak* in our own language. Opera is the best expression of Western classical music. In it the human voice achieves pinnacles of skill not known in our music. In Milan I was the guest of Alberto, my Milanese class fellow at Paris

University. He knew that I had lately developed a strong desire to learn to play the violin, so Alberto got me an old violin at a reduced price from a relative's shop. The shopkeeper advised me to look after the violin for it was a Stradivarius—a brand that would be worth thousands of dollars today. After my return to India, a relative borrowed it temporarily, and lost it permanently.

Although there is much to see in Italy, I will mention here only those sights that have left a special imprint on my mind. Among them is that unrivaled garden in Trivoli, where hundreds of fountains play simultaneously, sending jets of water into the air which suggest a heavy shower. Another indelible memory is of the famous square in Venice, on one side of which stand rows upon rows of old palaces. Yet another unforgettable sight was the building called San Michelle, which stands on the summit of a hill in Capri, and which was immortalized in a book called *The Story of San Michelle*. Actually, the book is the account of a Swedish doctor who had settled in Naples after the First World War, and created this building with ancient pillars and arches which he had collected. The view of the sea from this building is so spellbinding that I have never seen the like of it before, except once, in one other place—from the palace of the Somalian President in Mogadishu. As a matter of fact, one can appreciate the beauty of nature or art best when one regards it in the right setting. The Taj Mahal looks its loveliest not in the sunlight but in moonlight; but the beauty of a snow-covered mountain is at its most dazzling in the sunlight. To view any great piece of art, it is necessary to see it from the right distance, and in the right light. To appreciate the immensity of the ocean one should not look at the extent of its surface, rather, one should stand on high ground and see it stretching from all directions into the horizon.

In ancient times Latin was born in Italy, and in its turn it begot and enriched many of the European languages. Latin, like Sanskrit, is now regarded as a dead language, but its influence on the civilization, laws, and literature of Europe is very apparent. In the Middle Ages, a corrupted version of Latin began to assume the form of modern Italian. The first significant work of Italian prose is a collection of short stories called *Decameron*, which has been influenced by traditional Arab story-telling. About the same time Dante wrote his celebrated *Divine Comedy*. Many scholars believe that the basic concept of this work is an adaptation of Ibne Arabi's *Miraj Nama*. During my last visit to Paris I was reminded frequently of this poem. In the evenings, when I used to go out for a stroll, I had to pass the museum which is named after the greatest sculptor of modern times, Rodin. On its main gate are carved scenes from the part of Dante's poem entitled 'The Gate of Hell'. Rodin has rendered the 'seven circles of hell' with such consummate skill that the viewer begins to hate both life on earth and life hereafter.

I visited Italy on three different occasions, but it was in Somalia that I had to deal with Italians. For the first half of the twentieth century the Italians controlled the southern part of Somalia. At first, criminals from Rome were sent there to settle, just as British criminals were exiled to Australia. Later, during the Mussolini era, political dissidents were banished there. Thousands of these political exiles were present in Somalia during my stay in that country. Not known for accomplishing much else, the Italians did introduce modern modes of agriculture in a country of shepherds and herders. They did not treat the natives with the arrogance for which the British were notorious, which was the reason why the Somalians maintained a good relationship with the Italians even after they had gained independence.

An Italian by the name of Romano became a good friend of mine. He had been a schoolmaster in Italy and was forced to go to Somalia during the War. Gradually Africa spun such a spell over him that, like many white pioneers, he too settled down there. He established an agricultural school for Somali children just outside the town, and began to live there. His fields and gardens were inhabited by colourful birds, and harmless animals wandered there, safe and free. Romano went back to Italy but soon returned to his adopted home. He used to tell me that like other Western countries, Italy was a huge factory where machines dominated the human personality. The cultural values that were dear to him are becoming blurred in our lives like a dream from the past, but future generations will continue to hear their echoes.

14

Some Impressions of America

It is strange that the Indian tribes of North America did not inherit the slightest trace of that civilization which Columbus, and later Spanish aggressors beheld in South America, and the archaeological remains of which astound even modern viewers. On the one hand we are dumbfounded at the vestiges of thousands of years old civilizations such as the Aztec and the Maya, and on the other hand we are taken aback by the meagerness of the North American Indian way of life. For these were people who could not even count on their fingers, let alone be capable of the complicated skill of writing. In fact, they had not progressed beyond the level of primitive man. Therefore, when the Europeans, led by the British, invaded the continent they had no trouble eliminating the men and beasts whose home it was. The land now appeared as a new country, devoid of any signs or reminders of the past. Like the chronicle of Africa, the story of America too is a shocking example of how cunning white traders conned naïve tribesmen into selling them large tracts of land in return for necklaces of shining glass, and when they could not force the proud Indians into becoming serfs, they exterminated them and brought countless shackled negroes from western Africa to build the New World.

If one can ignore this gruesome history, one should applaud the industry and enterprise of the Americans for turning their land into the most advanced country in the world in the short span of two hundred years. This country is in reality a vast continent, its length and breadth running into thousands of miles, displaying everywhere the same pattern of discipline and progress. Travelling in America I was always very aware of three of its characteristics: uniformity, modernity and affluence. People of diverse races and nationalities are settled here, but neither in their lifestyles nor in their cuisine is there much difference. The strongest force in the country is the media. So powerful is it that individuals have lost the capacity to think and comprehend, and tastes and minds bear the stamp of radio, television or newspapers. Although this is a phenomenon common to all industrial countries, its culmination can be seen in America.

In 1776, when its victory in the War of Independence liberated the United States of America from British domination, democracy made a breakthrough in the world. Its influence on the French Revolution is an important fact of modern history. In a way, the American Constitution can be called an exemplary constitution. On the occasion of the general elections there, I was astonished to witness the election of government officials in addition to Congressmen. I was told that not only the legislature, but the administration too should be answerable to the people.

After gaining independence, America crossed all the stages of industrial advancement that Europe had been through, and then after the two great wars of the twentieth century, it emerged as the strongest power in the world from the material aspect. After the Second World War was over, it assumed the responsibility for stopping the advancing flood of Communism, in addition to overseeing the reconstruction of Western Europe and Japan. Its strategies directly affected Latin America, Africa and Asia, for its aim was to keep them running on the lines of capitalism while depending on it for their development. These policies were the basis of the rivalry between Soviet Russia and the US, cooperation between the US and Western Europe, and the turbulence in the Third World countries, which became our lot.

The greatest problem of American society is the gulf that prejudice has generated between blacks and whites. The hundreds of thousands of African Negroes who had been imported into America were forced into slavery, and it was the question of their emancipation that led to the American Civil War in 1865. After this event, though the Negroes were no longer slaves, yet their status remains that of second class citizens even in present-day America.

In 1950, when I was making a long tour of America on my first visit there, I happened to go to the southern state of Alabama. The principal of a Black university there invited me one morning, and sent a professor to fetch me from the hotel. At the agreed time I went to the hotel lobby and waited for the person who I was to accompany. Since Americans are punctual, I was surprised when the professor did not arrive at the given time and was about to call the university to enquire, when a tall hotel employee came looking for me and told me that a black man was waiting for me outside. When I asked him why the man did not come in, the employee replied disdainfully that no black man could enter the hotel. I went out and apologized to the professor, but he said, 'You are a newcomer, so how could you know what it is like here? I have been waiting outside for the last quarter of an hour and begging the janitor to inform you of my arrival, but he was not convinced that a guest of this hotel wanted to see a black man.'

In those days there were separate hotels, restaurants, schools, and hospitals for blacks and whites; even the seating in buses and trains used to be segregated. However, gradually such overt barriers were removed, and now the blacks are better off at least than the untouchables in India.

The speed with which America advanced was matched by the pace at which the hold of the Jews grew within the country. It is thanks to their miraculous growth in power that the expansion and strengthening of Israel became a cornerstone of American foreign policy, even if it was paid for with the enmity of Arab countries. It would be accurate to say that the institutions which influence American life most are the World Zionist Organization, and the Italian secret criminal organization, the Mafia. Originally, 'Mafia' is an Arabic word which was used for the Arab guerillas who operated in the island of Sicily. In the Middle Ages, when Christians snatched Sicily back from the Arabs, the latter fought them for a long time from the relative safety of forests and mountains. This was when the Italians gave them the name 'Mafia'.

There was a time when Europeans believed that the Americans were an uncivilized lot, but now, in addition to science and industry, Americans have become the leaders in Literature and Art. Their contribution to modern English literature is invaluable, and no cultural centre in Europe can rival New York. Moreover the character of the average American has an aspect of simplicity that makes him indifferent to everything in the world beyond his own country and society. This is borne out by the fact that of the two movements that gained popularity there after the World War, one was the anarchist revolt against conventions, perpetrated by youth who called themselves 'hippies', and the other was the dissenting voice of those who protested against America's intervention in Vietnam. Other than the proponents of these two points of view, the majority of the American population, thanks to the affluence in the country, had become part of a burgeoning middle class, which has no interest in anything except what concerns their own wellbeing, with the result that no movements of the kind that flourish in underprivileged economic conditions are likely to find a foothold in America. Once I had the occasion to visit Los Angeles, which is the centre of the film industry. There I met an old gentleman by the name of Hasan Khayyam, who had migrated from Peshawar a long time ago, married a retired actress, and settled in Los Angeles. He invited me to spend a weekend at his house. While I was there, I went out for my morning stroll. I had walked a short distance on the deserted road when I heard a whistle from a police patrol, and a police car blocked my way. It was with great difficulty that I explained to the policeman that I was staying in a particular house and was out only for a stroll. He explained to me that in this country nobody but a burglar goes out of his house on a holiday so early in the morning, which was the reason why the neighbours regarded me with suspicion, and informed the police of my presence. Generally in the West, there is no concept of early morning walks.

The same evening I accompanied Hasan Khayyam and his wife to a dinner party at the residence of an Iraqi lady. This lady was well known by her pseudonym of 'Princess Ameena'. I was introduced to her as a gentleman who was connected to a ministry of an Asian country. That good lady was so intoxicated that she proceeded to introduce me to everybody saying, 'He is a minister and this party has been thrown in his honour.' When I asked Hasan Khayam to clear up the misunderstanding, he replied, 'Young man, she is not a princess and you are not a minister, but this is Hollywood where this kind of introduction can help you rise to dizzying heights.'

Many years later I heard in Karachi that a famous dancer by the name of Princess Ameena was performing in some hotel. The memory of the dinner that night in Los Angeles came back to me, and I set off for the night club wondering if it was the same imp who had hosted the party. However there was such a great crowd, and in any case so much time had elapsed since I had last seen her, that I could not recognize her.

San Francisco is the most beautiful city in America. It is situated on the west of the country, on the Pacific coast. The Golden Bridge, which is the world's longest bridge, links the city to Berkeley University, which is possibly the most progressive of all American universities.

At one time San Francisco was the headquarters of the Ghader Party, and the famous revolutionary leader, Maulvi Barketullah Bhopali died there. Dr Sayyid Husain taught at Berkley for many years, and I even met some of his friends. California is the largest state in the US, but its capital is neither Los Angeles nor San Francisco, but a small city called Sacramento, around which Punjabi farmers who arrived here after the First World War, have settled.

Three thousand miles to the East is the country's largest city, New York. It is like a forest of human beings, and is so beset by skyscrapers and multitudes of cars that the individual feels himself altogether insignificant. But it is the financiers here who control the money-market all over the globe. It is no coincidence that a large population of Jews lives in New York. During my stay in this city, I asked a number of affluent New Yorkers if they were happy. In reply they told me, 'Happiness is a condition we are unfamiliar with. However we are comfortable since we can buy the paraphernalia for comfort in the market.'

The art of filmmaking was invented in America, and so far they have no equal in this field. The fact is that nowhere in the world is there so much assorted home entertainment as there is in America. There are dozens of television stations and hundreds of radio channels that can provide entertainment 24 hours of the day. Most of them offer tasteless diversion, but these days it is futile to insist on good taste. The same is true of books, magazines and newspapers of which millions are printed and sold. In short, the principle of quantity rather than quality on which the industrial society is founded, rules America. Iqbal was right when he said,

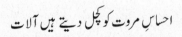

Machines kill the feeling of benevolence in life

Man started off by endeavouring to control nature with the help of machines, but is now himself dominated by them. At first he used machines for doing more efficiently the work that his hands and feet do, and now the ubiquitous computer has begun to make his mind redundant. Led by America, the whole world is now following this path, and therefore any mention of values, principles or courtesy seems like a cry in the wilderness. There is no doubt that machines are a boundless force in construction and creation, but their creator is man himself, and when man realizes that the purpose of machines is to serve humanity, not to dominate it, a major crisis of modern society will be resolved.

15

The Allure of Japan

There are many things in common between Britain and Japan. Both countries are small islands and lack natural resources. Nevertheless, just as Britain led the West in the industrial revolution and founded a vast empire, Japan was the first to show the way to Asia in the fields of industry and science. Surprisingly, although modern industry was initiated in Britain in 1760, and in Japan a hundred years later, in 1870, Japan organized its human resources in such a way that in only 35 years, that is in 1905, it was able to defeat Russia and capture a large area in the Far East. Then again in the early stages of the Second World War, the way it overpowered America, Britain, and other western powers in the Pacific Ocean, one after another, is an important event in modern history. In fact, Asia owes its political awakening in the beginning of the twentieth century mainly to Japan.

In the autumn of 1953, the government of Pakistan, in collaboration with the Ford Foundation, sent me to Japan for a month in order to study the reconstruction of the country. This happened a long time ago, but impressions of what I saw are still fresh in my mind. America had forced Japan to surrender by dropping atom bombs there, and signs of the destruction were evident everywhere. I had the opportunity to go to many Japanese towns and villages besides Tokyo, and was able to meet people from every class of society. What impressed me most was their pride as a nation. There is probably no individual there who escaped the ravages of war, yet none ever spoke a word of complaint. As far as possible they avoided discussion of the suffering they had endured and if a newcomer like me happened to mention it they would evade the subject by saying that there was a winner and a loser in every war. 'It was we who started the war and it doesn't matter if we lost it. We have the determination to rise again.' The fact that they redeemed this promise to history in a matter of thirty-five years is a miracle. Today, Japan is in the vanguard on the road to progress, and not just a fellow traveller of Europe. Rather than draw its inspiration from the West, a developing Asian country like Pakistan would do well to follow the example of Japan, which has condensed a voyage of centuries into a short span of time. Its success is all the more commendable because instead of blindly following the West it has preserved its own cultural heritage. My Japanese friend, Professor Isabuki was absolutely right when he said that modern science is no more than empirical knowledge, and it is wrong to suppose that there is a fundamental contradiction between it and the soul of religion or our cultural traditions.

The most appealing aspect of Japanese culture is its simplicity and elegance. A society in which culture is confined to the ruling class, and denied to the common people, cannot claim to be civilized. In Japan, the same standard of cleanliness and propriety prevails indiscriminately in the urban and rural areas. To assess the cleanliness of a house, its bathroom and kitchen should be inspected. In this respect Japanese homes have no equal. They contain very little furniture and other goods, and big or small, they are usually made of wood, with arrangements for sleeping and sitting on the floor. No Japanese enters his house with his shoes on. There is a row of slippers at the door, and everybody who comes to the house takes off his shoes and puts on a pair of slippers. There is another row of slippers outside the bathroom, exclusively for bathroom wear. After a day spent in earning his livelihood, when the Japanese man returns to his home, he straightaway takes off his outdoor clothes and attires himself in a silken robe, which is known as a kimono. He then observes the 'tea ceremony' which has a protocol all its own and is famous for it the world over. I had one interesting experience of this ceremony.

Tokyo is a city so treacherous that it could be called a jungle of humans. It has hordes of people, shops, cars, and no particular attractions. However Japan's old capital, Kyoto, offers many aspects of allurement. It is situated in the midst of hills and lakes, and is an old-fashioned town. On my first visit there I saw the embodiment of manliness in the Japanese 'Samurai' and the quintessence of womanly grace in the geisha. Both of these reflect the *joie de vivre* of the traditional Japanese culture.

A Samurai was a swordsman of ancient Japan who did not know the word 'defeat'. About to be routed on the battlefield, he would commit hara-kiri to avoid capture. This was a ritual known to Rajputs of long ago as 'Jauhar'. Japanese soldiers demonstrated this reaction to failure many times during the Second World War. Even now newspapers report from time to time that some isolated old Japanese soldier is still entrenched in a jungle, unable to believe that the war is over, or if he does know that, is unwilling to disarm without direct orders from the government of Japan.

A geisha is a lady who receives training to discharge the functions of a hostess. If you have no wife and you need to entertain, you can call the Geisha office and ask them to send you a suitable hostess. The geisha will handle the arrangements and the hospitality expertly. She will even entertain your guests with music and dance. In the olden days she used to be a respectable woman who people did not doubt would go home after the party.

An acquaintance in Kyoto, a Mr Eshikawa, invited me to dinner. When I took off my shoes and entered the house, a maidservant came towards me with a kimono. When I put it over my suit she laughed and explained to me in gestures that a kimono is worn next to the skin. To fulfill this requirement it was necessary that she made herself scarce, but she was bent on disrobing me and officiating as my valet. When my host understood the reason for the argument he delivered a speech on the Japanese phiolosophy of nudity, the gist of which was that it is not healthy to keep your body imprisoned in dress day and night, and that it is a sign of mental ailment to be shy of your own body. I encountered a similar episode in the Netherlands where I had gone from Paris to participate in a conference. Those were days when Western women had just taken to wearing the miniskirt. The quarter of a yard of cloth that covers the lover's chest, for which Ghalib yearns, seemed to have become the beloved's garment.

Among the participants of the conference was a Dr Ribka from Czechoslovakia. When the conversation turned to living styles of communist countries I mentioned the new fashion. He said, 'Women in our countries too are wearing the miniskirt.' When I expressed surprise, he commented rhetorically, 'Poets and artists have been imagining the woman's body for centuries. Now that women are voluntarily exhibiting it, what business do you have to object?'

However, I was on the subject of the Japanese lifestyle. The Japanese diet is simple, and in fact quite flat, but it is served and adorned so carefully, and there is such an uproar of thank yous and ecstatic cries with every morsel, that a simple meal could be taken for a wedding feast. Another good trait that the Japanese possess is their love of nature. There are plants and flowers in every house as well as fountains or little pools of water to rest the eye.

The most beautiful part of the country is the vast mountainous area, in the centre of which rises the famous volcano, Fujiyama. Earlier on I have mentioned the Fujia Hotel where I stayed. Although I have stayed in some excellent hotels of the world, none of them could match the Fujia in style and atmosphere. It used to be the palace of a Japanese aristocrat, and had fifty spacious rooms spread over two storeys. On 600 acres of land surrounding the hotel, hills, lakes, and gardens stretched out as far as the eye could see. The Fujiyama stood in front, its fiery body concealed beneath a robe of snow. The hotel rooms did not have numbers. Instead, each room had a name, for example, Orange, Pomegranate, Yellow; and the curtains, furniture, beds, and even the maid's uniform followed the colour theme suggested by the name. At night when I went into the hotel dining room, I was astonished to see that an image of the Pakistani flag had been printed on the menu. I was told on enquiry that I was the hotel's first Pakistani guest, and the gesture had been made to commemorate the occasion.

Until 1870 Japan was a closed book for the West, because no foreigner was allowed there. After this year samples of Japanese art and craft began to make their way to Europe, where they influenced the Impressionist style of painting in France. Japanese experiments in filmmaking after the Second World War, gave this art form new directions. Similarly, modern Japanese literature began a new movement, especially in the genre of the novel. As is universally known, in education as well as in industry Japan stands in the first row of highly developed nations. It is also worthy of note that Japanese is written in the same Chinese script that is considered the most difficult form of writing in the world.

It is strange that the yellow race of Asia is successfully competing with the white race in the West. The difference between the two is that Britain, which led the West in the war, is weakening despite its victory, while Japan, which is the most advanced country in the East, is soaring in spite of its defeat in the same war. Newly liberated countries in quest of progress cannot build a good future for themselves without understanding these subtle lessons of history.

16

Fading Memories of Some Other Countries

I am aware that in the previous pages I have not been able to do justice to the impressions and experiences gathered during my travels over almost half of the planet. Only a travelogue could adequately fulfil such a task. However, before I finish this chapter, I will try to recover some of my scattered impressions from the hidden drawers of memory.

Everybody has heard of the beauty of Sri Lanka's enchanting landscape. So, instead of repeating what has been said many times, I would like to talk about my encounter with the famous English writer Aldous Huxley, who I met there. Towards the end of 1961 I had to go to Colombo in order to make arrangements for an international seminar that was being organized by UNESCO. When I reserved about seventy rooms for the foreign delegates and UNESCO offices in a seaside hotel, the manager was impressed. He arranged for a separate table to be placed in the dining room for me, which afforded a fascinating view of the ocean. Meanwhile I heard that Mr Huxley was staying in the same hotel, and even saw him strolling in the yard once or twice. One morning, when I was having breakfast, I saw him standing pensively in the dining room. I realized that the waiters had not recognized him and he had not been able to find a place to sit. So I went up to him and introduced myself, and inquired if I could be of any help. He said he wanted to sit where he could have a view of the ocean, and since every other place was occupied I invited him to share my table. In this way, I was able to talk to him informally over breakfast for a week. If I wrote even a synopsis of what we talked about, it would be no less than an essay, so I will confine myself to describing two interesting dialogues that we had.

Ever since his childhood, Huxley's eyes had been so weak that despite numerous attempts, even some of the foremost eye specialists had not been able to restore normal eyesight to him. The only remedy that proved effective was a modern treatment, based on the principle of exercise. Thus Huxley regained his vision, and he even wrote a book about it. My own vision was quite good at the time. When he was telling me of his short-sightedness, he said that the problem is that 'Unless I see a face at close quarters I do not recognize the person. If I look at a woman closely she complains that I am staring at her, and if I turn away I am accused of rudeness.' Little did I know at the time that I would be facing the same problem.

Huxley achieved fame with his satirical novel, *Brave New World*. After I had read it at a young age, I expressed my view in an essay, that it had been influenced by a novel written a few years after the Bolshevik Revolution by a Soviet humorist, Zamyatin. When I mentioned this to Huxley he was surprised, and said, 'Your guess is right, but how did it occur to you?' A few years later when the Russian novel was translated into English and published in London, critics commented on the resemblance between the two novels.

I recollect another interesting encounter in Colombo. The Education Minister in Sri Lanka those days was a Mr Badeeuddin who used to be my neighbour in the Aligarh University hostel. Years later when I met him in Colombo, he extended to me all the help I needed in facilitating my work for my organization. Since Gagarin, the first astronaut had come to Sri Lanka on an official tour, Badeeuddin threw a party for him and invited me to it. We listened to Gagarin's interesting account of his voyage in space for a long time that evening.

I made a few trips to Burma as well, but my stay was confined to Rangoon on account of disturbances in the rest of the country. Rangoon has the Buddhist temple known as the Shimagan Pagoda. On its dome is a spire made of gold. However what interested me more was the dilapidated tomb of Bahadur Shah Zafar. It is located in the courtyard of the tiny house which served as the last abode of that ill-fated man. There it tells the student of Indian history its heartbreaking tale of decline and ruin. During my stay in Calcutta the first article I wrote in Urdu (in the year 1931), with the title, 'The last glimpse of the House of Tamerlane', concerned Mirza Bedar Bakht, Zafar's great-grandson.

An interesting incident happened on one of my trips to Rangoon. In 1964, when I arrived there from Bangkok, I found that not a single room was available in the only suitable hotel there. I was therefore forced to take a taxi to go to another hotel which was at some distance from town. Before the World War it had been the residence of a wealthy Chinese, but now the Burmese government had appropriated it. When I reached there I was told that a large party had arrived from China and had booked all the rooms in the hotel. When the manager of the group heard of my predicament he inquired where I came from. On learning that I was a national of Pakistan, he became kindly disposed towards me, and vacated one of the rooms that his party was occupying.

That night the seventy or eighty strong Chinese group took their places around the dining table, while I sat alone at a corner table. China was not a member of the United Nations in those days because the United States had vetoed each one of its attempts to enter the UN. I was therefore loath to have my connection with the organization revealed to the Chinese. But such things have a way of being discovered. Seeing me sitting alone in the corner, the Chinese interpreter came over and insisted on taking me to sit with the rest of his party, and so I joined the company of the delegates. In the course of the conversation that followed, the men asked me the reason for my arrival in Burma, and I thought it best to divulge my identity and my business. Although I did not understand the Chinese language, I could tell by the harshness of their tone that by making the disclosure I had touched a raw nerve. Their interpreter kept communicating to me their criticism of the United Nations for a long time but finally I managed to assure them that many people in the UN were, like me, well wishers of China. When at last they became convinced of my sincerity, they lavished such hospitality on me for the four days of my stay there, that I still remember it. Among the party were a few delegates from Chinese Turkestan. I was even able to speak with one or two of them in Farsi. Thailand, Malaysia, Singapore, etc, stand out among South East Asian countries for their prosperity and progress in education. Chinese minorities living in these regions have contributed more than the native population towards their development.

I visited Nepal just once, in 1964. Nowhere else in Asia have I seen such poverty. I still retain some striking images of Nepal. One of them is of Mount Everest, the tallest mountain peak in the world, which I observed through a pair of binoculars after climbing a hill that is situated a few miles from Kathmandu. Another is of the temple in the centre of the city, which was built by the daughter of an unsuccessful leader ('Nana Sahib') in the War of Independence fought against the British in 1857. On the walls of the temple are engraved curses and maledictions for the British. When the British brought the last leader of the Marathas, Baji Rao Peshwa, from Poona and incarcerated him here, he nominated a close relative, Nana Sahib as his successor. After Peshwa died, the British government of India refused to recognize Nana Sahib's right to succeed, for which he avenged himself on them in 1857. After his defeat he took refuge in Nepal. To the end of his days Azeemullah of Kanpur remained his sympathizer and friend. The latter lived to be 120 years, and died after Partition. He had written his memoirs, the manuscript of which I was told, was being perused by Maulana Abul Kalam Azad in 1952. I do not know whether it was eventually published. I was looking at the meagre collection of books in the Kathmandu University library, when somebody informed me that the best equipped library in the country could be found in the mansion of an old aristocrat, Rana Qaisar Shamsheer Jang. In fact, his library turned out to be a rare collection of its kind, which included almost 30,000 books in English, most of them dealing with history, politics, biography, etc. Rana Sahib was a venerable old gentleman, who spent most of his income on books and his time on their upkeep. The Christian priest Stocks, who became an Arya Samaji and went to live some distance from Simla, had a similar library. The name of Wajid Ali Shah's wife, Hazrat Mahal, is associated with the Kathmandu neighbourhood known as Begum Mahallah. In 1857 she bravely fought the British usurpers in Lucknow, and on being overpowered, perforce took refuge in Kathmandu. Finding no tombstone on her grave, I had the Archaeological department of Nepal hang a sign over it with her name inscribed in English.

Sometimes I see myself strolling on the bank of the Bosphorus—a site that could be called history's beat. In Switzerland, Lake Geneva offers an unmatched spectacle of nature's beauty. I am particularly attracted to places where the grandeur of history is entwined with the beauty of nature. To see an example of this, one need only behold the valley of the Loire in France, where chateaus of the Middle Ages pay homage to the genius of their architects and builders.

In Italy, near Naples, the ruins of Pompeii bear witness to the majesty of Rome, while close by, blazing in its rage, Mount Vesuvius spews out smouldering lava.

Sometimes my thoughts take me to the place where the frontiers of Austria and Hungary meet. To escape the fury of communism, gypsies sought refuge in this spot, and despite their poverty, their tents rang with the sound of song and dance. Memory then takes me in another direction and to another night. In Athens the Acropolis with its ruins of antiquated buildings reminds one of ancient Greece. This is the same place which was burned down by the Persian conqueror, Xerxes. Later Alexander took revenge for this act by destroying the Persian city of Persepolis which is still mourning its past near Shiraz. An acquaintance in Athens told me that some guesthouses have been built near the Acropolis, which are furnished and equipped in the style of that ancient Greek civilization which now seems so new to us. Such spectacles have left their imprint on my memory! I have described some of them here, and stored away others in the privacy of my heart. How well Bedil puts it:

Glad tidings, O heart! For I have discovered the past

17

The Past and Present of Literature

The evolution of civilization and language are closely linked. It is also recognized that poetry is the oldest and most popular form of literary creation. Historically, its oldest specimen is the epic, 'Gilgamesh', written in Babylon almost 7000 years ago and preserved to this day. The inscriber of the poem states that a part of it was taken from a piece of writing dated two thousand years earlier. In other words this poem was composed about 9000 years ago. It contains a detailed description of Noah's flood, and shows substantial merit in narrative and observation.

Masterpieces in poetry and other arts came into being as man's creative ability developed over thousands of years. A combination of the external influences of environment and the talent of gifted individuals was responsible for their existence. The act of creation is extremely complex and an explanation of it cannot be neatly gathered into any one hypothesis or view.

Poetry and prose are the two distinct forms of literature. Of the two it is poetry that has been accorded more importance so far. The reason for this is quite obvious. If words are musical, and are controlled by metre, they can absorb that quality of music which makes it reach the depths of the soul and impress itself on memory. Poetry is put to diverse uses. Whether it is communication with one's deity, eulogy of one's tribal chief, homage to one's ancestors, or expression of sentiments at a wedding, poetry is an efficient medium of expression for all such needs. Much of it is mere rhyming and versification, but nevertheless, even that is an early form of poetry.

Great poetry was first created in that cradle of civilization which is known as Greece. The epic poems, *The Iliad* and *The Odyssey*, said to be the work of Homer, were produced 3000 years ago. In Urdu 'epic' is translated as *razmia*, the accuracy of which is doubtful. Besides the *Odyssey*, Dante's *Divine Comedy* and Milton's *Paradise Lost* also fall into the category of epics, but they are not the versified chronicle of war indicated by 'razm'. Other than Firdausi's *Shahnama*, our culture has never produced any razmia poem of any significance. The *Shahnama* is indeed a razmia poem, but the epic cannot be called a razmia poem on the strength of it. The Sanskrit poems *Ramayana* and *Mahabharat* also fall into this [epic but not razm] category.

Subsequently, many exceptional examples of literary creativity in different languages came into being. The themes most prevalent among them are beauty, love, nature, the search for truth, and homage to the sovereign or patron. Compared to the East, Western poetry has not only a meagre tradition of the genres that eulogize personalities and render homage to God, but also lacks the mystical element.

Apart from poetry, drama and fiction were invented in creative prose. No one word in Urdu can render the entire scope of fiction. The English word 'fiction' encompasses everything, from narrative and short stories to the novel. Drama too is the invention of that wonderland of creativity that was Greece. It was there that 2500 years ago drama and the stage were developed and laid down the lines on which the future art of the theatre would be based and achieve great heights. The Muslims of the Middle Ages were so biased against acting, sculpture, painting and dance that these arts were never fostered in Muslim countries. That is why drama of any merit is absent in Muslim literature. However many plays were written in Sanskrit, of which *Shakuntala* is recognized as a masterpiece. A long time back I translated this play into Urdu. The shows that Hindus put up on the occasion of the Ram Leela ceremony, or the No theatre of Japan offer interesting spectacles, but they lack literary merit. Compare this creative poverty with the artistic greatness, the zenith of which is manifest in Shakespeare's plays. His plays place Shakespeare among the great artists of the world. If we then consider the works of Goethe, Moliere, Ibsen, Shaw, Chekov, etc., it becomes apparent that drama was enormously enriched in the West and was accorded no less acclaim than any other genre of literature.

The beginnings of fiction lay in story telling. Its earliest examples are tales of animals and birds, in the 1500 year old Sanskrit collection known as *Panchtantra*. Later they appeared in Arabic as *Kalila-wa-Dimna*. Up to that time prose had been used to write books on history, philosophy, medicine, etc. but it had not yet developed the capacity for conveying imaginative thought.

When we contemplate the clear and logical style of Aristotle and Plato's prose we are surprised to find that 2500 years ago such precision of language had been achieved for conveying subtle and complex ideas, which we are often wanting in, even today. The intellectual and artistic superiority of Greece was acknowledged by the West as well as by the Arabs.

The history of prose fiction is short compared to poetry and drama. Only in less than the past one thousand years has it achieved eminence. In Sanskrit its first instance is Katha Sart Sagar, and in Arabic it is the Arabian Nights. In the Middle Ages after the decline of Latin, when the European languages began to develop along modern lines, stories in prose were a source of guidance for them. The first examples of these in English are Chaucer's *Canterbury Tales*, in Italian it is Boccacio's *Decameron*, and in Spanish it is *Don Quixote* by Cervantes. All of these were written in the fourteenth and fifteenth centuries. Not only these but even the above mentioned Sanskrit work shows the influence of Arab storytelling.

At the end of the fifteenth century, printing took the place of calligraphy in Europe. Before this happened, the copies of hand-written manuscripts used to be few, and remained in the possession of selected individuals or libraries. With the advent of printing, thousands of copies were made of those same manuscripts, and were distributed far and wide.

About this time the Renaissance in Europe ushered in the modern age. The discovery of new countries, the growth of rational knowledge, and the translations of old and ancient works so stimulated prose writing in the European languages that by the eighteenth century they had developed qualities of style that equipped them as a fitting medium for *belles letteres* and other forms of sophisticated and complex writing. If France produced the powerful writing of intellectuals like Rousseau and Voltaire, England yielded the brilliant prose of Dr Johnson. The spread and popularity of prose is directly linked to the public's eagerness for education and knowledge. Against this background consider how the French revolution influenced Western literature when it separated church from state by apportioning religious and temporal affairs, respectively, to each. As a consequence of this the focus of society shifted from God and the state to the human being. Literature was bound to echo this new philosophy of life. Thirty years before the French political and intellectual revolution of 1789, the Industrial Revolution had begun in England. The nineteenth century has an important place in the history of the world, because with it began the decline of the Muslims, and the ascendancy of the West which soared with the rise of industry and science. This new state of affairs in the West was reflected in the fervour and gusto of the Romantic Movement, which was apparent simultaneously in the music, painting and poetry of the time. By contrast, a fog of gloom and helplessness cast its shadow over Eastern poetry. That, until the eighteenth century, Asia neither showed any interest in the printing press nor cultivated the capacity and potential of prose, which is essential for the spread of education and modern science, is an unhappy fact that should not be overlooked.

In the midst of these changes began the great era of fiction, a genre that forged ahead in the short space of two centuries and gradually overtook poetry and drama. For some time, under the influence of poetry, imaginative prose wandered in the vales and dales of romance and beauty, but in the nineteenth century, guided by novelists such as Dickens and Balzac, it discovered the highway of realism. In France specially, this literary movement produced many great writers whose influence proved to be enduring and far-reaching.

The Russian language imbued the novel with the environment and character of Russia. For example, the work of Tolstoy and Dostoevsky, who are considered doyens of novel-writing, leads in very different directions. Yet they share one common value, which is the search for truth and morality. Western realism confines itself to the analysis of good and evil in life. On the other hand Russian writers infuse realism with human and moral values. This is the distinction between reality and truth which the modern age has ignored, thus covering itself in hypocrisy, insincerity and duplicity.

This deeply ingrained moral sense led Tolstoy to the literary view which he expressed in his controversial book, What is Art? At the end of the nineteenth century, when Tolstoy wrote on the subject, he had already renounced his wealth and taken up the life of a hermit. The search for moral and human values that can be found in his novels, plays and short stories is present in his views on literature as well. For the West, his was a new voice. The aesthetic, technical, and scientific traditions that had permeated the West could not accept this new voice. But in Russia his influence prevailed even after the Revolution, though in a different form: the concept of morality moved away from the spiritual, towards the material aspect of life. Nevertheless, Tolstoy's basic perception remained unaltered, namely, that literature should not be aimless; and that the raison d'etre of literature is that it should always be seeking improvement in the plight of humanity.

Many other experiments were made in Western fiction in the beginning of the twentieth century, which cannot be disregarded. At the commencement of the century the great era of realism came to an end with Emile Zola, and the age of Romanticism with Pierre Louys and Oscar Wilde. From exploring the externals, the novel went on to probe the inner reaches of the mind. The influence of Dostoevsky was felt more in the West than in Russia, and Freud's theory of the subconscious brought about major changes in poetry and fiction. Moreover, we are witness to the effect on literature of wars that the colonies waged in order to gain their independence from imperial powers, and the awareness of social injustice that was created in the wake of the Russian Revolution.

The Second World War is a milestone in the history of the modern age. After this war, the world was no longer what it used to be. This change was so far-reaching that its influence can still be felt in our lives. On the one hand Communism spilled over from Russia and inundated China in the east, and central Europe in the west, and on the other hand, Africa and Asia were released from the stranglehold of European imperialism. There appeared on the map of the world, a new entity known as the Third World, which comprised the newly liberated colonies and the depressed countries of South America. The struggle between conservatism and progress for freedom from poverty and ignorance that is waging in this region, has involved all of us. The day by day advancement in science accompanied by the decline of human values in the Western capitalist system, the dominance of the state and the powerlessness of the individual under the communist regimes, and the conflict between old and new values in the Third World created a turmoil in literature just as it brought upheaval to every other intellectual and empirical field. That fervour and passion which had set in motion the fight for revolution and freedom was dying out, and those ideals in the light of which our prose had begun to seek the path to freedom, bit the dust. In Western literature this sense of drifting and disorientation is profound. The world has conspicuously failed to produce a single great writer or poet after the war. Sartre, Malraux, and Pablo Neruda are among those who were born at the beginning of the twentieth century and had reached the peak of their creative powers by the time the World War began. There is no doubt that the number of people who read books is now far greater than before, but most of them can easily be satisfied with trivial, facile writing, and can therefore be regarded as only semi-educated. While it cannot be said that the process of creation in literature has reached its end, it is a fact that along with the juggling of words in the name of experiments in technique, the conflict between thought and observation has created a tumult which has not yielded anything that can claim importance or significance.

Before the ascendancy of the West there was only a feeble tradition of creative prose in Asia. The emergence of the printing press and the proliferation of modern knowledge vitalized it. I will discuss this subject later, but for the sake of simplicity I will confine this discussion to Persian and Urdu prose. The poetry of these two languages has bestowed a precious gift not only on our own literary heritage but on that of the whole world, a fact that perceptive Westerners have now begun to acknowledge.

T.S. Eliot divides poetry into three kinds: the poetry of sound, of images, and of the intellect. The poetry of sound captures the heart with its harmony, music, and melody. The poetry of images is distinguished by its ability to achieve, by means of variety and vividness of words, such a vibrant exposition of war and festivity, of events, that it takes on the role of a painter or sculptor. Intellectual poetry describes reality and philosophy in such a novel way that the pedantry of philosophy is exposed.

Judging by these standards, our own poetry is in some ways unrivalled. In spite of the fact that everyone loves his own language, and it is difficult to translate poetry satisfactorily into another language, people who posses the ability to make comparisons of literary merit are in a position to make a fair judgment in this regard. If we take the genre of epic poetry, the *Shahnama*, *Ramayana*, and *Mahabharta* collectively are by no means inferior to the Western epic. It is also acknowledged that Rumi's place in mystic poetry is pre-eminent.

The distinctive feature of twentieth century poetry is its intellectual component, and in this context Iqbal can be ranked with Eliot and Rilke. Generally speaking, the real sphere of poetry is love, but it is not easy to make comparisons on this basis. In the Persian and Urdu languages love poetry has been mainly the domain of the *ghazal*, a unique genre that is found in no other language except Arabic. To indicate an emotion or idea on the theme of love and passion in a few words and a single couplet, within the confines of metre, rhyme, and post-rhyme, is a difficult test to pass. In good prose the word must reveal and not obfuscate meaning. On the other hand, in the language of the *ghazal*, words conceal meaning more than they reveal it. Even without brilliant intellectual content, the semblance of melody thus created can bestow on poetry the splendour of music. This association of word and meaning and the exquisite charm it engenders, pervades the work of Hafiz in matchless perfection. Among Urdu poets, Mir possesses this quality in the highest degree.

It is true that there is not much room for the exercise of imagination in the genre of the *ghazal*, and therefore the repetition of a few worn-out themes that generally characterize it, strain common sense. It is also a fact that most *ghazals* have nothing to offer except verbosity and rhyme. And yet there exists a large store of *ghazals* that splendidly render love. No other genre of poetry is blessed with the popularity that the *ghazal* enjoys. Its rendition in music has its own place in our musical tradition, and quoting its couplets appropriately is considered a sign of refinement in cultivated society. Beyond its blemishes and shortcomings, the popular acclaim that the *ghazal* has won, points to its importance in our cultural heritage.

In the East, as in the West, the theme of poetry changed during the twentieth century, and its focus moved from feeling to thought. In our language, Urdu, the hold of the *ghazal* was loosened by the influence of Hali and Iqbal. As the age of the great *ghazal* and *nazam* poets came to a close, experiments began to be made in free verse and the new ghazal. At present it is too early to express views about their future.

Real development in Urdu prose began in 1835, when the East India Company made English the official language in place of Persian. This is not to say that Urdu had lacked refinement before. Insha, in his story,

Rani Ketki, written at the end of the eighteenth century, and Mir Amman in *Bagh-o-Bahar*, written in the early twentieth century, had proved that storytelling in Urdu did not require rhymed prose. The scholarly books of Delhi College, and Ghalib's letters provide similar instances of a polished style in writing. However the real progress in Urdu prose began after 1857. The services of Sir Syed Ahmed Khan and his companions in this context are well-known, but we are prone to disregard the achievement of Ratan Nath Sarshar. Not only did he pioneer the art of the novel in Urdu, he also rescued Urdu prose from the maze of unending tales of sorcery that have now fallen into oblivion. Not only that, the way Sarshar exposed the decadant feudal society of Oudh is unrivalled. Only in Deputy Nazir Ahmed's novels can one find a glimpse of the same. No one has ridiculed the hollow societies of Lucknow and Delhi as Sarshar and Nazir Ahmed have, in the form of their characters Khoji and Zahirdar Beg.

When assessing the shortcomings of Urdu prose one should make allowances for its relatively brief existence. More than that, one should keep in mind that its growth may have been stunted by two powerful languages which flanked and impeded it—my allusion is to Persian and English, which, one after the other became the national, educational, and official languages. Until recently the language of Urdu poetry was so deeply influenced by Persian that it was to a large extent ignorant of the environment of its own homeland; and it chose a tone that recalled an Iranian expressing himself in Persian with some alteration in the order of words. Among the older poets I can think of only Mir and Nazir who guarded the distinctiveness of Urdu from being crushed under the weight of Persian.

With the development of the printing press, when all kinds of books began to be published in Urdu, the number of readers proliferated, and inevitably, the Urdu language left the palace and the pulpit and descended to the level of the common man. Two distinct tendencies were visible right from the beginning, among a variety of styles. On the one hand was the elegant prose style of Mirza Rajab Ali Beg Saroor, Mohammad Hasan Azad, Abul Kalam Azad, and Niaz Fatehpuri, with their concern for eloquence and fine writing, and on the other hand there was the flowing, idiomatic everyday language which was first employed by Mir Amman and Ghalib and continued to be used by Hali, Nazir Ahmed, and Abdul Haq.

At the beginning of the twentieth century people who were au fait with English literature began to join the ranks of literary writers in Urdu. This was the period when the Romantic movement in the West had come to an end but its echo could be heard in the hedonism of Oscar Wilde and Peter Louys. In Urdu this was a new voice, and it created new perceptions of beauty and new criteria of beauty in exposition. The Romantic masters of prose were headed by Mir Nasir Ali, who demonstrated such feats of colourful, idealistic writing in his magazine, *Sala-e-Aam* that a new chapter was added to Urdu prose. He was no less fastidious than Mir Taqi Mir. Consequently he wrote the contents of the magazine from cover to cover every month for twenty years, because no one else could meet his exacting standards. Not only had he employed a scribe, he had even installed a printing press in his house in order to ensure that there was not the slightest chance of error. As for Niaz, his manner of writing was so burdened with the influence of Arabic that it was unsuitable for the Romantic style. However the trend he set for free thinking and intellectual awareness in our prose will always be remembered.

Around the year 1935, the moonlight of Romantic writing paled before the sunlight of Realism and Progressive writing, but there is no doubt that it contributed to Urdu literature the capability to move away from conservatism and find new modes of expression. Its simple and lucid style influenced the school of realistic writing which was represented by Premchand, Krishan Chandra, Rajinder Singh Bedi Saadat Hasan Manto.

When a reviewer of fiction regards the earliest period of modern Urdu literature he is most impressed, first by Sarshar, and then by Mirza Hadi Ruswa. Between the oeuvres of these two writers there are hundreds of other novels, but except for the works of Nazir Ahmed and Sajjad Husain, few among them deserve attention. However the novels of Rashidul Khairi and Abdul Halim Sharar are noteworthy because they describe the Muslim past and present forcefully.

Premchand took fiction past this stage and commenced the great age, the effect of which is still felt. His important achievement was that, for the first time, he introduced rural life into the novel and short story. His characters are the common people, who speak a simple language, intelligible to all. Moreover, like Hali, he too created an awareness of human and moral values in literature. If Hali is known for heralding reform in poetry, Premchand will be acknowledged as the standard bearer of reformist literature. There is a high regard for his creations both in Urdu and in Hindi.

I have already described how in my youth, when I arrived in Calcutta, I was drawn to modern English literature along with Hindi journalism. Moreover, my sensibilities caused me to become deeply conscious of the powerlessness of the common people and reminded me that the inhabitants of the village that I owned belonged to the same exploited class. These people have figured in three of my short stories, which were published in 1932–33, one after the other, in the Hindi magazine *Vishwamitr*. It is not merely a boast, but a fact, that these stories won much fame in those days on account of their novel approach and unique perspective, and were translated into many languages of India. I translated one of them into Urdu and called it 'The blind beggar', but could not find the time to translate 'Two labourers' and 'Towards the future'. However, all three are present chronologically in my collection of Hindi short stories entitled Fire and Tears. My essay *Sahitya aur Kranti* (Literature and Life), which has been considered the foundation stone of Progressive criticism in Hindi, was published in 1935. It would not be true to say that there were no examples of realism in fiction before the start of the Progressive movement. As a matter of fact, Premchand had already initiated the trend. What Progressivism did was to use realism to protest against social injustice. Historically, this movement begins in July 1935, with an article that I wrote for Anjuman Taraqqi-e-Urdu's magazine, *Urdu*. Sajjad Zaheer has mentioned this in his book *Roshnai* [The Light] in these words:

> In 1936, or perhaps even a little earlier, Akhtar Hussain Raipuri wrote his famous article, 'Literature and Life', which was published in the quarterly, *Urdu*, brought out by Anjuman Taraqqi e Urdu. In my opinion it was the first essay in our language to present in a reasoned and detailed fashion, the necessity of creating new, Progressive literature, and elucidating and then condemning reactionary values. As the author of this important essay, Akhtar Hussain Raipuri is pre-eminent among the founders of the Movement for Progressive Literature.

This article is included in the collection of my essays, *Literature and Revolution*. Sajjad Zaheer founded the Association of Progressive

Writers in 1936, and Majnoon Gorakhpuri's book *Literature and Life* was published after that date.

Saadat Hasan Manto, Ismat Chughtai, etc. also adopted the realistic approach, although their interest was restricted to abuse and exploitation in sexual behaviour. Therefore it would be more correct to say that the literary group of those days which raised its voice in protest against imperialism and exploitation was that of the Progressive Writers. It is difficult to put the two trends into two clearly demarcated boxes, because writers of the two groups often overlapped in their work. Nevertheless, on the conscious level they accepted the principle that literature should represent life and must never hesitate to support the truth.

This movement had such a deep and enduring influence that it changed the character of the poetry and literature of the day. While it is true that during the turmoil of the struggle for freedom there was, inevitably, slogan chanting and expression of agitation and ferment, on the other hand there was no lack of durable writing. The Progressive school especially played a prominent role in every genre of literature in that period. After Partition, the Association of Progressive Writers weakened due to several reasons, but the Progressive trend so permeated literature that even those who opposed it had to accept it.

The debate between 'Art for Art's sake', and 'Art for Life' can still be heard. The real issue is the link between expression and communication. No doubt the artist has freedom of expression, but the feeling or event he is describing in prose or poetry is a conscious or unconscious reflection of his environment. When Ghalib claimed:

آتے ہیں غیب سے یہ مضامین خیال میں

These topics come to mind from the Unseen

he forgot that those topics were indebted to the traditions which the collective mind bestows on an individual. The writer's style of expression, whether realistic or visionary, does nevertheless influence the reader. This is the connection between reader and writer that lays social responsibilities on the writer. In any society, every individual is engaged in some occupation. So is the writer, and therefore, like the common man, he too is subject to rights and duties. Valuable literature cannot be created in an atmosphere of checks and restraints. Proof of this can be found in all those countries where there are curbs on freedom of expression and publication.

Of late, creative writing has had to face a new problem, aside from government censorship. This is the flood of popular publications catering to the growing number of semi-educated persons. While it is true that ultimately, like in the case of all other arts, the purpose of literature is entertainment, but, like creativity, entertainment too has different levels. A mature mind is affected by the kind of creative literature that sensitizes its readers to the noblest values of life. Movies, the radio, television and digests do provide temporary entertainment, but of the kind that is quickly forgotten. The machine culture that the industrial society is moulding requires that the common man be given no time to think and that he buy ideas as he buys commodities, from the ones advertised on the mass communication network. Consequently the artist's old links with publicity are broken and instead he has to deal with commerce, as though creativity were a commodity which is bought and sold subject to the market's law of supply and demand. This is why there are many buyers of cheap books and magazines in our language, while literature of a high standard has few purchasers.

Another problem is that most readers of serious literature are versed in English. Since the demand for such literature in Urdu is small, its publication is limited. When someone who is competent in English does not find books to his liking in Urdu, he turns to English publications, where he finds them easily. This situation has rapidly become graver than could have been imagined.

Serious literary creation requires a great deal of diligence and perseverance. It needs full-time application. Writing essays, short stories or ghazals is not subject to these conditions because they can be written sporadically, in a few sittings. But no great book can be written in this way. Just as no great films are made in our country, and even if they are made, they can find no viewers; similarly, even if good books are written there are few who will publish or read them. People who analyse the history of Pakistani culture should look into this state of affairs. It is not an issue of literature alone; it concerns the culture and moral values of the society as well.

The Muslims of the subcontinent have always been deeply conscious of their identity. It came under close critical examination in this century when they had to take the fork in the highway of history known as Pakistan. During this struggle they were spurred on by the recognition of the thousand-year-old cultural heritage which began with the arrival of the Arabs in Sindh. An important part of this heritage is literary, and this is what we are solely concerned with here. From the aspect of language this legacy can be divided into its constituents of Persian, Urdu, and several regional languages.

It is well known that Sindhi, Punjabi and Pashtu produced, respectively, the great poets Abdul Latif Bhitai, Waris Shah, and Khushhal Khan Khatak. But Urdu speakers are not familiar with the achievements of Muslim poets in Hindi. Of these, Kabir, Malik Mohammad Jaisi, and Abdur Rahim Khankhanan are counted among important Hindi poets. Kabir was the greatest Hindi Sufi poet, while Jaisi's *Padmawati* will be linguistically and artistically acknowledged as the forerunner of Tulsi Das's *Ramayan*. In Khankhanan's collection of seven hundred dohas, *Rahim Sat Sai*, are scattered pearls of intelligence and wisdom. Bengali produced the great poet Qazi Nazrul Islam, who was second only to Tagore. I do not wish to list more names, but it is a fact that if not in prose then at least in poetry the contribution of Muslims in these languages is an invaluable gift.

We can indeed pride ourselves on the wealth of Persian poetry produced in this land, beginning with Saad bin Salman, in the reign of the Ghaznavis, until Iqbal in the present era. In Iran when the inspiration for lofty verse dried up with the founding of the Safavid rule, the Mughal court at Delhi patronized the new school known as Sabak-e-Hindi. The names of Naziri and Saeb, who conceived this new style under the influence of the Indian environment, head the list of its founders. It is strange that before the collection of Faizi's poetry, *Nal-o-Man* arrived on the scene, no Persian poet in India had acknowledged the influence of his Indian surroundings. It was Akbar's encouragement of cultural tolerance between Hindus and Muslims that affected Persian poetry as well. The inventors of Sabak-e-Hindi called it *Taza Goi*, or 'New Expression'. Compared to Sabak-e-Iraqi or the Iraqi style more attention had been given in it to refinement of thought and innovation. So far Sabak-e-Hindi has not been made the subject of a thorough appraisal, but it seems likely that this style was influenced to some extent by the genre of doha in contemporary Hindi poetry. For one thing, the structure of the doha closely resembles the first two lines of a ghazal, which rhyme with one another and have the same weight. There is an assertion in the first line, which the second line substantiates with an example. The subject of a doha can be either love or edification. In my opinion, if someone studies Saeb in the context of Sanskrit and Hindi didactic dohas, he would be able to achieve a deep insight into Sabak-e-Hindi. Shibli Nomani concluded his book *Sher-ul-Ajam* (Poetry of Persia) with the poets of Shahjahan's era, asserting that the great period of Persian poetry did not outlast this era. However, nobody with any sense of justice can overlook Mirza Bedil. Likewise, the last chapter in the history of Persian poetry in India would remain incomplete without a mention of Ghalib and Iqbal. Owing to unfamiliarity with one or more of the languages involved, no one has done a comparative study of Sanskrit and Hindi poetry with Sabak-e-Hindi, so far. We have therefore been deprived of what is an interesting subject in itself.

Much of our literary heritage lies in Urdu. Along with Muslims, Hindus too have had a hand in the development of Urdu. It is the tyranny of politics that in the twentieth century, when both Hindus and Muslims were engaged in enriching Urdu prose and poetry, communal prejudice came in the way of its progress, and caused it harm. After independence the situation is such that the exchange of Urdu publications between India and Pakistan has almost come to an end. This has limited the dissemination and publication of Urdu books. During my employment with the Pakistan government and UNESCO I tried hard to do away with these restrictions, but was not able to do so due to political obstacles.

Invention and creativity are governed by the same deep bond that is present between analysis and the desire for progress. When layers of conventions crush a society, they can be removed only with the blade of critical analysis. But this operation can be performed only if the desire for progress is present. An imaginative and vibrant mind is attracted sometimes by artistic creation and sometimes by the discovery of nature's realities. Great literature and great art can be recognized by their hallmark qualities of analysis and desire for improvement, which are inherent in them.

The rise and fall of civilizations is directly linked to fluctuations in their intellectual life. When a nation makes blind imitation its rule of life, it begins to move backward instead of forward, and is deflected from the highway of history. This law applies to art and literature as well. The worship of convention that dominated our poetry until the early part of this century, and the prevailing practice of composing poems in the style of this person or that, injured the originality of many. Not only did words lose their meaning, they frequently became meaningless. We find that after the fall of the Mughals, whether it is prose or poetry, whether in Persian or in Urdu, there are the same old tired and clichéd ideas, the endless repetition of which makes the heart sink. There are countless religious magazines in which commentaries have been written on commentaries, and it seems that the padlock that Imam Ghazali placed on the doors of knowledge was never opened.

The realist movement that was begun in Western Europe in the nineteenth century, seemed to have taken on the form of a commitment at the beginning of the twentieth century. Earlier, the writer used to confine himself to analyzing the good and evil in society; now he has associated himself with the mission that is battling with the forces of oppression and injustice. Emile Zola was the first standard bearer of this trend, but it was Maxim Gorky who endowed it with the true stature of art. His autobiography is acknowledged to be a masterpiece, and I spent a good deal of time in translating its three volumes into Urdu. This trend dominated world literature until the Second World War, and the Progressive movement in Urdu was one aspect of it. To make the cry of the helpless and voiceless the subject of art, and absorb the voice of truth and justice into literature, are the goals that make the writer's pen the spokesman for humanity.

After the World War, when values and principles were sent to their grave in the West, writers began to suffer from a feeling of dissociation from society. This strengthened the trend of alienation which we now find in the literature of our own language. Immediately after the War ended, Colin Wilson in *The Outsider* and Camus in *The Stranger* gave such powerful expression to the feeling of alienation that it became a common theme. There is a difference between loneliness and alienation. In every age sensitive men have experienced intellectual and spiritual loneliness not only outside their home but even inside it. Shakespeare has painted a tragic picture of loneliness in Hamlet. In Urdu poetry

Mir's anguish holds in it, along with the moans of the wounded, the cry of the lonely. However loneliness and alienation are not the same thing. Alienation is a state that disassociates an individual from society. In Urdu, the presence of this trend is the outcome of the mental confusion that emerged after the events of 1947 and 1971.

When the artistic potential of these trends began to be exhausted, Europe turned once again to the tradition of storytelling which had given birth to fiction. Thousands of science fiction and detective novels are published every year. Famous writers even manage to extract material for hefty romances from the debris of history. Just as painting is no longer attracted to the body and the face, and instead, looks for inspiration in primitive and children's art, so fiction has lost interest in the monochrome of human life and has taken to exploring the lost world of dreams which had existed before the modern age. This is why sociologists have said that like religion, art had its beginnings in magic. This is the state of escapism that afflicts human beings not only in childhood but also in times of helplessness and vulnerability.

18

The Quest for Beauty

Although it is true that the mutual attraction and bond between beauty and passion is what enlivens life, yet it is but an excuse forged by nature to preserve the species. When Adam and Eve commenced the act of procreation, they could hardly foresee that today their descendants on earth would number several billions, and the greatest problem facing mankind would be how to check it.

Ghalib has called passion 'an unsoundness of mind':

کہتے ہیں جس کو عشق خلل ہے دماغ کا

What they call passion is but an unsoundness of mind

But Hafiz on the other hand calls it the gift of life:

خلل پذیر بود ہر بنا کے می بینی
بجز بنائے محبت کہ خالی از خلل است

Flawed is every foundation that I see
Except what is founded on love—that alone is flawless

Beauty does not have a universal standard. Some people have declared it merely an illusion. The famous French thinker, Voltaire, arrived at the conclusion that it is impossible to define beauty. Negroes like thick lips, but the white races worship thin ones; Iranians yearn for eyes resembling the narcissus flower, while Turks long for the same organ in the shape of almonds; Germans are enthralled by blond hair, whereas Indians are lovers of black hair. Beauty is therefore, nothing but a miraculous beguilement wrought by the eye. The ancient Greeks ascribed beauty to man rather than to woman, and so in the Greek statues of those days, the brilliance of art was more evident in male faces than in female ones. In Hindu aesthetics this problem was solved by the creation of a god who was half male and half female, and is known in Hindu mythology as Ardhnari Eshwar.

It should not be concluded from this discussion that I have never been aware of human beauty. However I have always found unselfconscious loveliness more appealing than beauty of the contrived, self-absorbed kind. I have had occasion to visit many abodes of beauty, the memory of which still burns bright in my mind, yet I did not find in them the splendour and allurement that dazzle the eye in the solitude of mountains and deserts.

It was before the Second World War that I had the opportunity to spend a few weeks in Kotgarh, a place about a hundred miles from Simla. My host's residence was situated on a hilltop from where one could view the snow-covered peaks of the Himalayas. Silence reigned all around, and was broken only by the whispering of leaves in the trees, birdsong and the melody of waterfalls. Such consummate peace had come my way after a very long time and I was happy that for the time being I had left behind the squalor of life. Close to this place was the fort-like house of a Christian priest named Stocks. He was an American preacher who had arrived here a long time ago in order to convert the hill people of this area to Christianity, but instead had fallen deeply in love with an Arya Samaj Hindu girl. The girl agreed to marry him on the condition that he convert to Arya Samaj. The magic of love did the rest. In the words of Mir, he:

قشقہ کھینچا، دیر میں بیٹھا، کب کا ترک اسلام کیا

Painted the mark of the Hindu on his forehead, sat in
the temple, and renounced Islam [or his own religion]

One day, when he had invited me to tea, I strolled along the winding mountain path in the direction of his house. On the way I came upon a fair that the hill people of the area had arranged. Business was lively and conjurers had created an atmosphere of fun-filled entertainment with their tricks. While I was watching this, three young girls dressed in pale green and adorned with flowers, stepped out of a rock in front. Their advent gave me the distinct sensation of seeing fairies from mythology. Actually they were Stocks' daughters. Their grace, coquetry and loveliness are etched in my mind.

I saw a similar sight once in Shiraz. It was the period between 1967-70, when I was working as the head of the UNESCO mission in Iran. Our organization was active in the fields of education, culture and science in different parts of the country, and comprised almost thirty foreign experts among whom were Americans, Germans, Frenchmen, and even Russians. The responsibility of ensuring cooperation between this motley group and the different departments of the government lay on me. We were also linked with an institution in Shiraz where female teachers were trained to teach in the tribal areas. This was the area of the Kashghai Turks who had inhabited the arid region bordering Shiraz for a very long period of time. Once when I had occasion to go to Shiraz on an official tour, the Director of Education there, Aqa-e-Behman Begi invited me to inspect the institution. When I entered the hall of the college accompanied by him, I stopped short in sudden panic at the door, because I had never before beheld such profusion of beauty in one place. I had frequently come across references to the 'Shiraz Turk' in Persian poetry, but it was only at that moment that the significance of it dawned on me. One can appreciate the elegance of Khwaja Hafiz's taste for offering Samarkand and Bukhara in exchange for such a face. He had said:

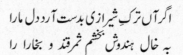

If that Turk of Shiraz would love me
I would give away Samarkand and Bukhara for the mole on his face

According to historians, Tamerlaine was so distressed on reading this couplet that after he had invaded Shiraz he summoned the frail and aged Hafiz, and rebuked him, saying, 'How did you dare to give away so liberally the cities that took me a lifetime to build?' Hafiz aptly replied, 'Had I not been profligate, would I have been so destitute today?'

While it is true that beauty takes many forms, what has always impressed me most is the beauty of nature. In particular, the panorama of snow-covered mountains, the eternal restlessness of the ocean, the fury of storms at sea, and the secrets hidden in the depths of the ocean have a quality of their own. Western poetry, music, and art have portrayed this in their masterpieces. They have used their creative brilliance to express also the majesty of mountains. In fact it would be appropriate to say that they have gone beyond short-lived human loveliness to discover the immortal springs of beauty. Hindu, Chinese, and Japanese art too depict this form of beauty, but one misses it in Muslim art.

I have had the opportunity to stay in some of the major hotels of the world, but nowhere did I find the kind of environmet that prevailed in the Fujia Hotel in Japan. It was situated opposite the snow-covered volcano known as the Fujiyama, and was surrounded by woods and waterfalls. I cannot remember how long I gazed at the mysterious loftiness of the volcano, in the shadow of which Japan's folklore took shape.

Unforgettable also is the mountain peak, Tirch Mir, in Pamir, which beckoned its admirers 25,000 feet above, to a place that was perhaps inhabited by fairies. I had seen this peak before Partition, from Chitral, where our host Nawab Nasir-ul-Mulk provided us with the opportunity to visit Kafiristan at a time when few people had heard of the place. One of my short stories, *The Princess of Kafiristan* (1942) was written in this setting.

Early in the morning on a clear day, one can view from Tiger Hill near Darjeeling, the towering Himalayan peak of Kanchanjunga. When the rays of the rising sun fall on it, creating a sort of rainbow the colours of which change so rapidly that the human imagination is flabbergasted, the scene that emerges before one's eyes is without equal. Compared to these mountains I found Iran's Koh-e-Damavand and Switzerland's Jung Frau quite disappointing, for they lacked the majestic stature of the Himalayan peaks.

Nor can I erase from my mind the beautiful spectacle that sometimes graces the sky. It is known by the hard Arabic word, *Qaus-e-Qaza*, but is described more agreeably by the Persian term 'Coloured Bow'. Most people must have seen it sometime or the other, but on my memory is imprinted a scene that I saw in Kashmir while travelling in a car with Nawab Jafar Ali Khan Asar. He was then the Home Minister and I had gone to Bara Mula from Amritsar to spend my summer holidays. Asar Sahib came to see me and persuaded me to go with him to

Srinagar. On the way when we happened to look at the sky we were stupefied. We stopped the car and gazed at the multicoloured cascade that had scattered the sun's rays from one end of the valley to the other.

I saw a similar magical scene in Tanzania's Nurdi Desert, during my stay in Africa. A number of intertwined colourful bows, spread across the sky to the horizon, presented an unforgettable sight.

My memory no longer retains a perfect image of visual beauty. However my ears still ring with the melodious chant that the nightingales of Shiraz poured into the night, giving the impression that somebody was reciting a ghazal from Hafiz. Or the passionate song of some unknown bird that echoed in the air of Simla. The voice of even a gifted singer does not possess the magic that suffuses the koel's song of passionate longing. However only those with an ear for music can appreciate it, just as it is only those with a grasp of poetry that can understand a good poem. There is a deep bond between the music of words and the sweetness of sound, and without a grasp of this connection no poem can achieve the melodious quality that is the soul of poetry. Similarly, unless the singer is practiced in the subtleties of the voice, his art will remain imperfect despite his knowledge of notes and rhythm.

What songstresses there were whose voices are now stilled for ever! But there is one voice that even now sometimes seems to echo in my ears. One evening a long time ago, I walked from my office in Paris to the entrance door of the large building which housed several apartments, including my own. As soon as I stepped into the courtyard of the building, I saw that the people in every apartment had opened a window and were listening spellbound to a song. I stopped short for a moment, as though what I heard was David singing the Psalms, or the voice of some bird in paradise. When I realized that the song was coming from my own flat I strode to the door of my apartment. On opening it I found the aged Madame Berger sitting in our kitchen and, oblivious to everything, singing an aria from some opera with utter abandon.

She was Bulgarian and had worked for a famous female singer for many years. But now she was homeless and friendless, barring a circle of admirers in Paris. Whenever the spirit took her, she would, without being invited, avail herself of somebody's hospitality, and after a short stay move on to another household. And so it happened that she was our guest every second or third month. She would tell the children stories or play the guitar to them. But it was only on that particular day I discovered that despite her age, the sweet strains of her voice could span the distance between the depths of the heart and the summit of human experience. It was a voice as sparkling as the ringing of silver bells. It was a voice, the like of which I never heard again.

The beauty of colour is expressed not in words but in pictures. Great artists of the world spent a good deal of time in observing the colours that nature has scattered generously in foliage. Our language names only a few colours, but European languages have words for hundreds of them. Yet the abundance of colours in nature is such that an artist can always find new potential for experiment and discovery. As the musician creates beauty from sound, and the painter from words, so the artist produces beauty from the harmonious blending of line and colour.

No one has been able to solve the mystery of the beauty in Mona Lisa's secret smile. And no one has been able to describe in words the pain of despair that Ophelia's eyes betrayed when she was about to commit suicide, as it is expressed in Monet's masterpiece.

Tagore likened the beauty of dance to the constant whirling in space that God has destined for the universe. The sun and the moon, the planets and stars have been dancing since the beginning of time. The same is true of the tides of the sea. To create a world of meaning with the movement of eye and eyebrow, and silent gestures of hands and feet in tune with music, is the pinnacle of creativity in art.

The ancient Greeks were unrivalled in hypothesizing. According to them music had its origin in the echo created by the constant whirling of planets. On the subject of dance, Tagore linked the circulation of blood in man to the spinning of earth and sky and tried to prove that trees and fruit, man and beast, sun and moon, are all in the same, and interconnected, state. A new scientific study, known as bio-rhythm confirms this poetic theory.

Everybody is susceptible to physical beauty, for by this means nature has ensured the propagation of the race. But to find pleasure in the abstract beauty of the intellect, a cultivated mind is a prerequisite. As Ghalib has said:

ہر بوالہوس نے حسن پرستی شمار کی
اب آبروئے شیوۂ اہل نظر گئی

Every rake has assumed the role of the asthete
No longer are the discerning esteemed for their talent

Just as there is a difference between spiritual and temporal love, so the mundane and spiritual aspects of beauty can be distinguished, one from the other. Great artists have tried to understand the beauty of character in their own way. Given a perceptive eye, even an ordinary person can easily assess this jewel among the qualities of man. The difference between the two kinds of beauty is that while physical beauty charms the heart, before spiritual beauty one bows in respect.

I do not remember the face of a single beautiful woman, but I have never been able to forget the Palestinian girl whom I saw absorbed in her book in an Israeli prison in Gaza. Only the perceptive can appreciate the value of the beauty of character that resides in some one who is at war with the forces of oppression and injustice. This is the point at which the outmoded views of aesthetics become silent, and the quest for beauty, according to Hali, flies from the temporal to the spiritual in its search for perfection.

When I take account of the gains and losses I made in my life, I count among my gains not a shred of fame or worldly eminence. What I consider as my real wealth is the benefit I derived from the study of great thinkers, writers, and poets. Similarly, beautiful sounds: of the vocalist's art, birdsong, or the humming of a waterfall in the mountains, still echo in my ears.

19

The Quest for Reality

Once, as a student in Paris, I met a Norwegian. He told me that after many years of hard work at the university, when he had acquired a degree in Philosophy, he realized that he was as ignorant of the reality of life as he was before he had begun to study for the university degree. It occurred to him that since one cannot learn about reality from books, perhaps knowledge of it can be gained from the battlefield of life. Consequently he became a sailor. He travelled for eight years, covering every corner of the earth, and during this time he asked everyone he came across what was his interpretation of reality. When he had collected all the answers to his query in many volumes, he returned to his homeland to analyse the material he had gathered and write a book. Who had created this universe and why? What part does our earth play in it? Why was life created, and where is it bound? What are the common traits between man and beast, and at what point did they part to become solely the characteristics of one or the other? Time, like space, is infinite. Has the future always existed but we are unaware of it on account of our own deficiency of perception? These questions, and others like them, have been asked in every age, and still remain unanswered. Views can differ about the beginning and end of time, but none can ignore the reality they encounter between their birth and their death.

If living beings knew before they were born the problems they would have to face during their lives, they would probably choose not to exist. But as the result of an inconsequential act they materialize into a world over which they have no control. After crossing all the vicissitudes of life when they arrive inevitably at the grim stage of death, no matter how strong their faith in the afterlife, they would rather draw back than move forward. But the inexorable law of nature that presides over the conflict between being and nothingness, survival and annihilation, allows no retreat.

I was sixteen years old and studying for my matric examination when questions of this kind began to exercise my mind. When I mentioned my doubts to my Science teacher he said, 'I am not a philosopher but I will try to prove to you that the universe does have a Creator.' He then hung a lamp from the ceiling of the laboratory, and placing a globe under it he rotated it in such a way that the light from the lamp fell alternately on its two sides. The teacher said, 'Just think, the earth has been moving in a predetermined direction for billions of years and there has never been an iota of change in its speed. Whatever exists on this sphere is kept in place by the force of magnetism in such a way that it is in no way affected by the perpetual rotation and revolution. Now tell me, what is the force that keeps a sphere of this size in constant movement?' This demonstration made my head spin, and for many days after it I used to gaze at the sky for hours in wonderment, trying to grasp the fact that I was stuck on the surface of a world that was ceaselessly gyrating like a top. My mind then accepted that the universe did indeed have a Creator; but what was his objective, and what was the purpose of life, were questions for which I never found satisfactory answers.

I remember an interesting incident that occurred in 1944, when, as I have mentioned elsewhere in this book, I was on an expedition in Kashmir accompanied by two friends. When we arrived in Pilgam from Srinagar in a lorry, bringing with us essential supplies for a long journey, porters refused to carry our stuff because the way ahead was fraught with danger. By chance we met Agha Safder there whom I had known in my college days at Aligarh, and who was the tehsildar in Pilgam. At first he tried to stop us from continuing on our dangerous journey, but my nature is such that I do not easily change a decision once made. So ten or twelve porters under orders from the tehsildar, picked up our baggage, and followed us willynilly in the direction of the Amar Nath Mountain. Disregarding the rules of mountaineering, we started on our journey that very afternoon instead of waiting for the next morning, to preclude the possibility of the porters deserting us. Our first camp was fourteen miles away at a place called Chandan Bari. Call it the madness of youth if you like, but stepping gingerly on an unfamiliar terrain in the darkness of the night, we somehow managed to reach the camp safely.

In the pitch dark we saw a distant light. The porters had been left far behind, and my two friends must have been censuring me in their hearts. Anyhow, in the middle of the desolation the brightly lit lamp proved to be a blessing for us. When we knocked at the door of the hut where we had seen the light, a Sikh opened it and asked us what we wanted. We were so enervated from the severe cold, exhaustion and hunger that he took pity on us and invited us in where we sat on stools by the fire. The Sikh told us that the season for the pilgrimage at Amarnath was over, and that no one would pass that way for months to come. All the shopkeepers had left, and he was the only one who was still there. While he prepared to cook something for us, we sat smoking our cigarettes silently in front of the fire.

Suddenly, we heard the growling of a beast along with a human voice shouting the name of the Hindu god, Ram. We turned around in astonishment in time to see a tall sadhu enter the cottage with a leopard. Each one of us had a spear in his hand, which we held tightly and drew back, away from the reach of the leopard. The sadhu laughed and said, 'Don't worry, he is my child.' At a word from him the beast went and sat quietly in a corner. However we remained vigilant, watching sometimes the man and sometimes his beast. The account the Sadhu gave us about himself was interesting:

Fifteen years ago he was the postmaster in Mirzapur. He was quite well-educated, to the extent that he was conversant with both Urdu and Persian. An epidemic of plague swept over the town, in which his wife died along with their two children. This occurrence made such a deep impression on him that the world for him lost its allure and life its purpose. He said good-bye to his job, took leave of his home and accompanied some sadhus to the Himalayas. He lived with them for many years until he found a mentor with whom he shared a spiritual and mental rapport. Our sadhu had been living in the area for many years. Currently his abode was the hollow trunk of a large chinar tree which had been struck by lightning. The sadhu used to lie there, lost in thought, with a deerskin under him and a blanket over him. He had found a leopard cub wandering around nearby, and had adopted him. The cub became so attached to him that he would come back to him every evening. I asked the sadhu, 'What did you gain by renouncing the world?' His reply was, 'What did you gain by enduring the world?' In actual fact, since life is ephemeral, every individual must find his own meaning and purpose in it, in keeping with his temperament and circumstances.

The mind is the precious core of human life. Scientific research on the mind is still in its initial stages, and all that is known about its infinite complexity is that there are about ten billion cells in less than a kilogram of brain, and that at present no intelligent man is able to use more than 15 per cent of it. Hundreds of thousand of years ago, man had not progressed beyond the level of beasts. With the development of culture his abilities grew, in the same way as a child's intelligence grows with age and he learns to comprehend, explore, analyse, and gain knowledge from trial and observation. In addition he keeps trying to pass on what he has learned to others, at first orally and then through writing. With the growth of such abilities, man not only became superior to animals, he was also able to benefit more from natural resources. In other words, evolution, which began at the time of creation, is even now in progress. Nobody knows how much latent power is trapped in the 85 per cent of apparently unused mental potential. It is simply a misinterpretation to say that there is a fundamental contradiction between religion and science. Science is the name given to knowledge that can be proved through experimentation. It does not claim to dominate all branches of knowledge, because knowledge under any name is the search for the boundless directions of space and time. Knowledge grows, and the intellect becomes more penetrating with passing time. The present age has covered so many stages in a single leap that the feat would have been considered inconceivable a hundred years ago. On occasion the intellect may disappoint, but to ignore it for that reason is the kind of ignorance that is responsible for the superstition and prejudice exhibited by mankind.

In every era, personalities appear whose intellectual calibre is higher than the average. Their character, hard work, persistent practice, as well as better mental endowment are factors that are responsible for their superior intellect, which is beyond that of average people. As an illustration of this, imagine that all of us are facing a high wall which blocks our vision. However one person finds a crack in it and putting his eye to it he can see what lies beyond the wall. Scientists now agree that natural sciences, which depend on the five senses, are not superior to all other branches of knowledge. This does not mean that a gulf exists between the two kinds. It is a question of developing the unexploited potential of the mind.

History is witness to the fact that until the eleventh century, for as long as Islamic society allowed religion and knowledge to coexist harmoniously, it was able to achieve eminence. But after that era, when Islamic jurisprudence blocked the path of science and philosophy, signs of deterioration became visible in the society as well as in scholarship. The consequences of this are now before us. How ironic it is that the followers of the very religion that gave the highest importance to learning, became the greatest enemies of reason, to the extent that rejection of reason, and frenzy, became popular themes in our poetry.

The most important issue for any individual is self-preservation. He is obliged to live as part of a group that by degrees takes the form of family, tribe, and nation. The principle of mutual dependence ties the individual to the group. Rousseau, the intellectual standard bearer of the French Revolution, explained this principle by saying that the age of despotism has ended and democracy has been founded. Rousseau said that the aim of government is the well-being of the people, and when a government chooses the path of alienating the people, it gives up the right to govern. According to Rousseau's philosophy of democracy, freedom is the birthright of every individual, and the law should keep a balance between his rights and duties. This voice of truth gave rise to the intellectual revolution that brought in its wake a struggle for a democratic constitution, which is still going on in many countries of the world.

Until the nineteenth century, the Christian Church in many Western countries insisted on the concept of the divine right of kings. Muslim rulers who came after the first four Caliphs adopted this same doctrine, so much so that later kings even bestowed on themselves the title of 'Shadow of Allah'.

When intellectual and political awakening among Muslims started one hundred years ago, it took two forms: one was to replace dictatorship with constitutional democracy, and the other was to fight against Western dominance. If he can turn away from the undesirables of life, every intelligent individual tries to comprehend the boundless extent of the universe. Every year the diameter of telescopes in the observatories grows larger, but meanwhile distance and depth in space grow more profound. According to the science of astronomy there are innumerable galaxies in space, and in each of them there are billions of luminous stars, endlessly spinning, while preserving the same distance from one another. It is only recently that the probe into this unbounded immensity has been started. Who can say when, where, and in what form signs of life will be detected. With time as the gauge we can estimate that light from a distant star left in our direction billions of years ago, and perhaps is still on the way. According to Einstein's theory, space and time are linked in this fascinating universe. The mysterious character of time has filled with wonder religion, philosophy and science, equally. Time is like the ocean that has no shore, and the waves of which are constantly in motion. The present is the past as well as the future, and nothing has permanence except movement. However all of us, at some time during our lives become aware of an impending event, whether intuitively or through the intervention of an astrologer. This is that complex puzzle of destiny or free will, that human intelligence has not been able to fathom. Has the path of life been preordained? And is man a puppet who believes himself to be independent but is in fact controlled by one who holds him on a string? This presumption was the basis of the outlook which could only lead to faith in the idea of predestination. Whatever the reality, it is laid down that man must wage a constant struggle in order to make this borrowed tenure of life meaningful. From the religious and materialistic points of view, human life is caught between two constantly conflicting forces. These are the forces of good and evil, which Islam calls Allah and Shaitan, Zoroastrianism calls Mazda and Ahriman, and Buddha has named darkness and light. In the dialectical philosophy of Karl Marx they are the economic forces that remain engaged in a class struggle in order to gain dominance over the resources from which wealth is created. The common objective of all these different theories is that the forces of good, justice, equality and egalitarianism should succeed and rid mankind of the curses of exploitation, coercion and injustice. History is the account of precisely this gory struggle. Despite the efforts of several thousand years man has acquired merely a patina of civilization, and has overtly become a champion of peace and justice, but no sooner do his personal interests encounter some obstacle in their path, than the fragile layer of civilization crumbles away and and he is revealed as the beast, of which he is an incarnation. We cannot be too amazed at this contrast of creation and destruction, intelligence and ignorance. On the one hand the extraordinary development of the intellect has resulted in discovering new forms of energy which transformed life by bringing about the industrial revolution, and has caused man to become acquainted with the depths of the ocean and the exalted abode of stars. It has also enabled man to discover ways to fight and control poverty and disease. Yet on the other hand such barbarism is exposed in the unprecedented perpetration of brutalities, carried out in the name of colour, race, and nationality. What is the treatment for this hypocrisy? Would it be correct to say that evil is the main component of man's conscience? According to Iqbal, Lucifer complained to God that:

اے خداوند ثواب و ناثواب
من شدم از صحبت آدم خراب

O Lord of Reward and Punishment
It is the company of man that has made me bad

When Jesus picked up the cross to wash off the stain of evil, or Mansoor cried out 'I am Truth' as he arrived at the gallows, did the Lord of the Day of Reckoning accept their sacrifice? Or is it basically not an issue of the individual's moral exaltation or baseness at all, but rather, a question of the economic imbalance in society? History is witness to the fact that any society has always been divided into those who rule and those who are ruled. The differences between them were always veiled, but their fundamental clash of interests cannot be denied.

According to scientists, the earth came into being a few billion years ago, after a violent upheaval in space. This view is known by the deafening name of the 'Big Bang Theory'. Anyhow, whether it was with a Bang, or with God's command to 'Be', the earth was created, and after millions of years of changes in climate it became a suitable habitat for life. Then, after crossing complicated stages of evolution, appeared the two-legged animal who, with the development of his mental faculties, came to be seen as the rightful claimant to the position of human being. From the lighting of fire by rubbing two flintstones together to the invention of atomic energy, from mimicking the arboreal leaps of monkeys to walking in space, from the age of bullock carts to that of supersonic jets, the progress humanity has made is mind-boggling! And yet, it did not preclude the immensity of ignorance and prejudice that makes the white man mistrust the black, and speakers of every language think their own language divine. As a matter of fact every individual of any standing believes himself to be the axis around which the world spins.

If one thinks about it one can see that a single individual has few wants. If he puts in a little work he can easily take care of his needs. The real issue is of involvement. An individual wastes most of his time finding solutions for the problems of those he is involved with. The trouble is that man cannot live in isolation. The approach of the modern age in its attempt to straighten out the mishmash of the overt and covert, the individual and society, needs to be analysed. This is the age of industry, science and technology, and whether it is capitalism, or communism, all follow this path. The difference between them lies only in the ownership of the means of production. Those countries that have adopted this route have advanced far in material progress, and South America, Africa, and Asia are now following in their footsteps. Tribal and agricultural societies graduating into industrial ones are obstructed not only by cultural traditions, but also by mental concepts and moral and cultural values. Every society fashions its own moral values, and characters change with environment. However in every age there are always some people who are the standard bearers of truth—people who lighten somewhat the dark night of history. From the beginning of Creation man has made his life a burden for himself by seeing his deliverance not in this world but in the next. Hence the Hindus and Buddhists believe in total annihilation of self, that is, not only of one's physical needs but also of one's soul. According to the Semitic religions this world is a transitory abode, and it is only after divesting oneself of it that one can pass the stages of reward and punishment and achieve eternal life. Contemporary man has begun to believe that modern knowledge has equipped him with the necessary abilities, so that there is no reason why he cannot transform the world into a cradle of peace and freedom. Four hundred years ago Sir Thomas More had portrayed in his book, *Utopia*, an ideal place where men had risen above prejudices of colour, race and religion, and were living in a society so peaceful that distinctions between master and slave, rich and poor did not exist. In More's days it was impossible to achieve such a society because the material resources for it were not available. But today, when the advancement of knowledge has brought about a great increase in wealth the issue is a just distribution of it. The responsibility for the destruction and advancement of humanity lies with none but man himself. Man is his own best friend and worst enemy.

The process of evolution still continues. And as long as there is no harmony between speech and action, the overt and covert, and the individual and society, this process will remain incomplete. In order to live in this world, it is neither necessary to become its abject follower, nor to renounce it. The middle way is better than the extreme abstinence and self denial of a monastic life. If one is afflicted by greed or avarice, even a gold mine is not enough to satisfy one's appetite. Tolstoy has illustrated this with an incomparable story: When the reign of the Czars was coming to an end in Russia, the serfs were emancipated. One landlord was very fond of his aged serf, so when it was time to free him, he asked him, 'What will you do now?' The old man replied, 'All I know is to till the land, but I have no land to till.' The landlord who possessed thousands of acres of land said to him, 'There is no shortage of land. You can have as much as you want.'

Finding the serf incredulous, his former master said, 'You can have as much land as you can cover in one day, by walking from morning to evening.' On hearing this, the erstwhile serf was overcome with greed. Early the next morning, despite the intense heat of summer, he ran for all he was worth in order to become the owner of many acres of land. But by the evening, defeated by the hot sunlight and thirst, all his strength ebbed away and he fell lifeless at his master's feet. In spite of his frenetic efforts, his destiny had sanctioned him no more than the six feet of land that every human being is finally entitled to.

How ironic it is that nature rescues the infant from the darkness of the mother's womb, only to bury him in the dark womb of Mother Earth. But though he is well aware of this truth, man still rushes around madly in his greed and avarice. When the sadhu asked me what I had gained by enduring the world, he had implied this same tragic loss of direction in the life of the world. This does not mean that like the sadhu one should renounce the world and live in the hollow trunk of a tree; for a middle path does exist between such an inactive life and the furious pursuit of livelihood. The greatest proponent of inactivity was the Chinese philosopher Li Ho who said these famous words: 'If you can walk don't try to run, if you can stand don't try to walk, if you can sit don't try to stand, and if you can lie down don't try to sit.' Between this sluggishness of the East, which is given the name of spiritualism, and the frenetic pursuit of wealth and property, wisdom and courtesy can create harmony and balance.

Man becomes a slave of his own greed for two reasons: Firstly, because he is egoistic by nature, and secondly, owing to the unpredictability of his circumstances. Religion teaches him self denial and gives him hope that if not in this world then in the next there will be an end to the anxiety caused by uncertainties. As far as society is concerned, the government uses restraints and punishment to keep the greed for wealth within acceptable limits. In order to do this, all kinds of methods are used. In ancient Greece, one ruler introduced copper or iron currency weighing approximately half or one kilogram, so that people would find it too cumbersome to carry or hoard such wealth. Alauddin Khilji's deterrent for those merchants who gave short weight to their customers was to cut off as much flesh from their bodies as the weight of the commodity they had deprived the buyer of. These strategies are no longer employed; if they were, we would have been able to get rid of the curses of inflation and black-marketing without loss of time.

To a large extent, the reason for the economic problems of today is that the government interferes in all kinds of matters, and the citizens too would like to leave all their responsibility to the government, but in the process they lose their own rights. If the government were told that not only should it provide protection for life and property, but that it should also shoulder the responsibility for Education, Health, Transport, Business and even the upkeep of maternity homes and cemeteries, the individual would be relegated to the status of a mere servant or a workman. He would begin to lose his individualism and would be no more than a humble cog in the formidable machine of mass production. The reaction to this condition is Anarchism, which does away with government for the reason that it imposes the curse of a permanent subordination on men; instead, this system persuades people to find solutions for their problems through mutual cooperation. The concept is right in principle, but it is extremely difficult to implement. So finally we have to recognize that democracy alone is a reliable way to keep a balance between the interests of individuals and the group.

The underlying reason for the material progress of the present age is that the physical labour of man and beast has been replaced by automated machines. Life without machines is unthinkable now. Indeed, in some fields machines have achieved so much that man is becoming redundant. Instances of imbalance caused by the conflict between good sense and the lack of it are numerous. In the developing countries if the number of quadrupeds would increase and the number of bipeds decrease, and in the developed countries the dominance of machines could be controlled, many of the problems of the present era would be solved. But civilization is an unbridled horse which, lacking the reins of faith and the saddle of good sense, is galloping away in an unknown direction. When nature brought this earth into being, it apparently did not intend it to be divided into hundreds of countries of different sizes. But the greatest tragedy of human history is racial prejudice and nationalistic chauvinism, which cast their hideous shadow over mankind like that of a brooding evil spirit. The hatred and bitterness, of which prophets and thinkers had tried to keep the human race free, are destroying those ideals everywhere under the banners of race, colour, points of view, and language. This endless conflict between wisdom and ignorance is either the herald of a new world order or the last gasp of the old one!

In the middle of the twentieth century when the famous researcher, Velikovsky, tried to prove that about 15,000 years ago a comet had struck our earth and given rise to upheavals on a massive scale, there was pandemonium in the scientific world. The scientists did not believe that the act of evolution had been interrupted by a cataclysm. To them the emergence of life on earth followed such an iron law of cause and effect that there was no room in it for any change. But Velikovsky tried to prove with meticulous hard work that some cosmic calamity did occur and its effects became apparent as Noah's flood and the sinking of the continent known as Atlantis which was first mentioned by Plato. In this tempestuous era the planet Venus played such an inauspicious role that people of the ancient ages remained fearful of it for a very long time, and even now it is associated with bad luck. According to Plato the continent of Atlantis sank in the ocean, and even today the search for it continues. The few of its

inhabitants who survived were impelled by the waves to the shores of
South America in the west and Egypt in the east. In this way this lost
civilization left its traces in these new lands. The ends of our own
cultural history can be found here. To learn about forgotten history
one needs to study the evidence painstakingly collected in his books
by Velikovsky.

In the early periods of history one does not find the propensities for
greed and lust, hatred and bitterness which later inundated mankind.
Romantic historians saw the period as a heavenly age, but it was a
heaven that soon vanished, and then began that association of master
and slave which is present in every society under a different name. To
quote Anand Narayan Mulla:

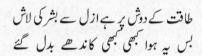

The corpse of the individual has always rested on the shoulder of power
Only now and then, it was a different shoulder

The slave may try hard to break this tie, but only those with a luminous
conscience can accomplish it, and for them no better word can be
found in the dictionary than *mujahid*, or 'warrior'. It is oppression and
injustice that give rise to the fervour for jihad, which under one form
or another impels society towards reform and progress in every age.
In modern times when the ruler of Ethiopia announced emancipation
of slaves in his country, they protested loudly, begging not to be freed,
for what good was freedom to them? Even Karl Marx's prediction that
workers would be the natural torch-bearers of revolution in the
industrial society has been proved wrong. On the contrary, in the
industrial countries of the West these same workers are loyal to the
capitalist systém.

It is necessary also to analyse the association between man and
nature. A few hundred years ago when man became capable of using
natural resources to his advantage, he began to exploit them carelessly.
The reserves of minerals that nature had built up over hundreds of
thousands of years were depleted by industrialists in no time.
Consequently there is now universal anxiety about how the needs of
future generations will be met. Nature had preserved a balance in

human population by maintaining a ratio between births and deaths. As soon as modern medicine eliminated the danger of epidemics, an unprecedented increase in population followed. The most important issue facing humanity today is how to keep its own population in check while increasing the number of plants and livestock. The future of progress in developing countries especially, depends on this factor. Reality, in short, has many aspects. First of all, there is the search for one's own identity, secondly, the recognition of principles that determine the relationship between the individual and society, and thirdly, an awareness of the correlation that can maintain harmony between the goals of humanity and those of nature.

The twentieth century has possibly not produced another thinker of Bertrand Russell's stature. I have mentioned before in this book how his writings influenced me in the days when I was a student, and continue to do so to this day. Russell wrote in his autobiography:

'Three passions, simple, but overwhelmingly strong, have governed my life: the longing for love, the search for knowledge, and unbearable pity for the suffering of mankind....'

Even to fully understand the significance of these goals requires intelligence and sensibility of a high order, leave alone the attainment of them. When the greatest scientist of the world, Newton, received intimations of his impending mortality, he said:

I don't know what I may seem to the world, but as to myself, I seem to have been only like a boy playing on the sea-shore and diverting myself in, now and then, finding a smoother pebble or a prettier shell than ordinary, whilst the great ocean of truth lay undiscovered before me.

It was Adam and Eve who started the custom of love. As for their children, nature has kept them busy in the quest for this mirage. Love is a passion that acquires nobility only when it discards physical satisfaction as its goal, and adopts a form that is the purpose of worship and the essence of art. The bond that exists between the restlessness for knowledge, the longing for love, and the empathy with suffering humanity, is the light that illuminates the dark abode of civilization. Indeed it is the destination towards which the weary caravan of life is headed.

20

Epilogue

In the Middle Ages it was customary to see faith and reason as two conflicting entities, and the Christian Church had given the impression that the two were incompatible. After a long struggle, when the hold of the Church became weaker, the rational sciences began to guide humanity towards the modern age. In Islamic society there was at first no discord between knowledge and faith, but with the decline of the Abbasid caliphate a conflict emerged between the two with such force that its echo can be heard even to this day. Clearly, just as religious people are not necessarily irrational, so rational people are not inevitably devoid of faith. If we look at history we find that until the nineteenth century education was confined to the privileged upper classes all over the world. Educating the masses became necessary in the West after the industrial revolution, because illiterate workmen were not able to use complicated and costly machines. Before this phase, the ruling class everywhere had kept the common people deprived of education. The worst instance of this is prescribed by Manu, the Hindu lawgiver, who said that if the words of the Hindu scripture, the sacred Ved, were heard by a member of the lower caste, molten lead should be poured into his ear. The purpose was to keep the common man deprived of the ability to think. In Pakistan the same attitude is expressed in the denial of education to their subjects by tribal lords and other landlords. In the villages generally women are barred from becoming literate. The truth is that the disapproval of insidious religious scholars for knowledge and intelligence among the common people is no more than an excuse to protect the interests of the ruling class. If we look at it from this perspective it becomes clear why adult education, education of women and scientific research are ignored in our country.

Another point that deserves attention is that after losing their political eminence in the subcontinent during the nineteenth century, the consequent lack of confidence among the Muslims gave rise to feelings of rootlessness and escapism. Despite their one thousand-year association with the subcontinent, they began to turn away from the concept of nationhood. The apparent reason for this was that they did not want to live as the subject race in a land that their forebears had ruled for centuries. This attitude was further strengthened by the political awakening that had been caused by Western dominance in the Islamic world. Finally, Muslims adopted the strategy, which by bringing Pakistan into existence, created the hope for the simultaneous satisfaction of the demands for nationhood and Islamic unity. However every ideological concept has to confront practical difficulties. The prime duty of a state is the advancement and protection of its citizens. Muslim population is spread over almost thirty-five to forty independent states, and the interests of all these countries are not identical. In practice none of them would risk their own existence for another. The forces of history had made the creation of Pakistan inevitable, but the geographical form it was given was not practical. Consequently, the two parts of the country split and became two countries. While two independent Muslims states had in fact been mentioned in the Pakistan Resolution of 1940, the Resolution was amended in the Muslim League meeting of 1946 which was held in Delhi at the insistence of the delegation from Bengal. Once again the psychology of rootlessness cast its shadow over every aspect of our lives. At the time of Partition, 15 million people were forced to leave their homes and seek refuge in India or Pakistan. Their rehabilitation was beset by problems that defy description. Subsequently the question of creating national unity arose in the newly independent state, to deal with which statesmanship and political perceptiveness were needed, but these qualities had become scarce in the country after Liaquat Ali Khan. In the fracas created by provincial, tribal and personal interests, the mentality of escapism and rootlessness intensified. Although according to a saying of the Prophet (PBUH) 'Patriotism is a part of Faith', people began to shun patriotism; there was even a group that proclaimed it to be opposed to Islam. The new scenario is that everybody is dying to leave the country and go abroad. Strangely enough, for the last ten years the government has not tried to stop even the members of the professional class from emigrating, though these are people on whose training and education the country spends billions of rupees every year. In the days when we were children, Muslims would often express their devout longing in the words, 'My Lord, call me to Madina'. These words still express their longing, though in a totally different context, and for a different end. Nobody is troubled by the question of who will help in the development of the country if there is no place in it for able people. When people speak about the economic and cultural crisis in the country and criticize the unruliness and lack of direction of the new generation, they should remember that by setting the example of rootlessness they are building an edifice on weak foundations. What is worse is that human relationships are confined to one's tribe or community, and are founded on the assumption that two different standards should be applied to one's own people and others. It is useless to touch on the hypocrisy that this double standard has engendered in society, but the explanation for the growing shallowness which our poetry, literature, art and music are acquiring with passing time should be sought in this very situation.

When a student of history regards the Muslim past, he is astonished by the fact that Muslims were unable to devise rules for handing over government by a ruler to his successor. The desire for power has created conflicts in every country in every age. However the West reduced the danger of civil war in this process by adopting the ancient Roman principle of transferring power to the eldest son. Muslims were not able to devise a similar system, which was the reason why, after the reign of the first four Caliphs had ended, every ruler's ascent to power was determined by the sword:

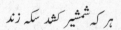

He who drew his sword was the one
whose name was stamped on the currency (was installed in power)

This is echoed on every page of our history. The effects of the damage that was caused to Muslims by this lack of political acumen can still be felt. A good example of this is that our political mind cannot distinguish between constitution and law. A democratic constitution is based on the principle that the ultimate power lies with the people, who elect their rulers for a fixed period of time, and divide power between the Executive, the Legislature, and the Judiciary in such a way as to maintain a balance between them. However the tradition of despotic monarchy in much of the world, and among Muslims in particular, has been so strong until recently that the ruling class in these regions does not easily accept the peoples' democratic rights. Consequently the movement for constitution-making and human rights which began at the start of the twentieth century has still not been able to succeed in its objectives. It must be acknowledged that the conflict between dictatorship and democracy still goes on in most countries of the world. The difference in the Islamic countries is that the anti-people elements use wrong interpretations of religious injunctions to protect their own position, thus making the issue more complex.

The other great weakness of Muslim society is that it has regarded trite and obsolete superstitions as its cultural heritage, and has failed in building institutions which are necessary for survival in the modern age. We are unable to run even ordinary institutions, such as the municipal and district councils, which used to function smoothly under British rule. Nothing can be accomplished easily without the intercession of influential people and personal clout. Citizenship alone does not guarantee the rights of an individual; rather, it is his affiliation with a particular family, tribe or province that matters. On the contrary, the secret of the developed countries' advancement is that all their citizens, without distinction, are entitled to the rights recognized by the law as theirs. For centuries people have been used to economic responsibility and cooperation on local matters. The concept of morality is based not on individual salvation, but on the well-being of society. The conscience does not demand that one remain endlessly absorbed in the contemplation of the hereafter, but that we order the world on foundations of justice and equality, which is the true will of God. Blackmarketing, profiteering, injustice and exploitation do not fulfil the intention of the true religion. It is also true that choosing the right people is necessary for running institutions efficiently, and this can only be achieved when the criterion for selection is not personal influence but sheer competence. In Pakistan, basing employment at the federal level on the provincial quota system has caused immeasurable damage to national unity. Worst of all, many highly talented people, who would head the list of successful candidates in federal examinations, completely lost their advantage because they did not qualify for the provincial quota. I remember an amusing episode in this connection.

About thirty years ago Mian Afzal Husain was the Chairman of the Public Service Commission, and Hasan Shahid Suhrawardy was a member of the same organization. When foreign scholarships were announced for higher education, a committee was formed for the selection of suitable candidates. I represented the ministry of Education on this committee. A young Urdu-speaking applicant came from East Pakistan, and appeared to be suitable in every way, but for some reason Mian Afzal Husain did not like him. When Mian Sahib could not find anything to pick on, he asked him, 'How long have you been living in Dacca?' 'My father took up employment in Dacca before Partition,' the boy replied. Mian Sahib was not satisfied. 'But you were not born there,' he objected. When the young man grasped the drift of the objection, he gathered up his papers and left the room saying, 'I didn't know that the scholarship was contingent on the geographical location of the sperm.'

The boy's remark sent Suhrawardy and me into fits of laughter, but Mian Sahib's face was ablaze with fury. I was an examiner for the Federal Public Service Commission for many years, and can say with certainty that every applicant who headed the list of successful candidates was rejected on the basis of not satisfying the requirements of the provincial quota. In the deathlike silence of the evening that follows a day of raging battle, vultures, who have been lying in wait, arrive in the battleground to tear at the flesh of dead and dying men. A similar scene could be observed at the dawn of Pakistan, when in the wake of the devastation of mass migration, after they had grabbed evacuee property, the opportunists invented such ingenious methods of plunder that in time deceit and shirking work began to be seen as skills and assets, while commitment and hard work were regarded as shortcomings. In no time the cities were dominated by the nouveau riche. These were people who were entirely unacquainted with moral, traditional and cultural values, but were so adept at making money that they picked the pockets of the country clean, and filled their own.

In the seventeenth century, a thinker named Malthus was born in Holland. He predicted that population would become the greatest problem for humankind in the centuries to come. There would come a time when the food produced would not be enough for all, and starvation would become the destiny of the human race. In the twentieth century, the population of the subcontinent has so far tripled, that is, from 300 million it has become 900 million, and is projected to total 1.5 billion in the next twenty years. The developed countries have curtailed births as well as deaths in order to keep the balance, which is in accordance with the law of nature. But in a developing country like Pakistan little attention has been paid to this aspect. On the contrary, abundance of progeny is considered a blessing. Until society gives the first priority to family planning no reasonable amount of progress is conceivable. If one examines the causes of corruption and acquisitiveness, one finds that production has not kept pace with consumers. To make this situation worse there is that nouveau riche mentality which intensifies the appetite with every morsel consumed.

I have expressed my views on a few specimen issues which we need to resolve. To burden the future generations with them, or hold foreign powers responsible for them is altogether unjust. The feudal outlook cannot build a new kind of life, nor can the demands of sturdy progress be met with foreign loans. Only the right leadership, good organization and love can help the nation overcome the problems it is facing. One can think of many serious mistakes that have been made by our authorities, but it is not possible to recount them in a few pages. When the atmosphere is conducive, and the historian finds the opportunity, he may be able to reveal those bitter realities. However a traveller in the dark continues his journey in the hope that somehow he will arrive at his destination. An artist has painted a picture called 'Hope', in which humanity, represented by a blindfolded woman, is sitting on top of a globe, [trying to draw music from the single unbroken string of a lyre]. We are in the same state of hope and dread.

In the fervour of the Pakistan movement, nobody had anticipated that linguistic and cultural conflicts would emerge in this country. But in a short time the struggle between Bengali and Urdu turned as bitter as the erstwhile conflict between Urdu and Hindi. This situation did not arise in West Pakistan despite the presence of regional languages, one reason for which was that they shared a common script with Urdu.

The national status of Urdu is assured, but along with it the regional languages too are advancing, and their literatures are developing.

For writers and readers literature is a thing of pleasure. However it is only in an atmosphere of freedom that good literature can be created. Strangely enough, under British rule the creative writer did not suffer from the claustrophobia that he now encounters. In addition to censorship there are checks on broadcasting and publishing today that would have been unimaginable in those days. However not only has the number of Urdu readers increased, there is now no dearth of popular books and journals. The situation is different with literature. Extended practice is needed for creating good literature, a fact that only those with a taste for it can comprehend.

Debates continue on the subject of Pakistani culture, which is not surprising. Until the partition of the subcontinent Muslims used to believe themselves heirs to a single culture; but this idea came apart after the partition of India, and a conflict began between history and geography. If one looks at it purely from the viewpoint of culture, civilization is not the monopoly of any one nation or country; but there is no room for such open-mindedness in national politics. Nevertheless, as long as Urdu stays alive in India, and has a role in the national solidarity of Pakistan, a sturdy bridge of amity will remain in place between the two countries.

The importance of the arts in cultural life is disregarded not only by the common people but even by our rulers. It is not just literature, but also music, painting and all those other arts which suppress the bestial in human nature and introduce humans to spiritual pleasures. The harshness and aggression that are expressed in our everyday life prove that we lack civility and forbearance. To some extent this malaise can be counteracted by appropriate changes in the school curriculum.

The search for reality which I began at a young age continues in my old age. My physical eyes have seen much in this theatre that is the world, and the eyes of my spirit have to some extent become acquainted with the depths of the soul. I have no yearnings now, nor desires. The past accompanies me like a loyal companion. There is now no difference between dreams and awakening. When I look at the sky at dawn the morning star smiles at me and whispers 'The Greek myths are right in supposing that when the spirit leaves behind its earthly attire it takes the form of a star in the heavens. Come close to me, you burnt-out star, a place has been chosen for you.'

It is said about Al Mansur, the vizier of the ruler of Andalusia, Abdur Rahman III, that whenever he returned from a campaign he would shake off the dust from his garment into an earthen pot. At the end of a life spent in combat, when he died, the accumulated dust from the pot was sprinkled over his shroud. Where can I find so much dust from my own path in life? But whatever there was has been shaken over these pages.

In Iran I had a friend called Dr Barjandi. His wisdom and sharpness of mind were acknowledged by all. Once, I said to him, 'How strange it is that good advice is lost on man, and every generation repeats the follies of its predecessors.' His reply was insightful. He said, 'All the advice that thinkers have given and all the experience acquired from history can be collected in one slim volume. But the destiny of every individual is that he should keep treading just the one circular path, like an ox driving an oil press, under the illusion that he is discovering something new. He keeps doing this until he reaches the very point where he started.'

In this book I have recounted my surroundings, and what I gathered through my observation and reading. In this respect the book is not an autobiography, rather, it is a work which is less about me and more about the world. After a long absence from the literary scene when I was able to return to it a few years ago, I wrote a series of articles for the magazine *Afkar*, at the insistence of Sehba Sahib. Ideas grew, and an outline of a book was forming in my mind when my eyesight, which had already weakened, fell victim to a surgeon's scalpel, and my pen deserted me. Without the support of my wife and sons I would have long been dead, but all through this anxious time I used to feel jabs of the desire to complete my book. For this, the cooperation of some lover of knowledge was needed. Fateh Farrukh was the first to undertake this work, but soon he left for Lahore. Leila Khurshid then transcribed the rest of the work with a great deal of patience and commitment. When the manuscript was finally ready, Sehba Sahib shouldered the responsibility of printing and publishing it. Jamil Jalbi Sahib undertook to read the last proofs. I will not be able to read this book after it is printed, but the fact is that once a book is published it belongs to the readers and not the writer, and it is they whose verdict counts. I have passed through the whole maze of hating and loving man, and have emerged at the phase of knowing man. This spiritual and intellectual journey was not easy, and I could not avoid resorting to brevity in giving an account of it. Unfavourable circumstances dictate that much of what I would like to narrate remains unsaid.

کفن بیار تو تابوت و جامہ نیلی کن

کہ روزگار طبیب است و عافیت بیمار

Bring the shroud and dye your garments blue (the colour of grief)
For time is the physician and well-being is the patient

Addenda

In Search Of Times Past

No writer is happy when concluding his last work; in fact he feels the kind of sorrow one endures when losing a dear friend forever. This is indeed the emotion that Gibbon experienced when he had completed his masterpiece, *The Rise and Fall of the Roman Empire*. When he bade farewell to the fruit of his reflection and study after fifteen years of continual hard work, he became in his own words so restless that it seemed that life had lost its purpose and the spirit had deserted the body.

The famous French novelist Marcel Proust was not willing to relinquish his grip on the process of creation and publication as long as he lived. He therefore decided to write a novel that would never come to an end. He worked at it ceaselessly for fifteen years, but before the twelfth and last volume was completed and before his youth had yielded to old age, he had breathed his last.

On the last page of my memoirs, *Gard-e-Raah*, I have acknowledged the constraints that kept me from recounting many subjects that were worth mentioning. Among them, besides my illness and my proclivity to concision, were the restraints that circumstances had imposed. Consequently, I shared with readers a sense of unfinished business in the book. So when it was time for a new edition and the publisher demanded more material, I had no option but to pick up my pen yet again, despite the feeling of inner void that I now experience. My pen is indeed a friend whom I have betrayed repeatedly in my life. Yet it remains faithful to me at a time when I have no other friends.

As long as the mind is active the chain of thoughts remains unbroken. Providing the heart is alive, the springs of sensibilities continue to gush forth. As long as the eyes possess vision, life is a rainbow. As for me, I am now like the lamp left burning at dawn, which has nothing to contribute except the smoke of last night's memories. These I will try to present in such a way that the readers of *Gard-e-Raah* can relate them to each chapter of the book. Things left unsaid previously will also be recorded.

یہ کس کا ذکر ہے قصہ خواں وہ جاگ اٹھے
یہیں سے جوڑ لگا دے میرے فسانے میں

Who have you mentioned, oh storyteller, for it makes them sit up
Insert this fragment into my story

Memories of Calcutta: About Gandhiji

Gandhiji had three sons: Hiralal, Devdas, and Ram Das. Their father's preoccupation with his work deprived them of a good education and upbringing. When Rajagopalachari, the first editor of Seth Birla's newspaper *Hindustan Times* left his post, he had it filled by Devdas, who was by then his son-in-law. Incidentally, as I have mentioned earlier, he had selected me for a sub-editor's position, but Seth Birla rejected his proposal with the explanation that he could not tolerate the presence of a Muslim on the staff of his newspaper.

However, it is Hiralal Gandhi, whom I saw during my stay in Calcutta, that I am about to recall. I used to occupy a room in a building which was located on Nawab Badruddin Street. Close to this building were tall mansions belonging to Marwari moneylenders. I am not sure how the leather merchant from Chiniot, Haji Maula Bakhsh's building escaped the clutches of this community of burgeoning property owners.

From his early youth Hiralal had fallen prey to alcoholism, and though his father tried hard to dissuade him, he refused to give up his addiction; and leaving his own home went to live as a guest in the house of a Marwari moneylender. His arrival there caused enthusiastic crowds of Marwari men and women to flock there, bringing with them bottles of alcohol, along with other gifts. Several times I saw Hiralal, inebriated and senseless, lurching through the gate of the mansion, supported by others. When Gandhiji heard of his son's misdemeanours he openly abused him, and disinherited him. This was a chance the Muslims had been looking for in their antagonism to Gandhi. Some of them approached Hiralal in his sober moments and began to preach

Islam to him. At such times he was attentive to the voice of reason and truth, and was therefore soon ready to convert to Islam.

One day I heard people shouting Allahu Akbar on the streets. When I came out to look, I found some pious individuals evacuating Hiralal from the moneylender's mansion and taking him in the direction of a mosque. Subsequently Hiralal announced that he had converted to Islam. Although Gandhiji warned Muslims that his son was not a reliable person, nor a principled one, his counsel was ignored. However soon afterward Muslims grew tired of his misdeeds, and then Hiralal faded away from the public eye and no one knew when and how he departed this life.

I detailed my first meeting with Gandhiji in *Gard-e-Raah*, but have just recalled an interesting incident, which I am recording here. It was mid-July of 1947. The partition of India had been announced and I was preparing to escape from Delhi where my life was at risk, and leave for Karachi the following month. About this time, Gandhiji and his camp followers came to stay in the Sweepers' Colony, which was located at a turning in New Delhi from where the road led in the direction of the neighbourhood where I lived, known as Qarol Bagh. One evening, as I was leaving my office to go home, the thought occurred to me that I should go to the place where, at sunset, Gandhiji used to conduct his prayer meetings. On those occasions, after singing religious songs, Gandhi would lash out at the audience with advice and admonition. When I arrived there I found Gandhi and his adherents seated on a platform in the sweepers' compound and swaying as they sang their religious songs, which would end with *Raghupati Raghav Rajaram Patit Paavana Sitaram*. There must have been about sixty persons in the crowd. When Gandhiji acknowledged my presence with a look, I too joined in singing the devotional song to Ram, for his sake. At the end of the last song Gandhiji told this parable to the gathering: A village *patwari* (tax official) was known far and wide for his cunning, deceit and ruthlessness. So notorious was he for his harsh and corrupt ways that people would cover their ears with fear when his name was spoken. But how long could such a man escape the wrath of God? One day he fell mortally ill. In the darkness of the night when he heard the footsteps of the angel of death, he gestured for his two sons to come close. He then directed them not to take his body to the cremation ground but instead, to hang it from a *peepal* tree (Sacred Fig or Bo tree). Having given his instructions the *patwari* gave up the ghost, leaving his sons baffled over whether or not to carry out his wishes. Finally they decided to do what he had desired, out of fear of being haunted by his ghost for the rest of their lives if they cremated him according to the prevailing custom. So, they wrapped their father's body in a shroud, and hung it by a rope from a branch of the *peepal* tree.

Next morning, the patwari's corpse swinging from a tree created a sensation among the villagers everywhere, and the police rushed to the scene. Some people said that there was no shortage of enemies that the scoundrel had made, and one of them must have suspended his body from the tree. As soon as this rumour spread, the police began to hunt for and pursue the patwari's foes; and thus the man proved to be a mischief maker even in death, leaving behind a new cause for strife.

Having related this parable Gandhiji said, 'I am sure you get my meaning. The British are like the patwari, and when they quit India they will leave behind some new trouble that will keep the inhabitants of this country in its grip for years to come.'

Every word of Gandhi's prophecy came true; however he forgot to tell us on that occasion that only a few days ago he had been to Kashmir on a secret mission, and there he had whispered a magic charm into Maharaja Hari Singh's ear which drove the latter to create what has so far proved to be an unbridgeable chasm between the two newly independent states, by unexpectedly announcing Kashmir's accession to India. It may not be out of place here to mention that about the same time, that is in July 1947, the 'Frontier Gandhi', Khan Abdul Ghaffar Khan, had been on a similar mission to Kabul, as a result of which the Afghan government challenged the newly independent state of Pakistan by declaring that after the British left, it would cease to recognize the international frontier, known as the Durand Line between the two countries.

The Temple Of Kali Mai

I had been hearing about the temple of Kali Mai ever since my childhood. So, after I arrived in Calcutta I often felt an urge to go and see it, but was restrained by the thought of going there alone. When my friend Basant Kumar came to Calcutta from Raipur I expressed my desire to him. He was staying in the neighbourhood of the temple and so he arranged for us to go there one evening.

Before I describe this bizarre temple, some information about the more important deities of the Hindu religion would be interesting. Although thousands of gods and goddesses are mentioned in Hindu mythology, the three most important among them are Brahma, Vishnu and Shiv. Two of these, that is, Vishnu and Shiv acquired more popularity under various other personae and appellations. Among the manifestations of Vishnu are Ramchandar and Krishan. Worship of these two is common from Bihar to Gujarat, and is regarded as Bhagti or mysticism. Shiv is also known by the title of Mahadev. While he is worshipped more in South India, his wife Parvati is worshipped in Eastern India under the name of Durga or Kali Mai. When Lakshmi pooja is observed during Diwali in northern India, the Hindus of Bengal organize Durga or Kali Mai pooja with great enthusiasm. In keeping with ancient legends, the idol representing this deity is given such a fearsome appearance that viewers are transfixed. The full impact of this can be had in the temple of Kali Mai, which was constructed in Kali Ghat, near the Hugli River and has probably given Calcutta its name.

When evening fell we joined Kali Mai's devotees and headed for the temple, the spires of which were beginning to be eclipsed by the growing darkness. Beggars, flower sellers and vendors of offerings to the goddess thronged the main gate. After I had managed to enter the temple, making my way through the crowd, I stood to one side, spellbound by the ambiance of the temple which was filling my field of vision like a nightmare. This happened sixty years ago, and if there have been changes since, I am not aware of them. In those days oil lamps used to be lit in the vast hall of the temple. So much oil was sprinkled on them intermittently that a cloud of smoke kept rising from them. Since this had been a continual practice, carried out over many years, the walls and ceiling of the temple were blackened by numerous layers of soot. On a platform at the end of the hall stood a life size statue of Kali Mai, who, with a garland of human skulls round her neck, her naked black body, and the blood red of her tongue and eyes, commanded homage from her worshippers. The priests kept ringing bells, blowing conch shells, and raising cries of 'Kali Mai'. Joining in the cries were the local devotees, come to worship at the temple, chanting their 'Jai' with such full-throated passion that it shook the building. Now and then someone would bring a sacrificial goat to a priest, and the latter would intone a mantra to Kali and follow it up with such a tremendous blow of the chopper on the animal's neck that it was instantly decapitated. When he sprinkled the gushing blood over the idol, many would enthusiastically replicate the dance that according to Hindu tradition, Mahadev will execute on the day when the world comes to an end. Readers may have seen pictures of Kali Mai or Durga demonstrating the dance, which is known as the 'Tandav nritya'.

Disciples of the priests were removing heads and torsos of the dead goats from the hall, the floor of which was bathed in blood. The blood-spattered idol looked even more menacing and uncanny in the fading light of the torches. I cannot say how long I watched this fearsome but fascinating spectacle. At last my friend prodded me and indicated with a sign that we must leave. The memory of this scene became etched in my mind, though the experience was never repeated. Not very long ago, in this temple as well as in some others, human beings used to be sacrificed, not goats. The garland of human skulls that Kali Mai wore served as a reminder of this custom.

In Hinduism's oldest holy book, which consists of the four Vedas, there is mention of *narmeda*, or human sacrifice. In fact, the practice of human sacrifice was common in ancient civilizations, and Hazrat Ibrahim's decision to sacrifice his son in compliance with the will of God is a vestige of this rite. How strange it is that though we find the idea of human sacrifice hair-raising, we belong to an age when the blood of countless innocent human beings is spilled in the name of nationality, race and colour.

Introduction To Communist Literature

My memoirs describe the political environment of Calcutta in December 1928. During this period the annual meetings of political groups like the Congress and Muslim League were creating turmoil in the city. Precisely at this time I was appointed Sub-Editor of the Hindi daily, *Vishwamitr*, and my training in journalism began with the political meetings. I have already mentioned that one day I happened to go to Albert Hall, glued to the door of which I found a notice for a meeting of the Kissan Mazdoor Party. There had been no sign of the Communist Party in India until then. According to the British government, when four young men, on their return from Soviet Russia, had attempted to organize the party secretly some years before, they had been tried in Kanpur and sent to jail. Apparently no more was heard of it for a long time after that. However the communists held a meeting under the guise of the Kissan Mazdoor Party. Among the people I saw at the meeting in Albert Hall was Jamaluddin Bukhari with whom I maintained contact for the rest of his life. After the creation of Pakistan he renounced politics and settled in Larkana. He died there recently.

It was the British government that began unintentionally to promote communism in India in March 1929, by arresting almost 25 communists from all over the country and trying them on a concocted charge of conspiracy. The proceedings continued for two or three years in a special court in Meerut, and were reported daily in newspapers. In this way people learned about the aims and objectives of communism. Later on this movement took the form of an official and organized Communist Party.

In March 1929 when the Meerut Conspiracy case began to be reported in the papers, I began to feel a desire to learn about communist literature. However in those days nobody had ever heard of such a thing, and neither books nor journals were available on the subject; as a matter of fact people recoiled at the mention of communism. I hunted for material in the libraries but all my attempts ended in failure. One day, while walking on the footpath along Zakaria Street, I came to a sudden stop in front of a building with the name of Dacca House, because on one of its doors hung a board which read, 'Mazdoor Kissan Party'. I entered the open doorway unhesitatingly, and found myself in a hall whose furniture consisted of a few scattered chairs, and two tables in front of which two people were reading newspapers. Both the men, whose names I later gathered were Abdul Haleem and Shamsul Huda, looked up at me questioningly and with some surprise. Abdul Haleem stared at me suspiciously, but Shamsul Huda, judging me from my youthful looks, thought that I was a student, and greeted me with a smile. When he learned that I was a journalist he began to discuss his party warmly with me. In the course of the conversation when I asked him for communist literature he was taken aback, and replied, 'Do you know what a rare species you are looking for? Don't you know that publication and import of communist literature are banned?'

Shamsul Huda had travelled to America as a common sailor, and laboured there for a few years. He returned to Calcutta as a member of the secret communist organization, of whose working he was very well informed. When I was taking my leave he invited me to drop by from time to time, and promised to give me the material I was looking for if it came his way.

After I had met him a few times and he began to trust me, he pointed out a shop from the window of the room, and said, 'The owner of that laundry is called Hakim. Wrap your dirty clothes in a newspaper and hand them to him saying you've come from Dacca House. He will return the laundered clothes to you wrapped in other papers, which you should take to your room and read when you are alone. Do not show them to anyone, for they are pages from English newspapers or journals brought now and then by foreign sailors to Calcutta and left at the laundry by some means or other. It is possible that you will find in them the material that you want. After you've read them give the papers to some like-minded individual, but be extremely careful because in the eyes of the government there is no bigger threat than the communist movement.' Hearing this I rushed to my room and having wrapped a few clothes in some newspaper, ran to Hakim the laundry owner. When I handed him the bundle and furtively mentioned 'Dacca House' I could see a meaningful gleam in his eyes as he told me that my clothes would be returned on such and such a date.

The precious gift of newspapers that I received in this way once or twice a month, used to include old issues of the British paper *Daily Worker*, and the American *New Masses*. There was also the Moscow based *Communist International Press Correspondence*, whose thought-provoking analyses of political and economic issues of the day I found quite incomparable. I used to put away the back numbers of this journal carefully for future use. Its Editor was the Hungarian economist Emile Varga, renowned in European circles. In the following decade, during one of Stalin's purges in Russia, Varga lost his life along with thousands of other intellectuals.

In my memoirs I have mentioned the fugitive revolutionary, Kundan Lal. After working with me for a few months he suddenly disappeared.

I have also written about Tagore's nephew, Samarendranath Tagore, an admirer of Trotsky, who had returned to India after completing his education in England and was residing in his ancestral home, Tagore Palace, in Calcutta. Thanks to these two, I was able to peruse some of the works of Karl Marx, Lenin, and other leading communist thinkers, and became acquainted with the basic realities of human society which are usually hidden behind curtains of ambiguities and superstitions. Later, I was able to spend a good deal of time on studying this philosophy of life, and had the opportunity to make contacts with its leading lights in different countries. I am grateful that nature has endowed me with the light of conscience, which has remained with me ever since my childhood. It teaches me that irrespective of ideological quibbling, the salvation of mankind lies in building a society in which exploitation and injustice have no place, where religious and racial prejudices cease to exist, and where hypocrisy does not thrive. This was not a new idea, but influenced by the changes that followed the Industrial Revolution in the nineteenth century and the political revolution of France, Karl Marx tried to prove through his momentous analysis that the class war that would inevitably throw up a communist society had begun. In other words, the triumph of communism lay not merely in its moral superiority but in the indisputable historical demand for it. The revolution of 1917 which erupted in Russia under the leadership of Lenin has achieved widespread and extraordinary results. It is an important chapter not only of the modern age but also of human history. Inevitably, there were many vicissitudes in this journey, and at the time of my writing this, it looks as though modern scientific inventions are helping capitalism to maintain the ability to exploit deprived nations. In contrast, communist countries have not been able to control their internal problems adequately, and are also in a state of indecision as to what kind of links to maintain with capitalism. However, these are the issues of today; they were not present when, as a student, I was studying communism and felt that in order to achieve salvation and ensure continuance, society needed to pursue the path of equality and egalitarianism, and this would only be possible when inconsistency between word and action was wholly discarded. My view is that the perfection of humanity lies in achieving this goal, but if it does not succeed in this endeavour, the Creator will have to review his decision of whether the world in which we live is competent to continue its existence.

Memories Of Calcutta: The Poetry Of Josh Maleehabadi Takes A New Turn

When Congress started its Civil Disobedience Movement against the British government in 1931, nationalist Muslims of Calcutta felt the need for a newspaper of their own. Maulana Abul Kalam Azad was their leader and a long time resident of the city. Among his circle of devoted friends was Abdur Razzaq Maleehabadi, an Arabic scholar and an experienced Urdu journalist. After collecting a small sum of money, a weekly journal, *Payam*, was started with Razzaq Maleehabadi as its editor, with the object of propagating the Civil Disobedience Movement. Although the wrath of the government did not allow it to continue beyond one year, yet even in this short time the journal had become quite famous, thanks to its high standard of political and literary writing. Abdur Razzaq Maleehabadi was not one to accept defeat easily. After the *Payam* was closed down, he, with the help of his sincere companions started a daily newspaper by the name of *Hind*, which is still being published under the care of his son.

Josh Maleehabadi was involved in those days with the Darul Tarjuma, or translation bureau, in Hyderabad Deccan. His poetry had not yet left the meadows of romance and entered the wilds of revolution. Since Abdur Razzaq was a close relative, the weekly *Payam* published one of his amorous poems every week. Whenever I had some time to spare, I would stroll into the *Payam* office and Abdur Razzaq would insist that I write something for his paper. One day he suggested to me that since Urdu speakers were unfamiliar with the poetic eminence of Qazi Nazrul Islam, and since I knew Bengali well, I should translate one of his poems for *Payam*. Accordingly, I chose Nazarul Islam's famous poem 'Badrohi'. The translation was published in *Payam* under the title of 'Baghi' (Rebel), and gained wide fame. A few weeks later, Maulana Abdur Razzaq received, in my presence, a poem from Josh Maleehabadi, named 'Baghawat' (Rebellion). He read it out to everyone commenting that the poem had been directly influenced by Nazrul Islam's 'Baghi' and that Josh's poetry seemed to have taken a new turn.

The following year I left Calcutta for Aligarh. Around this time Niaz Fatehpuri was for some reason displeased with Josh, and he started a series of articles in his magazine, *Nigar*. It so happened that concurrently, an exhaustive article on Qazi Nazarul Islam titled 'Bengal's rebel poet', authored by me and containing translations of several of Nazarul Islam's poems in addition to 'Baghi', was also published in *Nigar*. For somebody as discerning as Niaz it was not difficult to spot the resemblance between Qazi Nazrul Islam's 'Rebel' and Josh Maleehabadi's 'Rebellion', and he pointed out the influence of one on the other, with great clarity. After this incident Josh's poetry began to show a gradual change, and in 1934, after he was forced to leave Hyderabad as a consequence of incurring the Nizam's wrath, his romantic poetry metamorphosed into fiery verse and he began to be known as a revolutionary poet.

14 December 1989